THE DISCOVERERS OF
AMERICA

By Harold Faber (with Doris Faber)

WE THE PEOPLE
The Story of the U.S. Constitution since 1787

THE BIRTH OF A NATION
The Early Years of the United States

GREAT LIVES
American Government

GREAT LIVES
Nature and the Environment

THE DISCOVERERS OF
AMERICA
HAROLD FABER

CHARLES SCRIBNER'S SONS • NEW YORK
Maxwell Macmillan Canada • Toronto
Maxwell Macmillan International
New York • Oxford • Singapore • Sydney

Charles Scribner's Sons Books for Young Readers
Macmillan Publishing Company
866 Third Avenue; New York, NY 10022

Maxwell Macmillan Canada, Inc.
1200 Eglinton Avenue East; Suite 200
Don Mills, Ontario M3C 3N1

Macmillan Publishing is part of
the Maxwell Communication Group of Companies.

First Edition   10 9 8 7 6 5 4 3 2 1
Printed in the United States of America

Library of Congress Cataloging-in-Publication Data
Faber, Harold.
The discoverers of America / Harold Faber.
p.   cm.   1st ed.
Includes bibliographical references.
Summary: Chronicles the discoverers of America, from the Native Americans believed to have crossed the Bering Strait after the last Ice Age, through the Vikings and the major European explorers, concluding with Bering's discovery of Alaska and Cook's voyage to Hawaii.
ISBN 0-684-19217-9
1. America—Discovery and exploration—Juvenile literature.
[1. America—Discovery and exploration. 2. Explorers.]   I. Title
E101.F33 1992   970.01—dc20   91-17001

061241

To Doris

Contents

Foreword

Who discovered America?

The short and quick answer is Christopher Columbus—on October 12, 1492.

But is that true? Was he the first person to set foot on the lands of the Americas?

Not really. Other explorers, notably Norsemen from Norway, Greenland, and Iceland, touched the shores of America many years before Columbus.

More important, when Columbus first came ashore, he was greeted by people he called "Indians." How could anyone "discover" a land where people already lived?

Look at the definition of the word *discover*. It means to see or obtain knowledge of something for the first time. Columbus was obviously not the first person to see America. Although historians describe the voyages of Columbus as a turning point in world history, crucial to the European settlement of North and South America, they have long recognized the inaccuracy in describing him as the discoverer of America.

For instance, the eminent historian Samuel Eliot Morison in his two-volume work *The European Discovery of America* started with the Norsemen. Another historian, David B. Quinn, called his account of Columbus and the others who followed him *The Rediscovery of America*. J. H. Parry, an authority on Spanish explorers, said, "Columbus did not discover a new world; he established contact between two worlds, both already old."

ix

Soon after Columbus, mariners from Spain, France, England, Portugal, Holland, and Italy reached other parts of the Americas and helped define its geographical limits. Many of those who followed in the wake of Columbus made important discoveries, too, and should not be forgotten.

Among them were John Cabot, the first European since Leif Ericsson to set foot in North America; Pedro Cabral, who landed in Brazil; Amerigo Vespucci, who explored the coast of South America and gave his name to the Americas; Giovanni da Verrazzano, who mapped the eastern coast of the United States; Jacques Cartier, who sailed up the St. Lawrence River; and Juan Ponce de León and Hernando de Soto, who explored the southeastern United States while Álvar Núñez Cabeza de Vaca and Francisco Vasquez Coronado penetrated the southwest.

To native Americans, though, Columbus and the others were invaders trespassing on land that they already occupied. The real discoverers of America were the ancestors of the people who lived there when Columbus and the other Europeans arrived. Who were these native Americans and where did they come from?

Today it is generally accepted that they were descended from groups of prehistoric men and women who had crossed over the icy waters and lands of the Bering Strait from Asia into America about fifteen thousand years ago. Gradually, those early discoverers spread east to the Atlantic Ocean, south to Central and South America, and north to the Arctic Ocean. Although North and South America may have seemed empty to European eyes, the land was populated by millions of native Americans in communities that varied from hunting tribes to farming villages and major cities rivaling even some in Europe.

Columbus was the first to bring word back to Europe of that new land and its people across the ocean to the west, opening a great era of exploration, conquest, and colonization. The story of the discoverers who preceded Columbus, of Columbus himself, and of the discoverers who came after him is told in the pages that follow.

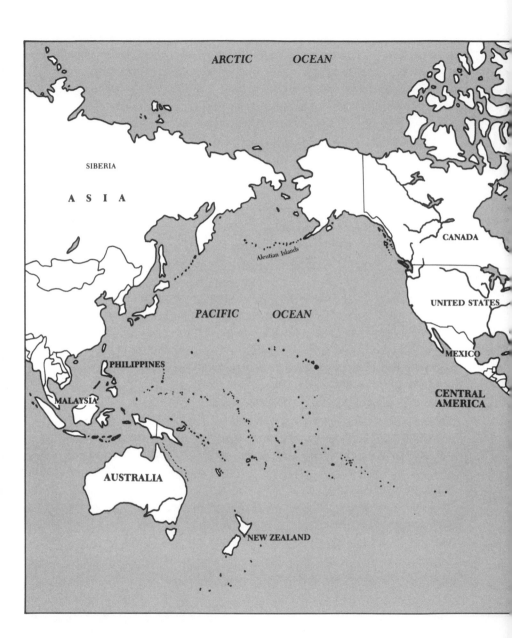

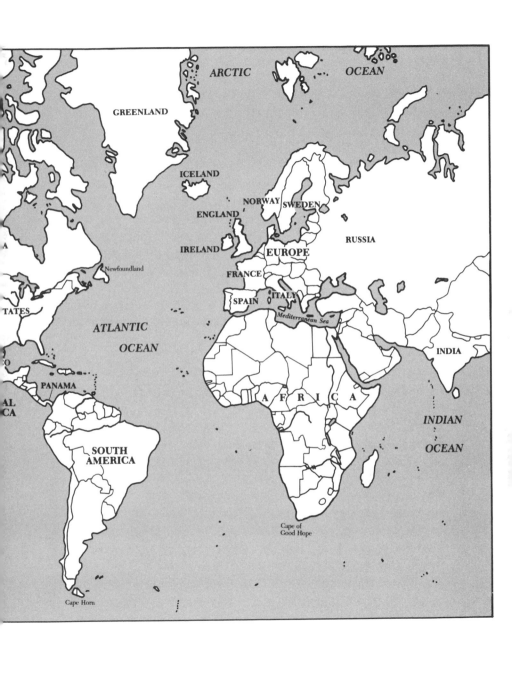

ARCTIC OCEAN

GREENLAND

ICELAND

NORWAY SWEDEN

ENGLAND

IRELAND

EUROPE

RUSSIA

Newfoundland

FRANCE

SPAIN ITALY

Mediterranean Sea

TATES

INDIA

ATLANTIC
OCEAN

A F R I C A

PANAMA

INDIAN

AL
CA

OCEAN

SOUTH
AMERICA

Cape of
Good Hope

Cape Horn

❧ 1 ❧

The First Americans

ON A SPRING MORNING IN 1908, GEORGE MCJUNKIN, A BLACK COW-
boy, rode his horse along the edge of a dry stream in New Mexico,
looking for a stray cow. He peered down at the sandy bottom of
the streambed, searching for hoofprints of the missing animal.
Suddenly he saw something glittering white in the blazing hot sun.

McJunkin got off his horse to take a closer look at what seemed
to be bones jutting out from the bank of the stream. He pulled
out his knife and worked the bones free. As he did so, a stone
fragment, looking somewhat like a point of a spear, also fell out.
To McJunkin, the bones seemed much larger than the bones of
an ordinary cow.

He carried the unusual bones and the spear point back to the
ranch house, not far from the town of Folsom, but no one paid
any attention to them then. There is no record of what happened
to McJunkin, but somehow, seventeen years later, in 1925, the
bones and the spear point arrived on the desk of Jesse Figgins,
director of the Colorado Museum of Natural History. Figgins, an
expert on fossil bones, identified them.

The bones came from an extinct form of a huge bison that had
roamed the plains of America thousands of years before at the
end of the Ice Age. But there was uncertainty about the spear

1

point. Was it used by prehistoric hunters to kill the bison? If so, it meant that people lived in America more than ten thousand years ago, longer than most archaeologists thought. Or was it of more recent origin, by coincidence in the same place as the bones?

To find out, Figgins went back to the Folsom site in New Mexico in 1926. He dug out more bison bones and more stone weapons. Still, other archaeologists were not convinced. They said it was possible that the stone spear points had somehow gotten mixed up with the bones long after the bison were killed.

Figgins returned to Folsom in 1927. This time when he found more bones and spear points he left them in place. He invited several colleagues to come and see for themselves. They flocked to Folsom and saw one of the spear points between two ribs of the animal skeleton. It convinced them that some ancient hunter had killed that ancient bison, more than ten thousand years ago.

"In my hand, I hold the answer to the antiquity of man in America," said Dr. Barnum Brown from the American Museum of Natural History in New York, one of the groups Figgins had brought to Folsom.

That landmark find opened a new chapter in the search for the first discoverers of America. Experts seeking answers to the questions of who they were, where they came from, and when they came began sifting clues like detectives in a mystery story. And more clues kept being uncovered as archaeologists dug up animal bones and primitive weapons at sites throughout North and South America.

A few years later, in 1932, a second great discovery was made. Two amateur collectors discovered some mammal bones and stone projectiles along the shores of a dried-up ancient lake near Clovis, New Mexico. Between the ribs of some of the animals were two-by-five-inch spear points, much larger than the Folsom points, and extremely sharp. Which were older?

The answer came through careful examination of the sites near Clovis by archaeologists. They found some Clovis-type points in layers of soil underneath layers containing Folsom-type points. Obviously, the Clovis type was older.

But how old? If scientists could tell with some degree of certainty how old those bones or weapons were, they could also fix the time when prehistoric people lived in what is now the United States. A precise method of dating was discovered in 1949 by Dr. Willard Libby in his laboratory at the University of Chicago. He developed a system for determining the age of organic materials like bone by measuring the decay rates of a radioactive form of carbon, carbon-14. The key lay in the fact that carbon-14 is not replaced when an organism dies. Thus by measuring the amount of carbon-14 remaining in a specimen, one can tell how old it is.

Using that method, scientists fixed the date of the Folsom points at between eleven thousand and ten thousand years ago. The Clovis points were older, dating between eleven thousand five hundred and eleven thousand years ago. From the proliferation of sites they have uncovered, archaeologists now know that the Clovis people flourished all over the Americas more than eleven thousand years ago.

But were the people who used Clovis points the oldest Americans? Some scientists argued then and still argue today that there were indeed other men and women in the Americas prior to the Clovis people, perhaps dating back fifty thousand to forty thousand years ago, or longer.

Recent discoveries in the Bluefish Caves in Canada's Yukon area have revealed flaked bones of mammoths, possibly indicating some toolmaking and butchering about twenty-four thousand years ago. In some excavations in Chile, archaeologists have found clay-lined hearths, stone tools, and bone implements thirteen thousand years old. Newly discovered rock shelters in Brazil have convinced at least one scientist that humans occupied them forty-five thousand years ago.

But the prevailing archaeological opinion is that there is not sufficient evidence to prove that people lived in the Americas before those who used the typical Clovis spear points and tools about eleven thousand five hundred years ago.

If the Clovis people were the first Americans, where did they come from? How did they get here and how did they develop into the great number and diversity of native American tribes that the Europeans found when they rediscovered America?

It is now generally believed that the story begins between forty thousand and thirty-five thousand years ago when small bands of Homo sapiens, men and women appearing much like those of today, suddenly appeared in Africa, the Near East, and Asia. With greater brain power and better tools than the primitive Neanderthals, they began to spread out, even into the inhospitable cold climate of Russia and Siberia.

They were essentially hunters, using stone weapons to kill mammoths, woolly rhinoceros, bison, and reindeer for food. They also trapped birds, caught salmon and perch, and gathered wild vegetables to eat. As local game herds disappeared under hunting pressure, bands of men, women, and children moved north and east in quest of food until they reached the area of what we now call the Bering Strait.

Today it is a natural sea barrier between Asia and America, but between twenty-five thousand and fifteen thousand years ago there was no water there. At that time, the period of the last great Ice Age, glaciers covered most of northern America, including parts of the United States. With so much water locked up in the ice, the level of the sea dropped more than three hundred feet. That exposed the landmass of Beringia, a dry plain between Siberia and Alaska.

Beringia was a frigid, inhospitable land, treeless and sparsely vegetated, with strong winter winds that made it seem even colder. But it did support a population of woolly mammoths, bison, reindeer, and other grazing animals that ate the scattered grasses and vegetation.

The scenario, as outlined by some leading experts, holds that bands of primitive people from Asia gradually wandered into Beringia in pursuit of big game. It is not surprising that no evidence of human habitation—weapons, stone points, or even animal bones—has been found there, because since the end of the Ice Age it has been covered with water again.

From Beringia, most of the experts say, bands of these hunting people trickled south and east about fifteen thousand years ago—first into what is Alaska today, and then farther south, always searching for food. However, recent evidence indicates that some of the first Americans may not have been primarily big-game hunters, but maritime people, living on a plentiful supply of fish, sea mammals, and birds in the Pacific Ocean.

Either walking or using boats made of skin, these maritime people followed the coastline of Siberia and Beringia into Alaska. Traces of them have been found in fishhooks and harpoons uncovered along the coast and on the islands in the Pacific Ocean off Alaska.

Whether along the coast or on ice-free passages inland, those migrant hunters and wandering fishermen were truly the discoverers of America. It was then a virgin land occupied only by vegetation and Ice Age mammals, such as the mammoths, mastodons, ground sloths that reached twenty feet in length, beaver with huge teeth, giant bears, lionlike cats, antelope, and long-horned bison.

As the Ice Age ended and the climate moderated, those early Americans found themselves in a changing environment. On a game-rich continent providing an abundance of food, they flourished, but as their numbers increased rapidly, they killed so many animals for food that the available herds dwindled. Some of the proliferating bands of hunters moved steadily onward to other areas, ever searching for more big game.

Over the centuries, the migrants from Asia pushed south into Mexico, Central America, and South America, until their descendants occupied the western hemisphere from the Arctic Circle to the Strait of Magellan. Archaeologists have traced their early expansion by uncovering the distinctive Clovis points—the sharpened stone points used as weapons—throughout Canada, the Great Plains of the United States, Mexico, Panama, and farther south.

While the prevailing scientific opinion is unanimous about the Asiatic origins of the first Americans, over the years other explanations have been presented. Most Indians in the United States today do not accept the theory that their ancestors came across the Bering Strait thousands of years ago. They believe that specific tribes were placed on the land they lived on by their Creator in the distant past. That is why, over the years, they have strongly resisted being moved from their lands by encroaching white settlers.

And then there are other less plausible theories. One held that the Indians are the descendants of the ten lost tribes of Israel. Another that they came from the lost continent of Atlantis in the Atlantic Ocean. Still another that they are descended from wandering Scandinavians, Ethiopians, Chinese, Polynesians, Egyptians, or Phoenicians.

While no one can say for sure that a boat containing people from Asia or Africa or the Polynesian Islands could not have been driven to the Americas by storms at any time, it seems reasonable to assume that no such chance landing could be the basis for a large native population. Nor is there any scientific evidence to show, much less prove, that humans could have originated in any part of America. Almost everyone accepts as a fact that the first Americans were those wandering bands of prehistoric men and women who came through the now-lost land of Beringia.

But how could they multiply and spread so rapidly?

First, the population grew over ten thousand years, which is a long time in the history of the human race. Add to that the discovery of a land where food was abundant in the form of a wide variety of animals and where the soil was fertile enough to support agriculture.

Second, some scientists have calculated that if some of those ancient people moved south at the rate of four miles a year, they could have easily reached the southern United States in about five hundred years. At the same rate, some of the Indians could have reached the southern tip of South America in about one thousand years. Indeed, evidence of human habitation dating back to 9300 B.C. has been uncovered in caves at the southern tip of South America.

About eight thousand years ago, the climate of the Americas stabilized into roughly what it is today. Ice remained in the Arctic areas, the eastern part of the United States became forested, grasses covered the Great Plains, scrubby vegetation struggled in the southwestern deserts, and rain forests thrived in the tropical areas of South America.

As the descendants of the original wanderers spread out over two continents—North and South America and the islands around them—they adapted to different climatic and environmental surroundings and blossomed into a spectacular diversity. But all of them retained traits of their Mongoloid ancestry: brown skin, dark eyes, and straight black hair.

Separated by geography and distance, the native American tribes developed different and complex systems of religion, government, agriculture, astronomy, and architecture, as well as language, pottery, weaving, and ceramics. When their daily lives are compared with their contemporaries in Europe and Asia at the time of the rediscovery of America, they come out very well. Mostly they lived in harmony with their natural surroundings.

The Indians spoke more than four hundred different languages. They constructed houses of stone and complex irrigation systems in the American Southwest. In the frigid north, they developed technologies of survival that are truly marvelous. In many places they invented farming techniques that enabled them to store surpluses for survival in the winter or lean times. And in Mexico and Peru, their cities rivaled those of Europe in size and complexity.

From the simple hunting-fishing people of the Arctic Circle to the complex empires of Mexico and Peru, the descendants of those first Americans built relatively stable societies, with governments suited to their local needs. Without money, they lived in communal societies, with religions and elaborate codes of ethics that met tribal purposes, although they sometimes confused Europeans. Without written languages, they created complex legends, song, dance, ceremonials, and art to remind them of their past, traditions, and gods.

By the time the first Europeans came, tens of millions of native Americans occupied the land. No one knows how many there were, but the Europeans found large numbers of people wherever they went. The prevailing opinion of historians is that there were at least forty million people, possibly fifty million, in the Americas when the first Spanish discoverers came.

Who were they and where were they?

✌ 2 ✌

The Native Americans

WHEN THE WHITE REDISCOVERERS OF AMERICA CAME, THEY FOUND two continents and numerous islands occupied by hundreds of different Indian tribes. Some were simple hunter-gatherers of food, but many had developed communities dependent on farming. A few had built mighty empires, with large cities as their capitals and complex societies that rivaled any in Europe. The native people of America were anything but the savages described by some of the first Europeans.

From north to south, here is a brief overview of the inhabitants of America at the time of the arrival of the Europeans.

THE ARCTIC

The northern rim of North America stretched in desolation, covered with snow and ice fields reaching to a horizon without end, surrounded by ice packs and frigid water. Yet its seas provided an abundance of whales, seals, walruses, sea lions, and fish. On its shores were caribou, musk oxen, and migratory birds, food for the Aleuts, who settled down along the Bering Strait in Alaska.

Farther east, another group of primitive people—the predecessors of the modern Eskimos—had started out as hunters of caribou and musk oxen. They spread over thousands of miles of the northern Arctic until they reached Greenland. With so much water nearby, they became skilled walrus and whale hunters, using harpoons. They also developed a remarkable technology of survival with warm clothing, mostly of animal skins, and housing of snow and ice.

Their descendants call themselves Inuits, but others know them as Eskimos. In that rigorous climate, they developed the skill of storytelling to help pass the long winter nights. Their art, too, became an integral part of their life. Their tools, for example, were not only useful, they were beautiful. As one scientist put it, in the far north where life is reduced to the basics for survival, it turns out that one of those essentials is art.

THE SUB-ARCTIC

A vast area of more than two million square miles stretches from Alaska to Labrador in what today is northern Canada. The ancient peoples who discovered that land sustained themselves on the herds of caribou that wandered over its vast areas of tundra, bogs, forests, and mountains. They also hunted moose, snowshoe rabbit, and other game wherever they could find it. Above all, they prized the black bear, because its abundant fat was a necessity in the cold climate, where the winters were long and dark.

With little vegetation available, hunting became the primary occupation of the men, while making clothing—mostly of animal skins—and providing for the family became traditional women's work. Over the centuries, these people lived in small hunting bands because the barren areas had little capacity to provide for wandering animals. With the coming of the first whites, the natives' economy shifted somewhat to supplying furs for traders, but they remained in small hunting units.

THE NORTHWEST

An area of relative plenty, the Northwest coast stretches fifteen hundred miles from Alaska to Washington and Oregon, bounded on the east by thickly forested mountains. The earliest inhabitants discovered an abundance of sea mammals, land animals, and fish, notably the salmon racing up coastal rivers to spawn. Unlike most other native Americans, who had to work hard to survive in hostile environments, the Northwest peoples found the living comparatively easy and enjoyed a rich ceremonial life.

They lived in permanent, substantial rectangular wooden houses, accumulating and displaying their wealth. Conspicuous consumption was a primary objective of Northwest society in a ceremony called potlatch, an Indian word for *giving*. Potlatches were held when a tribal chief celebrated an important event—a marriage, the death of a predecessor, the birth of a son. Not only were there speeches, songs, and dance, but elaborate foods were served and many gifts were given to the guests to demonstrate the chief's status, as well as that of his kin, tribe, and village.

THE PLAINS AND PRAIRIES

From the Mississippi River to the Rocky Mountains, the prairies and Great Plains stretch as far as the eye can see. Largely dry, they sustain short buffalo grass in the west and mixed taller grasses farther east. The plains supported large numbers of bison (often called buffalo later) as well as deer, antelope, elk, and other animals. At the end of the Ice Age, hunters and their families followed the mammoths and a now extinct form of the early bison to the plains.

In the northern part of the region—in what is Wyoming, Montana, and Alberta today—the prehistoric people were wanderers. Using light tepees made of bison hides, they made camp quickly as they moved through the country, settling temporarily near streams and sheltered areas where bison congregated.

THE NORTHEAST

In the vast area between the Mississippi River and the Atlantic Ocean, many different Indian bands discovered lands in which they could live and thrive. In Ohio, the Adena people built villages and evolved elaborate ceremonies to remember their dead, burying them in mounds that are still being excavated today. They were followed by the Hopewell and Mississippi cultures, which produced the most complex American societies north of Mexico. At Cahokia, in what is now Illinois, a city of perhaps ten thousand people developed, surrounding a gigantic mound about ten stories high, presumably used for religious purposes.

Along the forested eastern seaboard, many tribes made maximum use of its natural resources, the sea for fish, the forests for animals, and even used fire to clear fields to grow crops like corn and squash. Some, particularly the Iroquois of New York, lived in villages of longhouses, each more than a hundred feet long, depending on hunting and agriculture for food. Many of these tribes waged war on one another, until a chief called the Peacemaker persuaded the five major Iroquois tribes to unite in a confederation, just before the Europeans arrived.

THE SOUTHEAST

All over the Southeast, mounds built of earth dot the countryside, remnants of the culture of the early inhabitants of the area. Temple mounds served religious purposes, and burial mounds were raised over the bodies of chiefs and other leaders. Some of the elite built mounds for their homes, while other mounds served as defensive forts. Today archaeologists find these mounds treasure troves of artifacts, indicating how the people of the Southeast lived in prehistoric times.

About six thousand years ago, farming began to supplant the mere gathering of acorns and other natural products for food. Soon agriculture became the basis for life, with villages and cities becoming the centers of thriving societies. In western Alabama, for example, the town of Moundville served as the religious, political, and economic center for about twenty thousand people who lived nearby. Farther east, the Cherokees numbered more than sixty thousand people in at least one hundred different settlements.

THE SOUTHWEST

Perhaps the most remarkable example of adaptation to hostile environment was that of the prehistoric Americans who discovered the arid desert lands of what is now the southwestern United States. The ancestors of those early southwestern people arrived in the area as far back as eleven thousand years ago and somehow survived, hunting and gathering food until they developed an agriculture that used scarce water resources carefully. Today many Americans know them and their descendants because of their magnificent pottery and their cliffside pueblo dwellings.

Three major cultures developed in the late prehistoric period: the Mongollon, the Hohokam, and the Anasazi. The Mongollons, who were master potters, lived in southwestern and eastern Arizona. In the Sonoran Desert to the west, the Hohokams—"the vanished ones" in modern Pima language—built hundreds of miles of canals to channel water for their agriculture. To the north lived the Anasazi—"the cliff dwellers"—who congregated in villages in higher elevations. They were the builders of Mesa Verde and Pueblo Bonito, with great cliff houses, some of them containing as many as several hundred rooms.

THE FAR WEST

From desertlike Utah to the rich California coast, the early Far West became the home of a diversity of peoples and cultures. In the arid Great Basin in and around Utah, primitive peoples survived with difficulty from year to year, living in small bands and wandering in search of food. They hunted for small animals such as rabbits but depended more on gathering nuts, seeds, and insects as a food supply. Unlike the southeastern people who made beautiful pots to store their food, the Great Basin people wove intricate baskets of reeds and other vegetation.

In the more hospitable climate of California, with its seacoast, mountains, and central valley, a variety of cultures emerged. Along the southern coast, the people lived on the bounty of the sea—a rich source of sea mammals, tuna, and sardines. Inland, they hunted for deer and gathered pine nuts, seeds, and acorns. California's population of Indians grew rapidly—to as many as three hundred fifty thousand at the time the Spanish arrived. But they remained in small, independent communities, speaking as many as one hundred different languages.

MEXICO AND CENTRAL AMERICA

The archaeologists call it Mesoamerica—the area south of the United States, including Mexico and most of Central America. It lies largely within the tropics but contains a diversity of climates and environments, ranging from jungles to icy mountain peaks. Rich in wild plants, the lush land provided abundant food for prehistoric tribes. They cultivated beans, pumpkins, squash, chili peppers, and, above all, maize, or corn. Primitive corn was very small compared with the corn we eat today. But it became a major crop and, together with other plants, a primary factor in converting the early hunters into farmers.

The development of agriculture made possible the growth of villages, cities, and, finally, the great empires of Mexico. Although many less advanced peoples lived in the lowlands of Mexico and Central America, on the coastal plain near the present-day city of Vera Cruz the Olmec civilization suddenly emerged. Today it is remembered by the massive carved stone heads that can be seen in museums, but in its time, about 900–400 B.C., the Olmec civilization exerted political and military influence from central Mexico south to El Salvador.

As the Olmecs faded, the astonishingly rapid rise of the city of Teotihuacán in central Mexico began. It supported a population of two hundred thousand in about A.D. 500, rivaling, as one writer has said, the glories of ancient Rome and Greece. It grew because of an extensive irrigation system, which made it possible to raise crops to feed a large urban population. But as suddenly as it rose, Teotihuacán began to fall. For reasons unknown today, its population gradually moved away.

At the same time, the Mayan civilization to the south began to rise in the Yucatan Peninsula and Guatemala, flourishing in the six centuries between A.D. 300 and A.D. 900. The Mayan cities of Chichén Itzá, Copán, Uxmal, and Tikal became great centers of art and commerce. Of all the people in the Americas before the arrival of the Spanish, the Mayans reached the highest levels of science, devising very accurate calendars, for example. In addition, the Mayans developed a fully literate culture, carving into their stone monuments hieroglyphic accounts of their accomplishments.

Once again, that civilization collapsed, and no one really knows why. As the Mayans declined, the Toltecs of the city of Tula to the north expanded. They, in turn, were succeeded by the Aztecs, who constructed the most spectacular of all pre-Columbian civilizations in North America. They came into the central valley of Mexico from the south and by 1345 began to build the fabulous city of Tenochtitlán on an island in a lake where the present Mexico City stands. At the time of the Spanish conquest, Tenochtitlán, with a population of two hundred thousand, was the largest city in the world except for London.

At the beginning of the sixteenth century, the Aztec empire stretched from the Atlantic Ocean to the Pacific and as far south as Nicaragua, controlling a population of perhaps ten million people. A commercial and manufacturing center, Tenochtitlán was supported by an elaborate system of farming on raised beds in swampy areas in the Valley of Mexico. At the top of the political pyramid was an emperor, supported by a large army of warriors and tax collectors. To Europeans, one of the barbaric customs of the Aztecs was human sacrifice, a sacred religious rite for them. The Aztecs waged war to collect captive warriors to be sacrificed to their gods.

The Aztec empire expanded through aggression. The Aztecs

warred against and conquered their neighbors. But their subject peoples constantly rebelled. Although these rebellions were put down by force, the Aztec neighbors retained a fierce hostility against their conquerors and later, when the Spaniards came, made an alliance to topple the cruel tyrants.

SOUTH AMERICA

From the islands north of South America to the Strait of Magellan, the continent filled with a diversity of peoples, ranging from the naked Indians of the tropical islands found by Columbus to elaborately dressed Inca nobles. The largest area occupied by the Indians was the basin of the Amazon River, covered by tropical forests. Even though the Indians there lived in widely scattered villages, the population of Amazonia around the time the Europeans arrived has been put at about five million.

The Indian discoverers of South America came down the narrow Isthmus of Panama as early as eleven thousand years ago. Some spread east toward modern Venezuela and then south into present-day Brazil. Along the northern coast, a few used primitive vessels to discover and occupy the small islands to the north and Haiti and Cuba. But the major dispersal was south along the Pacific coast, hemmed in by the towering snow-capped Andes Mountains to the east.

Recent discoveries have shown that complex societies appeared and flowered between five thousand and thirty-five hundred years ago in the area of today's Peru. Archaeologists working in the narrow river valleys that plunge to the Pacific have found the remains of stepped pyramids and huge U-shaped temples, some more than ten stories high. They predate the Mayas in the Yucatan by more than two thousand years and the Aztecs in Mexico by three thousand years.

But the highest level of cultural development in South America was reached later in the central Andes Mountains, in a long narrow strip encompassing the modern nations of Ecuador, Peru, Bolivia, and northern Chile. There the Incan empire flowered for a brief time in the 1400s and early 1500s, with splendid buildings, including a vast temple to the sun, where thousands worshipped before the Spanish conquest.

Based in the valley of Cuzco, the ancient Incan empire was ruled by a mild despot, supported by a large number of nobles. At its height, the population reached ten million people. The Incas built elaborate roads of stone to tie their empire together, as well as magnificent bridges of wood and stone, aqueducts and canals for water, large stone buildings for worship, and terraces for agriculture.

Like the Aztecs, the Incan empire expanded through aggression, gradually conquering its neighbors in all directions. It was an endless struggle to maintain the empire because of constant revolts by the subject peoples. Although these revolts were put down cruelly, the hatred persisted, as did rebellion. The Inca rulers fought for an empire; their subjects fought for small plots of land on which to grow food to live.

On their irrigated terraces, the Incas grew what one modern writer called an "agricultural wonderland," with more than seventy different crops. Among them were the now-familiar potato and lima bean, but also exotic white, yellow, and purple roots, beans that pop like corn, grains rich in protein, and a wide variety of papayas, pineapples, and bananas. Overlooked by the world for centuries, many of these crops are now being investigated to see if they can be used today.

The Incas were also rich in precious metals—gold and silver, which they used as jewelry and decoration. That led to their downfall, for when the Spanish discoverers of America heard about the vast riches of the Incas, they came and conquered.

⮞ 3 ⮜

Norsemen

ABOUT FIVE HUNDRED YEARS BEFORE COLUMBUS, A NORSEMAN NAMED
Biarni Heriulfson set sail in a small ship from Norway to visit his
father in Iceland. It was the year 986, when Scandinavia was the
leading seapower of Europe. At a time when Spanish, French,
English, and Portuguese ships dared not sail out of sight of land,
hardy sailors from Norway and Sweden ventured boldly in all
directions—to Ireland, to Iceland, to Greenland, and as far south
as the Mediterranean Sea.

Not much is known about Biarni. He was a young merchant,
only twenty years old, accustomed to spending each winter with
his father. In a ship laden with cargo, he sailed to Iceland but
found that his father had gone on to the new Norse colony of
Greenland, some distance to the west. Biarni had never been to
Greenland, but he and his crew decided to follow his father there.

They set sail for the unknown land, but a storm blew them off
course. When they saw the sun again, they continued on their
course to the west. Several days later, they saw a level land covered
with woods in front of them. It could not be Greenland, they
decided, because there were no mountains.

So they went on, this time to the north. Once again they saw
flat land in the distance. It could not be Greenland, said Biarni,

18

quoted in an old Icelandic saga, "because in Greenland there are said to be many great ice-mountains." His crew suggested that they land to take on both water and wood, but Biarni, apparently impatient to complete his journey, refused.

Turning away from the land, he sailed to the east and made landfall several days later in Greenland, where his father lived. Although he had not set foot on the far shore of the lands to the west, he had discovered America—Labrador and Baffin Island—and did not know it.

Today the name of Biarni Heriulfson is forgotten except in the sagas of the Norsemen. But, as the historian Samuel Eliot Morison has said, "Let us give Biarni Heriulfson his due as the earliest, Number One, indubitable European discoverer of America."

Even though he did not know that he had discovered a new world, Biarni talked about his voyage. One of those who heard his tale was Leif Ericsson, son of Eric the Red, the man who had discovered Greenland. Eric, known as "the red" because of the color of his hair, had a dramatic past.

A fighting man, he was exiled from Iceland after a quarrel in which he killed two men. Having heard from a friend that there might be land to the west of Iceland, he sailed toward the setting sun and discovered an island with good harbors and some pasture land. He called it Greenland because, he said, people might be attracted there "if the country had a good name."

On his return to Iceland, Eric organized an expedition to found a colony on the west coast of Greenland. He and his wife, Thorhild, built a home in one of the more pleasant and fertile areas and called it Brattahlid. They had three sons, Thorstein, Leif, and Thorvald. Eric also had a daughter, Freydis, by another woman.

Leif sailed to Norway in the year 999 and paid his respects to the king, Olaf Tryggvason. One day, according to the saga, the king asked him, "Is it thy purpose to sail to Greenland in the summer?"

"It is my purpose, if it be your will," replied Leif.

"I believe it will be well and thither thou shalt go upon my errand to proclaim Christianity there," the king ordered.

When his ship was ready the following year, Leif sailed. Following the orders of the king, he proclaimed the Christian faith in Greenland. His mother, Thorhild, warmly embraced the new religion and built the first Christian church in Greenland, but his father, Eric, remained a pagan until he died.

Back home, Leif heard about the discovery of Biarni Heriulfson and determined to learn more about those strange new lands. He had a good reason: The settlers of Greenland had no wood because no trees grew there. Perhaps those new lands that Biarni had found could provide timber for houses.

Leif visited Biarni, listened to his story, and bought his boat. No one knows what it looked like, but other ships of the same period were small and crude. Most of the Norse sailing ships were about fifty-four feet long and fourteen feet wide, made mostly of oak. Each ship had one big square sail mounted on a large mast. It had no cooking facilities; presumably the crew ate cold meats and bread and drank beer.

After collecting a crew of thirty-five men, Leif asked his father to become leader of the expedition. As they rode from their home toward the ship, Eric fell from his horse, injuring his leg.

"It is not designed for me to discover more lands than the one in which we are now living," he said, taking the fall as an omen not to go on a new journey.

Leif, then twenty-one years old and "a big strapping fellow, handsome to look at, thoughtful and temperate in all things," took command and sailed in the year 1000. Unlike Biarni's voyage, by all accounts this one was uneventful.

After a few days at sea, he and his crew spied land. Anchoring their ship, they went ashore on flat rock and saw in the distance great ice mountains. Clearly, it was a land without any good qualities. Leif gave it the name of Helluland, meaning "country of the flat stones." Today historians believe that Leif's first landing in America was on Baffin Island, off the east coast of Canada.

Turning south, Leif and his crew sailed a short distance and found another new land. They landed on a broad stretch of white sand in front of a level land covered with trees. Leif decided to call it Markland, or "land of the forests." It was the eastern coast of Labrador.

Not satisfied, Leif once more sailed south and landed on a shore where a river flowed out of a lake. His crew took their leather sleeping bags ashore and built shelters. The words of the ancient saga then describe what happened:

They afterwards determined to establish themselves there for the winter, and they accordingly built a large house. There was no lack of salmon there either in the river or the lake, and larger salmon than they had ever seen before. The country thereabouts seemed to be possessed of such good qualities that cattle would need no fodder there during the winters. There was no frost there during the winters and the grass withered not. The days and nights there were of more nearly equal length than in Greenland or Iceland. On the shortest day of the winter, the sun was up between breakfast time and late afternoon.

When they had finished building their houses, one of their crew, called Tyrker the German, disappeared. A search party found him a short time later in high spirits.

"I have something to tell you," he said. "I have found vines and grapes."

"Is this indeed true?" Leif asked.

"Of a certainty it is true," Tyrker replied. "For I was born where there is no lack of either grapes or vines."

Then, according to the saga, Leif and his men loaded the boat with grapes as well as timber and sailed back to Greenland. Because of the plentiful growth of vines and grapes, Leif named the new land Vinland.

Unfortunately—because it is a good story—we know that grapes do not grow as far north as Newfoundland, where Leif landed. One botanist has suggested that they might have found wild red currants or gooseberries or mountain cranberries. Whatever Tyrker found, Vinland has remained to this day the name of the new land that Leif discovered.

Three more voyages to Vinland followed in the next few years, according to the Icelandic sagas. The first of these was led by Leif's brother Thorvald, who sailed to Vinland with thirty men in the year 1004. They found Leif's huts and spent a winter there, living mostly on fish.

During the next summer, they explored the area—and encountered the first native people. The Norsemen spotted three "skin boats"—what we call kayaks—each occupied by three men. For no apparent reason, the Norsemen attacked the natives, killing eight of them, but one escaped.

That aroused the local people. Armed with bows and arrows, they came out in a fleet of kayaks to get their revenge. The Norsemen, behind shields on their ship, repelled them. One arrow found its mark in Thorvald's side. When they pulled the arrow from his fatal wound, he said, "I notice I have put fat on my body. We have found a fruitful land, but we shall have little joy of it." He asked his crew to bury him there with a cross at his head and another at his feet, and they did so.

The Norsemen described their opponents as ugly black men with shaggy hair, large eyes, and broad faces. They called them Skrellings, a word meaning "barbarians." Scholars are still divided today about whether the Skrellings were Eskimos or Indians.

After burying Thorvald, the remaining Norsemen returned to Greenland and told the story of the strange Skrellings to Leif and the others. A few years later, another expedition was organized by Thorfinn Karlsevni, a rich man who had married Gudrid, the widow of Leif's other brother, Thorstein.

In 1009, in a serious attempt to establish a colony, he sailed to Vinland in three ships, with 160 men and a few women and many head of cattle. Among the women was Freydis, Leif's half sister, who showed that she was as tough a fighter as any of the Norse men.

Once more the Skrellings appeared, apparently in a fighting mood. On a pole, they raised a peculiar object—a large ball about the size of "a sheep's belly," according to the saga. They flung it at the invaders. It hit the ground with a loud explosion, frightening the Norsemen so much that they fled.

"Why do you flee from these wretches?" Freydis cried out. "Had I but a weapon, methinks, I would fight better than any one of you."

Picking up a sword lying next to a slain Norseman, she faced the approaching Skrellings. She slapped her breast with the naked sword and screamed like a hellcat. That frightened the Skrellings so much that they turned and fled back to their boats.

That autumn, Gudrid gave birth to a son, Snorri. Although he is not remembered today, he was the first white child born in America, back in the year 1009.

After the first winter, as the weather got warmer, the Skrellings came again, this time apparently in peace. The saga describes their visit:

A great troop of men came forth from out of the woods. The cattle were hard by, and the bull began to bellow and roar with a great noise, whereat the Skrellings were frightened and ran away, with their packs wherein were gray furs, sables, and all kinds of peltries. They fled toward Karlsevni's dwelling, and sought to effect an entrance into the house but Karlsevni caused the doors to be defended. Neither could understand the other's language. The Skrellings put down their bundles then, and loosed them, and offered their wares, but Karlsevni forbade his men to sell their weapons, and taking counsel with himself, he bade the women carry milk to the Skrellings, which they no sooner saw than they wanted to buy it, and nothing else. Now the outcome of the Skrellings' trading was that they carried their wares away in their stomachs, while they left their packs and peltries behind with Karlsevni and his companions, and went away.

Despite that peaceful exchange, trouble broke out when the Skrellings returned the following winter. One of the Skrellings was killed when he attempted to seize a Norse weapon. A battle followed in which many Skrellings were killed before they retreated. However, the incident convinced Karlsevni that he could not live there in peace, so he and the colonists returned to Greenland.

The third and final attempt to colonize Vinland came in the year 1014. It was organized by Freydis, the half sister of Leif Ericsson and the wife of a man called Thorvard. She convinced two brothers, Helgi and Finnbogi, who had just arrived from Iceland, that they could make a profit by voyaging to Vinland together. She and they, each in their own ship, would take thirty men and a few women, work together, and share the profits.

After they had landed in Vinland, Freydis became jealous of her partners because they had a larger ship than she had and began to quarrel with them. One night, after a discussion with them about the possibility of exchanging ships, she returned to her home. The saga continues:

She climbed into bed and awakened Thorvard with her cold feet and he asked her why she was so cold and wet. She answered with great passion: "I have been to the brothers to buy their ship, for I wished to have a larger vessel, but they received my overtures so ill, that they struck me and handled me very roughly . . . Poor wretch, wilt neither avenge my shame nor thine own?"

Unable to resist her taunts, Thorvard summoned his men and marched to the brothers' house. He seized the sleeping men, tied them up, and brought them outside. Freydis ordered them killed, and Thorvard did so. Five women were left, and Thorvard's men would not harm them.

"Hand me an ax," Freydis cried out.

With her own hand, she killed all the women. After the dreadful deed, Freydis, as the saga says, "was well content with her work."

When spring came, they loaded the brothers' ship with timber and other products and returned to Greenland. Although Freydis had warned the crew to say that the brothers and their men remained behind, some of them did tell the truth.

Leif thought it was a most shameful story. But he said, "I have no heart to punish my sister, Freydis, as she deserves, but this I predict of them, that there is little posterity for their offspring."

That ended the Norse effort to colonize Vinland. Although there may have been occasional ships that sailed to Vinland to gather wood to take back to Greenland, there is no historical record of any more trips there.

For years, historians have debated whether the Icelandic sagas were merely good stories or true accounts of the discovery of a new land. Some writers claimed that the Norsemen may have landed along the eastern coast of the United States, on Cape Cod, or at Newport, Rhode Island, or on Martha's Vineyard. But there is no evidence of that. As far west as Minnesota, a farmer once uncovered a stone bearing what was described as Norse writing. That was declared to be a hoax.

It wasn't until 1960 that real evidence emerged proving that the Norsemen had actually set foot in North America. A modern Norwegian named Helge Ingstad, who had done some research in Greenland, became convinced that Vinland did not mean "land of the grapes" but rather "land of the meadows," from the ancient Scandinavian word *vin,* meaning "meadow."

With his wife, Anne Stine, an archaeologist, Ingstad set out in 1960 to find Vinland. He explored the eastern coast of North America, starting with Rhode Island. Slowly traveling north, first to Maine and then to Nova Scotia, he found nothing. Eventually he came to Newfoundland. There at its northern tip, he saw a landscape matching the one described by Biarni at a place called L'Anse aux Meadows, a modern name meaning "the bay between the meadows."

Digging into some mounds yielded ancient foundations of several houses of various sizes, but that was no proof that they were of Norse origin. It wasn't until 1964 that Ingstad found conclusive evidence that Norse men and women had actually lived there. The evidence was only a simple bone needle of carved soapstone, the kind used in Norway and Greenland, but it was enough to convince the archaeologists. Added to that were carbon-14 readings of the age of the charred wood. They showed that the buried houses dated back to about the year 1000—the same date given by the Icelandic sagas for the first voyage of Leif Ericsson.

Ingstad concluded:

To judge by all the material available to us, it is probable that the Northmen who stayed in L'Anse aux Meadows about a thousand years ago are identical with the Vinland voyagers of the Icelandic sagas. It is also probable that it was there that Leif Ericsson built his big house. We must assume that the Vinland of the saga was northernmost Newfoundland.

At about the same time, a so-called Vinland map was bought by Yale University. It showed "the island of Vinland discovered by Biarni and Leif in company" west of Greenland. However, scholars doubted that it was authentic, and subsequent inquiries showed that the map was a fake.

Today no one doubts that Biarni and Leif did "discover" America. The Norsemen came, they lived in America for a short time, and they left behind the sagas of their adventures. But they made no lasting impact either on America or on Europe. It wasn't until almost five hundred years later that the rediscovery of America changed both it and the world.

〜 4 〜

Young Columbus

WE KNOW HOW THE STORY ENDED: CHRISTOPHER COLUMBUS "DIS-covered" America on October 12, 1492. But how did it start? Who was Columbus? Where did he come from? How did he make his voyage of discovery?

For the beginning, we have to go back into the ancient municipal records of the city of Genoa, on the northwest coast of the Italian peninsula. In the fifteenth century it was a major maritime republic, one of four in Italy (along with Venice, Pisa, and Amalfi). Ships arrived and left the protected harbor of Genoa to ply the Mediterranean Sea to and from Africa, the Near East, and the Aegean Sea.

In those days, long before Italy became a nation, its people always referred to themselves as citizens of the city-state in which they were born: Rome, Venice, Florence, Siena, or Genoa. Columbus was always proud of his Genoese heritage. In his will, for example, he charged his heirs "always to work for the honor, welfare and increase of the city of Genoa."

In Europe, Genoa was particularly known for its mapmakers, who supplied charts for most of the ships of the Mediterranean Sea. Even the bold sailors of Portugal went to Genoa for the most accurate new maps of the world they sailed in.

27

Columbus came from a family of weavers. His grandfather, Giovanni Columbo, made cloth in a village not far from Genoa. At the age of eleven, Columbo's son, Domenico, was apprenticed to a weaver in Genoa. Domenico became a master weaver himself and in 1445 married Susanna Fontanarossa, the daughter of another weaver.

In October of 1451, a son was born and named Cristoforo, after St. Cristoforo (who we know as St. Christopher). In later years, he was also called Christoferrus de Columbo in Genoa, Christobal Colom in Portugal, Cristobal Colon in Spain, and Christopher Columbus in England and America. Today he is known as Christopher Columbus in the United States but Cristobal Colon in the Spanish-speaking world.

Soon after his birth came more children in the Columbo family: a son, Bartholomew; still another son, Giovanni, who died as a young man; a daughter named Bianchinetta, about whom little is known; and, much later, a son, Giacomo, called Diego, who became one of Christopher's favorites.

Not much is known about Christopher's mother, but from the dusty records in the municipal archives, historians have dug out some facts about his father. He owned his own looms, bought wool, wove it into cloth, and sold the finished product.

But he apparently failed as a businessman. For example, the records show that the cheese merchant who married his daughter, Bianchinetta, had to sue Domenico Columbo for the dowry that had been promised for her wedding. In 1470, Domenico moved to the nearby coastal village of Savona, where he hoped his fortunes would improve by opening a small tavern to sell wine as well as weaving.

Little is known about Christopher in his growing years, but we catch traces of him in a few legal documents that have been preserved. In late 1470, then nineteen years old, he signed a paper acknowledging a debt for wines delivered to his father. In 1472, he witnessed a will in Savona and later that year with his father contracted to purchase a quantity of wool and pay for it in cloth.

By that time he was twenty-one years old, a grown man who

had had very little formal education. He was slightly taller than average, with a light complexion, blondish-red hair, blue eyes, and an aquiline nose. He was faithful in his religious duties, and he helped his father in the weaver's trade.

Like many young men of the seaport city of Genoa, Columbus dreamed of great deeds at sea. There are conflicting stories about when he first became a sailor—when he was fourteen years old, when he was twenty-one, or even later. We don't know, but it was probable that his father would send him along the coast in a small sailing vessel back to Genoa to buy wool, wine, and cheeses, and to sell cloth.

It seems likely that he made his first real sea trip in 1472 on a Genoese ship sailing in the Mediterranean Sea. His first long voyage was made either in 1474 or 1475, when his native city sent out an expedition to trade with and defend the Genoese colony of Chios, a far-off island near the Turkish coast. An ordinary sea hand then, he learned how to sail, manage a boat, estimate distances, and other elements of seamanship.

That trip ended peacefully. But in 1476, when most of the Mediterranean states were involved in war, Columbus's next voyage turned into disaster. He went to sea as a sailor on a convoy of five Genoese ships to trade with Portugal, England, and France. Off the coast of Portugal, they were attacked by a much larger fleet of French pirates.

By nightfall, three of the Genoese ships, including the one on which Columbus sailed, were in flames. Caught in the fire, many of the sailors jumped into the sea. Those who could not swim drowned. But Columbus, an expert swimmer, grasped a piece of floating wood. Alternately pushing and resting, he swam about six miles to the Portuguese shore. He made his way to Lisbon, where members of the local Genoese community cared for him until he recovered.

At that time, the small kingdom of Portugal was one of Europe's leading seafaring nations. It occupied a strategic position, facing west into the Atlantic and south toward Africa. Its ships traded with the Muslim cities of North Africa, ventured south along the western coast of Africa, north to England and France, and a little bit into the unknown ocean to the west to Madeira and the Azores, about seven hundred miles away.

Columbus arrived in Portugal only a few days after the death in 1460 of Dom Henrique, called Prince Henry the Navigator in English. At his headquarters in Cape St. Vincent, which was not only the southwestern tip of Portugal but of Europe as well, this remarkable man had organized a school for maritime discovery. He collected maps and sailing instructions from all parts of the world, hired pilots to organize geographic information, designed more seaworthy ships, and then sent them out on voyages of exploration in all directions.

Thus by chance, Columbus was washed ashore in a nation in a ferment of discovery. Year by year, Portuguese ships returned from dangerous trips farther and farther south along the west coast of Africa, seeking a new way to the riches of the Far East, especially spices and gold. They sailed into unknown waters, because the known routes to the Indies through the eastern end of the Mediterranean Sea were blocked by the Moors and the Turks.

Columbus, an unknown, penniless seaman from Genoa, had to find some way to earn a living in Portugal, so he shipped out again as a sailor in 1477 on a trading ship bound for Ireland and Iceland. In the following year, a merchant in Lisbon hired him to sail to Madeira and to purchase sugar for delivery to Genoa, an indication that the young sailor, then twenty-seven years old, was rising in the world.

Like many of his fellow Genoese, he found a congenial home in Lisbon, then as now one of the most beautiful seaports in the world. After his brother Bartholomew opened a chart-making establishment there, Columbus joined him as a partner. He developed into a skilled mapmaker, but, more important, he became acquainted with the latest information about the world and its geography from letters, books, and charts from all the European nations.

He also learned to speak Portuguese and Castilian Spanish, the languages of the leading explorers of the sea, as well as Latin, which was the tongue of learned men of the past and of educated people of his world. Although he had little formal education, he studied basic mathematics and astronomy, essentials for navigation. As a mapmaker, he talked with other seamen and ship captains about their voyages and findings.

He also fell in love while attending Mass in a church in Lisbon. Not much is known about the woman he met there, who became his wife, except her name, Dona Filipa Perestrelo e Moniz, the daughter of a noble family in reduced circumstances. She was about twenty-five years old at the time of their marriage, but we do not know the date or time of their wedding. The record of the marriage has disappeared, but historians have concluded that the ceremony took place in 1479, when Columbus was twenty-eight years old.

At first, he and his wife lived with her widowed mother, Dona Isabel Moniz, who told them stories about her life with her husband on the island of Porto Santo near Madeira. She also gave Columbus writings and sea charts left by her husband. Soon thereafter, Columbus and his wife went to live in Porto Santo, where her brother was the governor. Their only child, Diego, was born there in 1480.

Little is known about what the Columbus family did in the next few years. After his wife died some time in that period, Columbus made another voyage, still only as a seaman, south to La Mina, a Portuguese trading post in a gold-mining area on the Gulf of Guinea on the west coast of Africa (in what is Ghana today).

Columbus was greatly impressed by the gold mines there and by the riches they supplied to Portugal. He also learned much from his Portuguese shipmates, observing the pilots at work navigating the ship. He also learned how to handle a ship in heavy winds, what kinds of stores to take on a long voyage, and how to trade with primitive people. Above all, he gained confidence that with a good ship under him and with the help of God, he could sail anywhere.

On his return to Lisbon, Columbus was thirty years old, an experienced seaman ready to make his mark on the world, even though he had not yet commanded a ship at sea. Somehow during those years in Portugal, Columbus became convinced that he could reach the Indies by sailing due west into the unknown Atlantic Ocean. Once there, he expected to find spices, pearls, and gold, enough to make him rich. Neither he nor anyone else expected to find a new continent.

For Europeans of that time, the Indies included China, Japan, and the islands to the south. Everyone knew the story of Marco Polo, who had returned from China with stories of its fabulous wealth and of the gold-roofed and gold-paved palaces of Japan (which he had not seen).

Just as important to the Europeans were the products of the Spice Islands, a group of six small islands south of the Philippines near the equator (now part of Indonesia). Their cloves, cinnamon, nutmeg, ginger, mace, and pepper had become almost necessities in Europe. In those days, long before food could be preserved by refrigeration, spices were used to mask the unpleasant odors of rotting food, as well as to add flavor to many cooked meals.

Most of the spices from the Indies came in Arab ships, which carried them to the Persian Gulf. Then they were transported overland by animals, probably camels, to the eastern edge of the Mediterranean Sea. Before the Turks conquered the area, Genoese and other ships picked up the precious cargoes there and carried them to European ports. But now the eastern Mediterranean was controlled by the Turks, who had captured Constantinople in 1453, blocking European access to the region. Not only were they unfriendly, but—worse, to the religious kings of Europe—they were "infidels" who did not believe in Christianity.

At that time, the idea of sailing west to the Indies began to grow. It was not a new idea. All educated people and sailors knew that the earth was round and that, therefore, by sailing west one could reach the Indies. The major questions were how far west and how long it would take. Most of the geographers of the day thought such a voyage would be beyond the limits of their sailing ships.

By venturing into the Atlantic, the Portuguese had discovered islands like the Azores, and it was generally assumed that there must be more islands farther west. One eminent scholar, Paolo del Pozzo Toscanelli of Florence, had even written to the king of

Portugal suggesting that ships sailing west could reach Cipangu (Japan) and China after a voyage of perhaps five thousand nautical miles.

Columbus wrote to Toscanelli, requesting more information. In reply, the Florentine scholar praised Columbus's "great and noble ambition to pass over to where the spices grow." He also sent a chart showing his concept of the width of the ocean, but, unfortunately, that chart has been lost.

Using that material and the maps of Claudius Ptolemy, the ancient Greek cartographer, Columbus made his own complicated calculations of the distance between Europe and the Indies. According to Ptolemy, there were only three continents: Europe, Asia, and Africa. On Ptolemy's map, the world was only eighteen thousand miles around, with the three continents closer together than they really are. By that mistake, Ptolemy put the distance between the westernmost point of Europe to the easternmost point of Asia at twenty-five hundred miles.

That error was one of Ptolemy's great contributions to history. Columbus cited Ptolemy and other learned experts to support his arguments that the western ocean was not all that broad and forbidding. He shortened the actual distance that he would have to sail to reach the Indies and came up with a most optimistic result. His conclusion: By sailing only 2,400 nautical miles, he could reach Japan; and it was only 1,155 miles farther to China. (The actual mileages are 10,600 to Japan and 11,766 to China).

In the year 1484, Columbus presented his plan for a voyage to the Indies to King John II of Portugal. The king's maritime advisory committee rejected the proposal on several grounds: Columbus had grossly underestimated the distances to be traveled, the stories about Japan might not be true, and Columbus had demanded too much for himself—a title of nobility and a share of the riches to be found. There was another major reason, too: Portugal had committed itself to finding a different route to the Indies—by traveling around Africa.

So Columbus left Portugal in 1485, with his five-year-old son, Diego. His wife had died, he was in debt, and he was disheartened by the rejection of his plan. He sailed from Lisbon to the small port city of Palos in southern Spain, where relatives of his wife lived. His purpose was to offer his proposal to King Ferdinand of Aragon and Queen Isabella of Castile, the rulers of Spain.

Palos suited Columbus. His young son, Diego, would be housed with the Franciscan friars at the monastery of La Rábida, on a hill overlooking the sea. Moreover, there he met two monks who helped him. He talked about possible voyages into the Atlantic with Father Antonio de Marchena, who had a passionate interest in nautical studies. Columbus also made a friend in Father Juan Perez, who was the personal confessor of Queen Isabella. Just as important, Father Juan knew how to operate in the political thicket of the royal court.

For Columbus, a proud and sensitive man, the next few years were the hardest of his life. He had arrived in a country in ferment, not prepared to listen to a visionary idea. At that time, Spain was emerging from a period of civil unrest, trying to restore domestic peace and to expel the Moors from the country. Even though Columbus succeeded in approaching the two monarchs in Córdoba in 1486, they were not ready to finance such a bold and controversial expedition.

For Columbus, his trip to Córdoba had a happy personal result. He met a young woman named Beatriz Enriques de Harana, the daughter of a peasant family engaged in growing grapes and making wine. Although they did not get married, they had a son, Ferdinand, born in 1488, who later became the biographer of his father.

In Spain, Columbus made some converts to his cause but was unable to convince the king and queen, who were preoccupied with their war against the Moors. He sent his brother Bartholomew to England and France in an attempt to win support in those two countries, but they, like Spain, were not interested.

How did he manage to live during that troubled time for him? In later years, Columbus refused to talk about that period, but we know that he did have friends in Spain and that the Spanish monarchs did grant him small sums of money at various times. Perhaps he sold books and maps that he made.

Things began to change in late 1491. Once more he appeared before King Ferdinand and Queen Isabella, who apparently liked and respected the determined seaman. They referred his plan to a committee of astronomers, mariners, and pilots, but again it was rejected. Perhaps it was because Columbus asked too much in return—titles and riches—as the result of his expected discoveries.

The year 1492 dawned with a momentous success for Spain. On January 2, Grenada surrendered, freeing Spain of the foreign power that had occupied that city for seven centuries. Columbus was invited to march into Grenada along with the Spanish monarchs, an indication of their high regard for him personally. But, summoned before the king and queen later, he heard the bad news: Once again, they rejected his enterprise to sail to the Indies.

Outraged after wasting six years in Spain, Columbus decided to go to France, where he might be treated better. He saddled his mule, packed his bags with his clothes, books, and maps, and left for Palos, where his family lived.

His friends, the Franciscan fathers, still had confidence in Columbus and his proposal. Together, they went over all the details of his charts and maps. Then they called in one of the most experienced seamen of the area, Martín Alonzo Pinzón, to ask his opinion and advice.

In Palos, Pinzón was considered the best seaman along the coast. A rich man, he owned ships of his own. He also had a wealth of experience at sea—all over the Mediterranean, down the Atlantic coast to Guinea, and even into the open seas to the Canary Islands. Pinzón became a believer.

But could they make one more approach to the king and queen? Father Perez, who knew the queen, wrote a letter to her. In reply, she invited him to court. If Spain refused Columbus, Father Perez told the king and queen, certainly another country—perhaps France, perhaps Portugal—would eventually support him, and Spain would be the loser.

In the royal court, another of Columbus's friends, Luis de Santangel, the king's treasurer, appealed to Queen Isabella as well. He pointed out how so much glory and gold could possibly be obtained for the very small cost of financing Columbus's expedition. If money were the major consideration, he said, he would finance the trip himself. The queen, who had been impressed by Columbus's determination and persistence, changed her mind. She sent a messenger, asking Columbus to return.

It was in connection with this conversation with Santangel that the legend arose that Queen Isabella had volunteered to pawn her crown jewels to finance the trip. The queen apparently did mention that she could pledge her jewels to raise money, but Santangel assured her that it would not be necessary.

How much money was involved? From the best estimates of historians, the cost of Columbus's first expedition has been put at two million maravedis (the Spanish money of the time), or about fourteen thousand dollars in American money. It seems rather small, but it was enough for those days. Santangel borrowed most of the money from bankers, advanced a small sum himself, and Columbus furnished a small amount, too, which he must have borrowed from his friends and supporters.

With the great enterprise accepted in principle, it took three months, until April 1492, to negotiate an agreement between the monarchs and Columbus. In it, they agreed to all of Columbus's demands. He would become the admiral of the ocean sea around all the islands and mainland that he might discover and their governor. In addition, he would receive a hereditary title of nobility and be called Don Cristobal Colon, and he would be entitled to a tenth of all the riches—gold, silver, spices, pearls, and other merchandise—found there.

Even after that agreement, it took four months more to outfit an expedition. By coincidence, the queen selected Palos, the same city where Columbus had first set foot in Spain, as the home port for his fleet. For some minor violation of the law, she fined the city and ordered it to furnish two ships for Columbus. When he arrived back in Palos, he chartered a third ship as well.

Not much is known today about the details of those three small wooden ships, even though many people have built models of them over the years. Like most oceangoing vessels of the day, they were three-masted, with a large square sail on the main, or center mast, and smaller sails on the foremast and the mizzen, or rear mast. Each ship had a captain, a pilot, and a small crew, recruited for Columbus with the help of Martín Alonzo Pinzón and his younger brother, Vincente Yáñez Pinzón.

The elder Pinzón, a master mariner and community leader in Palos, agreed to work together with Columbus, but they never did become friends. Columbus, who had never commanded a ship at sea, was, of course, the leader of the expedition.

But Pinzón would take care of the practical details of navigating, battling the seas, and steering the vessels. With Pinzón's influence, the sailors of Palos flocked to enlist for the forthcoming voyage.

These were the ships:

Santa Maria

The flagship, eighty-five feet long, capable of carrying one hundred tuns, each about forty cubic feet, of wine (the standard measure in those days for the size of a ship). Captain, Christopher Columbus. Master and owner, Juan de La Cosa. Pilot, Peralonso Niño. Total crew, forty men.

Pinta

Sixty-nine feet long, sixty tuns. Captain, Martín Alonzo Pinzón. Owner, Cristobal Quintero. Master, Francisco Martín Pinzón. Pilot, Cristobal Garcia Sarmiento. Total crew, twenty-seven men.

Nina

Fifty-five feet long, fifty tuns. Captain, Vincente Yáñez Pinzón. Master and owner, Juan Nino. Pilot, Sanche Ruiz de Gama. Total crew, twenty-one men.

At last the fleet was ready for sea. At break of day on August 3, 1492, the *Nina*, the *Pinta*, and the *Santa Maria* floated down the Rio Tinto from Palos into the open sea and began a voyage of discovery that changed the world.

❧ 5 ❧

The Discovery of America

COLUMBUS WAS FORTY-ONE YEARS OLD WHEN HE SAILED INTO THE unknown Atlantic Ocean. No portrait of him was painted in his lifetime, but contemporary accounts describe him as tall and well built, with reddish-blond hair turning white, blue eyes, a ruddy and freckled complexion, with a hawklike nose and high cheekbones.

His second son, Ferdinand, added this in a later biography of his father:

> In eating and drinking and adornment of his person he was always continent and modest. Among strangers his conversation was affable, and with members of his household very pleasant, but with a modest and pleasing dignity. In matters of religion, he was so strict that for fasting and saying all the canonical offices he might have been taken for a member of a religious order.

Columbus was a stubborn and ambitious man, as he demonstrated in his persistence in following his dream of a passage to the Indies. Proud and sensitive, he never forgot or forgave those who made fun of him and his plans. On land, he was a good courtier because he knew that he had to obtain backing from the king and queen. At sea, he showed that he was a master mariner, skilled in navigation and able in command. He lost his temper frequently, but his most angry oaths were mild. When provoked, he would say "By San Fernando!" or "May God take you!"

Above all else, he was a religious man, believing that God had chosen him to find a new way to the Indies. He read the Divine Office daily, gave thanks to God constantly, and believed in spreading Christianity wherever he went. He started his voyage of discovery with prayers at the Church of St. George in Palos.

His plan was to sail south to the Canary Islands, off the coast of Africa, and then due west to the Indies. In his previous trips to Africa, he had observed that the ocean winds there blew from the east, just right for a voyage to the west. And even on the primitive maps of the time, Japan was shown to be at the same latitude as the Canary Islands. Thus by sailing west, he believed he could easily reach Japan, China, and the Spice Islands.

It took six days of sailing to reach the Canaries, where the first major problem of the voyage was solved. The *Pinta*'s rudder had slipped out of its pivots, requiring a major repair job. While that was being done, the other two ships filled their water casks and bought additional supplies of bread, cheese, and salted beef—enough to last for a year. Obviously impatient, Columbus nevertheless had to wait almost a month, until September 6, before he could sail once again.

His course was simple: "West, nothing to the north, nothing to the south," he ordered.

It sounds simple, but how did Columbus know where he was and where he was going?

In those days before electronic devices and radio, he used a process called dead reckoning. With a primitive compass that pointed north, he could determine the westerly direction. His officers estimated the distance traveled each day by watching the flow of water as the ship glided through the sea or by throwing a small object off the bow of the ship and measuring the time it took to go by. Those distances and the direction traveled were then marked on his charts.

With fair weather and following winds, the *Nina, Pinta,* and *Santa Maria* sailed on, 60 miles one day, 174 on another when the breeze was fresh. The crew settled into a routine, with their chores changing every four hours. Time was measured by a sand glass, which looked something like a transparent egg cup. It contained enough sand to run from the upper chamber to the lower in just a half hour. One of the boys would call out the change, reversing the glass, and the half hour would be marked on a board.

At noon, the sailors ate their only hot meal of the day, cooked on a fire resting on a bed of sand. For Spanish sailors, the food consisted usually of salt meat or salt codfish, hard sea biscuits, perhaps some cheese and beans, or even salted sardines, washed down with wine or water. At night, only Columbus had a cabin. The others went to sleep on the deck, wherever they could find a sheltered spot.

Day by day, the ships sailed on, a little more slowly in mid-September as the winds died down. The slow progress led some sailors to grumble that they would never reach land. When some of the officers began to suggest that perhaps Columbus should turn back, he replied that they might kill him if they could, but it would do them no good, because the king and queen would hang them if they returned without him.

In the first week of October, the ships' speed picked up, averaging 142 miles a day due to favorable winds. On October 9 and 10, the sailors became discontented even though they observed flocks of birds flying overhead. Historians have used the words "near mutiny" to describe the sailors' feelings that Columbus should give up and return home.

In his log, Columbus noted the episode. Using the third person to describe himself, he wrote: "Here the people could stand it no longer, complained of the long voyage; but the Admiral cheered them as best he could, holding out the advantages they might have, and he added that it was useless to complain, since he had come to go to the Indies, and so had to continue until he found them with the help of Our Lord."

Under strong winds, the ships sailed on. On Thursday, October

11, the sailors saw green reeds, canes, a carved stick, and even a branch covered with berries in the water—all sure signs of nearby land. At sunset, Columbus conducted a religious service and promised a special reward for the first man to sight land.

Late that night, Columbus thought he saw a light ahead and called some of his men to take a look, too. But he wasn't sure. A few hours later, as the full moon rose in the early morning hours of October 12, the lookout on the *Pinta* cried out, *"Tierra! Tierra!"* ("Land! Land!") The captain, Martín Alonzo Pinzón, came forward and verified that it was land indeed.

Columbus ordered the ships to shorten sail and wait for daylight before attempting to go near the shore and inspect what he firmly believed to be an island in the Indies. The first land sighted in the Western Hemisphere was, in reality, the eastern coast of one of the Bahama Islands, northeast of Cuba.

At daybreak, the ships sailed around the island to a shallow bay on the west coast. Columbus went ashore in his ship's boat, together with the captains of the *Nina* and the *Pinta*, Vincente Yáñez Pinzón and his brother, Martín Alonzo Pinzón. On the sandy beach, they planted the banners of the expedition, flags bearing a green cross with the letter *F* (for Ferdinand, the king) on one side and a *Y* (for Isabella, the queen, sometimes spelled Ysabella) on the other.

Columbus knelt on the ground and gave thanks to God for having reached land safely. He rose and gave the island the name of San Salvador ("Holy Savior"). Then he announced that he took possession of it for Spain in the name of the king and queen.

At first the native people of the island fled into the jungle behind the beach when they saw what appeared to them to be three winged monsters in the water. Then, curious about the strange things and the people, they flocked to the beach to see what was going on. Columbus, believing that he had reached the Indies, named them "Indians"—and the native inhabitants of the Americas have been called that ever since.

That famous first encounter between Spaniards and Indians was described by Bartolomé de Las Casas as follows:

The Indians, of whom there were a large number, gazed thunderstruck at the Christians, looking with wonder at their beards, their clothes, and the whiteness of their skins. They directed their attention towards the men with beards, but especially toward the admiral, who they realized was the most important of the group, either from his imposing physical presence or from his scarlet clothing. They touched the men's beards with their fingers and carefully examined the paleness of their hands and faces.

Here is Columbus's description of what happened after that, in his own words:

I, in order to form a great friendship, for I knew that they were a people who could be more easily freed and converted to our faith by love than by force, gave to some of them red caps and glass beads to put around their necks, and many other things of little value, which gave them great pleasure, and made them so much our friends that it was a marvel to see. They afterwards came to the ship's boats where we were, swimming and bringing us parrots, cotton threads in skeins, darts, and many other things; and we exchanged them for other things that we gave them, such as glass beads and small bells.

Those first Indians that Columbus saw were Lucayans, members of the Arawak language group. Their ancestors had discovered the islands, now called the Bahamas, by migrating north from the mainland of South America many years before. They grew corn, yams, and other roots for food, they spun and wove cotton, they made pottery, and they worked thin gold plates into ceremonial belts and ornaments.

A gentle people, the Lucayans were anxious to please. Expert woodworkers, they lived in large communal houses made of wooden frames and palm thatches. Some of these houses, circular in shape, were large enough to accommodate ten families. The interiors, divided by woven partitions, were well swept and clean.

Columbus described their physical appearance in his log:

They go as naked as when their mother bore them, and so do the women, although I did not see more than one young girl. All I saw were youths, none more than thirty years of age. They are very well made, with very handsome bodies, and very good countenances. Their hair is short and coarse, almost like the hairs of a horse's tail. They wear hairs brought down to the eyebrows, except a few locks behind, which they wear long and never cut.

The Indians who lived on the island where Columbus landed called it Guanahaní, a native word for "iguana." Once common, that reptile is now extinct there. For two days, Columbus explored the island, which he described as "very big, and very level and the trees very green, and many bodies of water, and a very big lake in the middle, and the whole of it is so green that it is a pleasure to gaze upon."

For years, historians have differed about which island in the Bahamas was the one discovered by Columbus. Many different landfalls have been suggested. The eminent historian Samuel Eliot Morison, who was an admiral in the United States Navy, identified the site as Watlings Island (officially renamed San Salvador in 1926 in the belief that it was the first landfall of Columbus).

But in 1986, a team from *National Geographic* magazine traced Columbus's voyage from his log and came to a different conclusion. Its candidate for the original landfall is Samana Cay, a small island southeast of San Salvador. It fits all the entries in Columbus's log, the team said, as well as the distances and directions to and from the other islands he discovered later.

Still another expedition in 1987 decided that Conception Island, just northwest of Samana Cay and west of San Salvador, was a likely landing site. Other investigators have named at least eight other islands as the site of Columbus's landfall: Grand Turk, Caicos, Cat, Crooked, Mayaguana, Eleuthera, Egg, and Plana.

Obviously, there is no agreement today about which of those islands was actually where Columbus landed, and we may never know positively. Back in 1492, though, Columbus was sure that San Salvador was one of the Indies, even though he saw no spices growing and the only gold visible was in small ornaments worn by the Indians. That was disappointing.

Columbus knew he had to bring back strong evidence that he had reached the Indies in order to convince skeptics in Spain that his voyage was successful. By hand language, the natives showed him that there were many more islands to the west and the south. Perhaps that was where the gold came from.

"I intend to go see if I can find the island of Japan," Columbus wrote in his journal on October 13, the day after he landed.

Taking along six Indians as guides, he sailed south on the afternoon of October 14. He touched on a series of small islands— Rum Cay, Long Island, Crooked Island, and the Ragged Islands. He discovered many new things—the first maize ever seen by a European, hammocks woven of cotton strung between trees for sleeping, and yams. But there were no signs of gold.

By now the Indians had learned that the strange white men were obsessed with finding gold. They pointed in the direction of a large island they called Colba (Cuba), where there might be gold. Columbus decided that Colba must be Japan and sailed there.

When he arrived at the eastern coast of Cuba on October 28, once again he admired the beauty of the scenery. Seeing no evidence of gold-roofed buildings or ships in the harbor, he reluctantly came to the conclusion that he had not yet reached Japan.

Optimistic as ever, though, he believed it when the Indians told him that he could find gold inland at Cubanacan. Columbus mistook that word to mean El Grand Khan, the emperor of Cathay. So he sent a delegation bearing a letter to the khan, announcing his arrival.

After tramping in the hills and valleys of Cuba, through fields of corn, beans, and sweet potatoes, the diplomatic mission reached its destination. Instead of a rich city with gold-roofed buildings and officials in brocaded gowns, they found a village of fifty palm-thatched huts and more naked Indians.

Despite that disappointing report, Columbus still felt, based on his charts, that he had arrived at the edge of Asia and its riches.

When asked about gold, the Indians pointed to another island. At Babeque, they said, there was gold.

Once more Columbus set sail, exploring the coast of Cuba as he went, sailing across the Windward Passage to an island he named La Isla Española ("the Spanish Island") and that we now call Hispaniola. There, at last, Columbus found evidence of the gold that he sought.

When he anchored off the mouth of what is now Trois-Rivières on December 15, the local *cacique*, or chief, wearing gold jewelry, came to dine with Columbus on board the *Santa Maria*. A week later, another chief sent Columbus a magnificent belt with a gold buckle. But just as Columbus seemed to achieve one of the major objectives of his voyage, disaster struck.

On Christmas Eve, when most of the crew had gone to sleep, the *Santa Maria* drifted gently onto one of the many coral reefs off the coast of Hispaniola. As the tide came in, she was swept higher and higher on the coral, which ripped holes into her hull. In the darkness of Christmas morning, Columbus ordered the ship abandoned, and he and his crew went aboard the *Nina*.

And so the first Christmas celebrated in America by Columbus and his men consisted of hard labor to float the *Santa Maria* and to save her supplies, instead of Masses, carols, and feasting. But the ship was too damaged to be saved. With the help of friendly local Indians, the Spanish ferried the *Santa Maria*'s cargo to shore.

A deeply religious man, Columbus pondered over the meaning of the accident. He concluded that it was the will of God that he should establish a settlement at that spot so that he could discover gold mines nearby. He ordered a fortified camp to be built from the salvaged timbers of the *Santa Maria*, and he called it Villa de la Natividad ("Town of the Day of the Birth of Christ").

Founding the new town solved many problems for Columbus. For one thing, the *Nina* and the *Pinta*, both small ships, could not handle the forty additional crewmen stranded from the *Santa Maria*. Staying behind suited some of the men, because they were eager to prospect for gold and get rich themselves. The local Indian chief, Guacanagarí, welcomed the new settlement, too, because he saw the Spaniards as allies in his wars with rival tribes.

Thus on the morning of January 2, 1493, as Columbus boarded the *Nina* for the start of the trip home, thirty-nine Spanish men stayed behind. At Natividad, on the north coast of what is now Haiti, they founded the first colony in America since the Norsemen. In command was Diego de Harana, a friend of Columbus's from Córdoba.

As the *Nina* and the *Pinta* sailed west along the coast of Hispaniola, Columbus stopped at the Rio Yanque del Norte and found there gold nuggets as big as lentils. The ships anchored near the mouth of Samana Bay, where Columbus met the first unfriendly Indians, armed with bows and arrows.

Finally, on January 16, Columbus started homeward, taking ten captive Indians with him. He knew he could not sail back the same way he had come, because the prevailing winds blew from east to west, directly against him. So he sailed to the north somewhat, hoping to catch a west wind.

Without knowing, for no one else had done it, Columbus chose the best possible route home from the Americas. After a short jog north, he caught the westerly winds that he hoped would bring him directly to the Azores. But in mid-February, he ran into a strong winter gale that almost destroyed his two ships.

Blown apart, the *Nina* and the *Pinta* separated, never to see each other again until they arrived in Spain. A few days later, the storm moderated and the *Nina* sailed west until Columbus caught sight of one of the islands of the Azores. When his sailors went into a church to thank God for a safe return, instead of being greeted cordially, they were thrown into jail.

The governor of the islands thought they had violated a Portuguese ban on trading with Africa. When he learned the true story of their voyage, he released the prisoners. With the *Nina* supplied with fresh provisions, Columbus set his course to Spain.

Once again a storm tossed the tiny *Nina* about, so much so that it blew her sails to ribbons. Afraid that if the ship went down no one would ever know of his successful voyage, Columbus wrote a brief account of his voyage on parchment, wrapped it in oilskin, and threw it overboard in a barrel. That account has never been found.

The storm broke after three terror-stricken days at sea. The *Nina* moved slowly east, using the one small sail that had remained intact. On March 4, Columbus spotted the rocks of southern Portugal ahead and entered the harbor of Lisbon.

Columbus sent a letter to King John II of Portugal, asking permission to land at Lisbon. In return, the king invited him to visit at the royal court. Taking with him some of his crew and three Indians, the first American Indians to visit Europe, Columbus traveled to the king's court. So it was that King John, who had refused to back Columbus's voyage, heard about his discoveries sooner than King Ferdinand and Queen Isabella, who had financed Columbus's trip.

With the Portuguese formalities complete, Columbus sailed from Lisbon for Spain, arriving in Palos, the harbor that he had left 224 days before, on March 15. By coincidence, the *Pinta*, which had been blown away from the *Nina* a month before, arrived in Palos later on the same day.

In Palos, Columbus and his sailors were received as heroes. People came from all around to see the strange Indians and to hear the tales of the returned sailors. The only one who did not take part in the festivities was Martín Alonzo Pinzón, disappointed at not being the first to return. He went straight home, obviously ill at heart and in body. He died five days later.

Columbus sent an official report on his voyage to the king and queen:

Thirty-three days after my departure, I reached the Indian Sea, where I discovered many islands, thickly peopled, of which I took possession without resistance in the name of our most illustrious Monarch, by public proclamation and with unfurled banners.

He reported that he had captured some Indians in order to learn their language. "These men are still traveling with me," he added, "and although they have been with us now a long time, they continue to entertain the idea that I have descended from Heaven."

Then he got down to the business that interested the Spaniards the most—gold. He told of an island that "abounds in gold." He concluded:

> Finally, to compress into a few words the entire summary of my voyage and speedy return, and of the advantages derivable therefrom, I promise, that with a little assistance afforded by our most invincible sovereigns, I will procure them as much gold as they need [and] a great quantity of spices.

The king and queen wrote back, addressing their letter to "Don Cristobal Colon, their Admiral of the Ocean Sea, Viceroy and Governor of the Islands that he hath discovered in the Indies." By using those titles, which they had promised him if his voyage were successful, they certified to the world that Columbus had indeed reached the Indies.

Columbus had not reached the Indies, of course. He had done more than that. Even though he did not know it, he had discovered—or, to be more precise, rediscovered—a new world, America. As we have seen in previous chapters, he was not the first European to set eyes on American soil. But unlike the Norsemen, whose voyages to America had long since been forgotten, Columbus's voyage sparked a golden age of exploration and settlement. It also resulted in intense rivalry among the seafaring nations of Europe, leading eventually to war.

∾ 6 ∿

Triumph and Tragedy

ALONG THE ROAD FROM SEVILLE TO BARCELONA, A SPLENDID PROCES-
sion approached. Christopher Columbus, dressed in new garments
reflecting his eminence as Admiral of the Ocean Sea and a nobleman of Spain, rode on a horse in front. Behind him came some
of his officers and men from the *Nina* and the *Pinta*, and, most
astonishing of all, six Indians brought home from the newly discovered islands.

On the dusty roadside, the people gaped at the strange-looking
red men. Carrying brightly colored parrots in cages, they wore
garments and belts held together with polished fish bones. According to one account, their clothes were "fashioned with ad-
mirable art, together with a great quantity and samples of finest
gold, and many other things never before seen or heard tell of in
Spain."

In Barcelona, as Columbus knelt to kiss their hands, King Ferdinand and Queen Isabella arose and motioned him to sit beside
them. They asked many questions about his trip, examined the
gold and other things he had brought back, and discussed plans
for another voyage. Columbus had obviously found favor with the
king and queen.

"Every day the import of the affair becomes greater," the queen wrote to Columbus. "You have rendered an immense service."

For weeks, Columbus took a prominent part in royal activities, attended state dinners, consulted with the king and queen on diplomatic matters, and talked to many who wanted to accompany him on a second voyage. The highlight of his stay came when the king and queen and their son, Prince John, acted as godparents to the six Indians when they were baptized as Christians in a colorful ceremony.

Outside the court, the news of Columbus's discovery traveled slowly. In those days before newspapers, radio, and television, news was transmitted by letter—not by a post office but carried by travelers or couriers on horseback or on ships. It took weeks and sometimes months before even important news reached the capitals of Europe.

Many letters went forth from Spain, reporting Columbus's discovery. The text of Columbus's letter to the Spanish monarchs was printed in Latin in Rome in April 1493. Later in 1493 and 1494, officials could read it in other European cities. But it took many months more before Columbus's brother Bartholomew, who lived in Paris, heard about the voyage.

From contemporary accounts, it seems that the public of the time was fascinated not by Columbus's discovery of the islands but by three other things he reported: gold, naked men and women, and the opportunity to convert them to Christianity.

Then as now, any gold strike and the lure of riches for the taking had a universal appeal. In a Europe that was strongly religious, the idea of bringing the word of Christ to the heathen Indians received warm support, too. But Columbus's description of natives who wore no clothes attracted the most attention. It reminded Europeans of the stories of Adam and Eve in the Garden of Eden, of a more innocent world long since gone.

Strangely, there was little immediate comment on Columbus's report that he had reached the Indies. Most learned men accepted the fact that he had landed on some islands to the west, but some questioned whether those islands were really the Indies. Among the skeptics was Peter Martyr, an Italian resident at the Spanish court, who later became a biographer of Columbus. He said that the size of the globe seemed to indicate that Columbus did not travel far enough to have reached the Indies. Perhaps he had found a new and yet unidentified world.

Still, Columbus had convinced the most important people in Spain—the king and queen—that he had indeed reached the Indies. They rewarded him handsomely. He received permission, as a new nobleman, to put on his coat of arms the gold castle of Castile and the purple lion of León, a rare honor. In addition, they made the admiral's two brothers, Bartholomew and Diego, noblemen as well.

They also issued the following order:

> We do by these presents confirm to you and your children, descendants and successors, one after another, now and forever, the said offices of Admiral of the said Ocean Sea, Viceroy and Governor of said islands and mainland that you have found and discovered, and of the other islands and mainland that shall by you or your industry be found and discovered henceforward in the said region of the Indies.

But they were not ready to let Columbus sail back quite yet. They needed his knowledge and advice in the realm of international politics. Important negotiations were going on with Portugal, the major rival of Spain, to secure Spanish rights to the islands that he had discovered.

At that time, Portugal and Spain were the two leading seafaring nations in the world. Lured by the prospect of riches from the Indies, both nations sought sea routes to those distant lands. For years, Portuguese ships had ventured south little by little down the coast of Africa until they had rounded the Cape of Good Hope in 1488, opening a sea route to India. Now the Spanish believed that Columbus had shown a better way by sailing west.

As was the custom of those years, the Catholic monarchs of Europe turned to the pope in Rome for title to lands not already possessed by another Christian nation. Already Portugal had obtained a ruling confirming its rights to the west coast of Africa. Now Spain wanted legal rights to the islands discovered by Columbus.

In those days, no one considered the rights of the native people. Spain believed that it had a just title to any new-found lands because of what it considered to be its obligation to convert heathens to Christianity. If the Indians did not become Christians, they were to be regarded as savages without the rights of other people.

For eighteen months, diplomatic negotiations were carried on in Rome, Lisbon, and Barcelona. At first, the rulings of the new pope, Alexander VI, who was a Spaniard, favored Spain. He drew a line running from the North Pole to the South Pole, about one hundred leagues, or three hundred miles, west of the Azores. West of that line all discoveries belonged to Spain, east of the line to Portugal.

But King John II of Portugal, with a powerful navy, a large merchant marine, and a history of successful exploration, was in a strong negotiating position. He rejected the pope's decision and embarked on direct negotiations with the Spanish. The result was the Treaty of Tordesillas in June 1494. In it, the north-to-south line between the two nations' possessions was pushed three hundred seventy leagues, or about eleven hundred miles, west of the Cape Verde Islands.

That agreement had a major impact on the future development of the yet-undiscovered continent of South America. Unknown to the negotiators at the time, the line ran through what is today Brazil. Under the agreement, Portugal gained title to Brazil, which is why it is a Portuguese-speaking nation today, while the rest of South America is Spanish-speaking.

Meanwhile, Columbus had already sailed on his second great voyage of exploration. He left Cádiz on September 25, 1493, with a fleet of seventeen vessels, crammed with twelve hundred enthusiastic volunteers. They included soldiers and sailors as well as many who saw a voyage west as the road to riches.

What kind of people were they?

Most of them came from poor families, the have-nots of Spain.

They left home to better themselves—not by work, but by finding riches for the taking. Their intention was not to make a better life in the new world but to return to Spain enriched, where they could live as gentlemen, respected by their neighbors. The quickest way to do that was to discover gold or to take it from the Indians there.

Before Columbus left, King Ferdinand and Queen Isabella issued the following instructions to him: to convert the natives to Christianity, to establish a permanent colony, and, of course, to bring back as much gold and spices as he could.

After a quick, pleasant voyage, Columbus landed on November 1 on an island that he named Dominico. It lies in the center of the island chain of the Lesser Antilles, which run in a gentle arc from South America to Puerto Rico. For days the ships sailed slowly up the arc, discovering island after island jutting up from the Caribbean Sea.

Two weeks later, Columbus anchored off what is now St. Croix (the first future United States territory that he discovered). There he and his men encountered the fierce Caribs, a warlike people unlike the gentle Lucayans whom he had met on his first voyage. Although outnumbered, the Caribs fought the intruders with bows and arrows. That skirmish taught the Spaniards respect for the fighting ability of the Caribs, who were believed to be cannibals.

Columbus left St. Croix hurriedly, exploring a group of small islands to the north that he called the Virgin Islands, before reaching the shores of Puerto Rico. A few days later, he returned to the island of Hispaniola, where he had left behind thirty-nine men in the fortress he called Natividad back in 1492.

Not one of them was alive. Greedy for gold and women, they had alienated the Indians in the interior of the island. The Indians responded first by wiping out a raiding party of Spaniards and then by attacking Natividad itself, killing everyone there.

Abandoning the site, Columbus sailed east along the northern shore of Hispaniola about thirty miles. There, in January 1494, he established a trading post he called Isabela, after the Spanish queen. Men dug a canal to bring water from a nearby river, cut trees, and built two hundred temporary huts for shelter. Almost immediately, an armed party went out into the interior to look for gold.

Columbus named Alonzo de Ojeda as commander of the prospecting party. One contemporary writer said of Ojeda, "He was very devoted to the Virgin Mary, but was always the first one to spill blood whenever there was any dispute or conflict."

Even though Ojeda returned with some nuggets, Isabela turned out to be a disaster. Several hundred men fell sick, food supplies ran low, and many of the colonists, those who considered themselves gentlemen, refused to work because it was beneath their dignity. The internal dissension was so strong that Columbus made a command decision: he sent twelve ships back to Spain, carrying many of the unhappy men, some spices, sixty parrots, twenty-six Indian slaves, and an appeal for more tools, livestock, Spanish food and wine, and arms.

Confident that he was near the riches of the Indies, Columbus was not discouraged. He decided to push on to Cuba, which he still thought was a Chinese province. Leaving his brother Diego in command at Isabela, he sailed on the *Nina*. Once more he explored the coast of Cuba, but once again he found no signs of China or its people. With supplies running low, he turned back.

By sailing a short distance south, he discovered a new island, Jamaica, with friendly people, but that was not enough to raise his spirits. He fell sick from lack of sleep, not enough food, and frequent drenchings from the sea. He was so sick that he had to be carried ashore when the *Nina* returned to Isabela in September 1494.

There the news was both good and bad. The good news was that his brother Bartholomew, whom he had not seen for seven years, had arrived. The bad news was that Hispaniola was in an uproar. Several of the Spaniards, discontented because they had found little gold, had seized some of the ships and sailed home. In Spain, the dissidents called Columbus incompetent and arrogant, and they denied that gold was readily available.

They did not report that, in exploring the interior of Hispaniola, the Spaniards had demonstrated extreme cruelty toward the Indians. On the island, the newcomers stole food, extorted gold, carried off boys as slaves and girls as concubines, and even put one of the Indian chiefs in chains when he protested. All this despite the order of the king and queen to treat the Indians kindly.

Here Columbus made a major mistake. Instead of stepping in and halting the cruel practices, he supported them. One historian explained his decision: "Pride compelled him to try to master the local situation and to provide a profitable export to Spain."

But it wasn't only greed that motivated Columbus. He and the other Spaniards of his time truly believed that natives could be enslaved if they were captured in a just war. They defined a just war as one in which the Indians refused to admit the Spaniards to their territory, or attacked Spanish settlements, or rebelled against Spanish rule. Thus, in the peculiar Spanish logic, if the Indians fought back against the invaders of their lands, it was legal, and even moral, to conquer and enslave them, because they were not Christians.

Soon afterward, when four ships arrived from Spain with more supplies, Columbus decided to send some of the enslaved Indians back on the same ship. By February 1495, Columbus and his men held fifteen hundred Indians and began to load them aboard. But the ships could only handle five hundred, so the others were released, fleeing into the jungle as fast as they could run.

For the Indians, the results were catastrophic. Aboard the Spanish ships, two hundred of the Indians died at sea. When the survivors landed in Spain, they were put up for sale, "naked as the day they were born," in the words of one observer. Soon, almost all died.

In Hispaniola, war broke out. A chief named Guatiguana collected an army of Indians to attack Isabela. But the Spaniards attacked the advancing Indians first, using horsemen, dogs, and soldiers on foot, protected by armor and firing primitive muskets. The cavalry rode into the naked Indians, with the savage dogs barking furiously. The Indians fled.

In less than a year, the Spanish had conquered all of Hispaniola and built forts in the interior. Armed men forced the Indians to deliver as much gold as possible as tribute. For food, the Spanish remained dependent on supplies from home, because many of them felt it was beneath their dignity to work the land. On an island that was rich and fertile, no one wanted to plant crops or pick them; they were only interested in getting rich quickly. Farming, they thought, was an occupation for peasants.

Instead, a system of land division, called *repartimientos* in Spanish, began, under which a Spaniard was granted ownership of a tract of land, including the Indians who lived there. (This system was followed by all the Spanish conquests in the New World.)

The natives became the property—in reality, slaves—of the owner, who had the legal right to use, punish, and even torture them, despite a Spanish law that proclaimed kind treatment. In Hispaniola, the cruel policy begun by Columbus and disease brought by the Spaniards resulted in genocide—the mass deaths of the kindly, peaceful Taino people. In 1492, the population of the island was estimated at two hundred fifty thousand. By 1538, only five hundred Taino people were still alive.

Back in Spain, the king and queen, alarmed by the stories of dissension, sent an officer to investigate. When he arrived with four ships in October 1495, he found the island in a shambles. The Spanish population had fallen to 630. Many of the original enthusiastic gold seekers had died of disease, more were sick, and all were discontented.

Columbus realized that only by returning home could he convince the king and queen once again that the lands he had discovered were indeed the Indies. But he made another major mistake. He named his newly arrived brother Bartholomew, whom he could trust, as governor, in his absence. That angered the other colonists, who had suffered through hard times before Bartholomew's arrival.

Columbus sailed on the *Nina* in March 1496. After a slow voyage home, he arrived back in Cádiz in June 1496—almost three years after he had left. But it was not a triumphant return, as it had been after his first voyage of discovery. Almost everyone was disappointed with the results.

He did not bring back large quantities of gold, nor had he discovered any sign of China or Japan. Some of the Spaniards who
came back with him told stories about mismanagement of the new
colony of Isabela. They reported that Indians, instead of being
grateful for the intervention of the Spanish, were beginning to fight
back. And they even made fun of Columbus, calling him the "admiral of the mosquitoes."

Columbus himself was not discouraged. He organized another
impressive parade—just as he had done after the first trip—to
report to the king and queen. In front rode servants with cages of
brightly colored parrots. Behind them came two Indian chiefs on
muleback, each wearing a gold collar and a crown, "very big and
tall, with wings on its sides like a shield and golden eyes as large
as silver cups."

The king and queen received Columbus politely, but they were
obviously not enthusiastic about outfitting a third expedition to
the islands, as Columbus requested. They changed their minds,
though, when they heard disquieting news that rival nations were
making plans to explore new routes to the Indies.

King Manuel of Portugal, who had succeeded King John, had
authorized Vasco da Gama to sail around Africa to the Indies.
And a nation that up to now had not shown any interest in exploration, England, emerged as a competitor. King Henry VII had
just approved a voyage of discovery across the North Atlantic
Ocean by John Cabot.

✍ 7 ✍

The Discovery of North America

FEW PEOPLE KNOW THE NAME OF THE MAN WHO "DISCOVERED" NORTH America, and very little is known about him. In most history books, his name is given as John Cabot, truly a sturdy-sounding English name. But in contemporary accounts, he is also called Zohanne Caboto, John Cabotto, John Kabotto, Giovanni Caboto, Ioni Caboto, Johanni Caboto, Johanni Cabetto, Zuam Calbot, Zuan Caboto, John Gabota, Ioan Caboto, John Gabote, and John Caboote.

As we have seen, Leif Ericsson was the first European to touch the shores of America, back in the year 1000. But that voyage of discovery was remembered only in the Norse sagas. Not until the age of Columbus almost five hundred years later did the rediscovery of America make a lasting impact.

At that time, the first European discoverers still thought they had reached the outer islands of the Indies. They had not yet come to the conclusion that they had indeed discovered a new world, the Americas. That revolutionary concept—that a large and hitherto unknown landmass stretched from north to south in the ocean between Europe and the Indies—came later.

Still, the idea of searching for a short ocean passage to the riches of the Indies persisted. It was not restricted to sailors of Spain, then the most powerful country in Europe. While Columbus had shown that it was possible to sail west to what he thought were the Indies, Spain's smaller neighbor, Portugal, sent pioneer mariners south around Africa's Cape of Good Hope toward the same objective. In England and France, too, merchants and sailors heard the news of Columbus's discoveries and began to consider how they could take advantage of the new sea routes.

In England, then emerging from a bloody civil war, King Henry VII listened to the proposal of an Italian sailor, John Cabot. Years before, King Henry had turned down a proposition for a voyage westward by the Columbus brothers. Now he was ready to back an exploratory trip, especially because Cabot's proposal meant no expense for the crown.

But who was John Cabot?

No researcher has yet found any portrait or personal description of him, no letter, no example of his handwriting, nor any signature on a document. He did not leave a journal of his trip, as Columbus did. Nor did any of his crew write accounts of his voyage, as some of Columbus's men did. What we do know of Cabot is pieced together from third-hand accounts, mostly in letters from diplomats of the time.

Cabot was born in Genoa, Italy, probably in 1451, the same year as Columbus. No one knows if they ever met in Genoa. Unlike the Columbus family, the Cabot family is not referred to under any of the variations of its name in the municipal records. The first official trace of John Cabot is in the documents of the city of Venice. On March 29, 1476, he was granted citizenship in Venice after a residence there of fifteen years or more, as required by law. He was then twenty-five years old.

Venice, like Genoa, was a major seafaring city-state. Historians have deduced that Cabot went to sea like many other young men in those two cities. One clue is that he told a friend that he had made a voyage to Mecca, the holy city of the Muslim world in Arabia near the Red Sea, then the greatest market in the world for the exchange of goods from the East for those of the West. A later letter from an Italian diplomat in London called him "a man of fine mind, extremely skillful in navigation." In another letter, Cabot was described as a "very good mariner."

The next clue to Cabot's life comes in the archives of the city of Valencia in Spain, where it is recorded that a Venetian named Johan Cabot lived between 1490 and 1493. Johan Cabot attempted to interest King Ferdinand of Spain in building a jetty at a seaport, but the project fell through for lack of money. If Johan Cabot was John Cabot, he certainly would have been in Spain when Columbus returned from his first voyage of discovery. Like other mariners, he would have been fascinated by the news.

Somewhere in that period, Cabot married a Venetian woman, Mattea, about whom nothing is known. They had three sons, whose names we do know because they are mentioned later in English documents: Lewis, Sebastian, and Sancto. Presumably, all of them were born in Venice before Cabot left for England.

Cabot arrived in England with his family no later than 1495, settling in Bristol, a major seaport. Second only to London as a port, Bristol was a thriving commercial city on the southwest coast of England, near the mouth of the Severn River. Many Genoese and Venetian merchants and seamen made their homes in London and Bristol, working in a three-cornered trade: to the eastern Mediterranean to buy spices, transporting them to Italy, and then shipping them to England, where they were in great demand.

Because of its geographic position on the west coast of England, Bristol engaged in trade with Iceland as well. Its ships brought codfish back from the waters around Iceland, taking the fish and woolens woven in western England south to Spain and Portugal. The ships returned with olive oil and wines, especially sherry, called at the time "Bristol milk."

A city of ten thousand people, Bristol prospered. It exported more cloth, imported more wine, and handled more goods subject to import taxes than any other city in England except London. It had become a major port despite its location eight miles from the sea, at the junction of the Avon and Severn rivers. That distance protected the city against attack by pirates but made it difficult for ships to enter or leave the harbor because of exceptionally high tides.

In the early 1490s when the Cabots arrived, Bristol was not only interested in expanding its trade but eager to find a better and more economic route to the Indies. Obviously, it occupied a strategic location among English ports if a new short route to the Indies lay to the west. "To discover a short, northern route to the land of spices would make a fortune for Bristol and for England," one historian wrote.

Because of the spherical nature of the earth, all mariners of the day knew that the longest way to Asia was at the equator, where the circumference of the world was twenty-five thousand miles. But the farther north one sailed from east to west, the shorter the distance would be. England was farther north than Spain or Portugal and so, the Bristol mariners concluded, they could arrive in Asia in a shorter time than even Columbus spent at sea.

No one knows when and how the idea of making such a voyage came to Cabot. By 1496, only three years after Columbus returned from his first voyage, Cabot had prepared a plan to sail west to the Indies, too. With the help of some merchants of Bristol, early in 1496, Cabot sent a petition to King Henry, asking permission to sail to Asia. It read:

To the Kyng our sovereigne lord.
Please it to your highness of your moste noble and hadbondant grace to graunt unto John Cabotto citizen of Venes, Lewes, Sebestyan and Sancto his sonneys, your gracious letters patentes under your grete seale in due forme to be made according to the tenour hereafter ensuying. And they shall during their lyves pray to God for the prosperous continuance of your most noble astate long to enduer.

In remarkably quick time, the king replied. On March 5, he granted to "our well beloved John Cabot, citizen of Venice, and to his sons, Lewes, Sebastian and Santius," the following:

Free and full authoritie, leave, and power, to sayle to all partes, countreys, and seas, of the East, of the West, and of the North, under our banners and ensignes, with five ships, and as many mariners and charges, upon their own proper costes and charges to seeke out, discover, and finde, whatsoever iles, countreyes, regions, or provinces of the heathen and infidells, whatsoever they bee, and in what part of the world soever they be, whiche before this time have beene unknownen to Christians.

In approving the voyage, the king took no risks. He supplied no money, only verbal support. It was up to Cabot to finance his own trip, probably with the help of some of the Bristol merchants. If he found anything, however, Cabot was required to return one-tenth of his profits to the crown.

Despite the king's authority to take five ships, Cabot obtained only one for his voyage, the *Mathew* (sometimes spelled *Matthew*). It was a small ship, capable of carrying about fifty tuns of wine (and so was called a ship of fifty tons), about the same size as Columbus's *Nina*. Like the *Nina*, she had three sails, square ones on the foremast and the mainmast and a triangular, or lateen sail, on the rear mast.

Only fifty to sixty feet long, the *Mathew* carried a crew of eighteen men, mostly Englishmen, but apparently none of Cabot's three sons. Not much is known about her crew, except that it included two Bristol merchants and two friends of Cabot, a Frenchman and a barber from Genoa.

The *Mathew* sailed from Bristol on or about May 20, 1497, down the Severn River to the Bristol Channel and then to the open sea. Unfortunately, like most material about Cabot, the ship's log and his notes have disappeared. Historians, however, have reconstructed his most likely course, based on contemporary accounts and the logical route any experienced mariner would have taken.

Cabot sailed west toward Ireland, sighting Dursey Head, one of the westernmost points there. Then he turned north for a short time to take advantage of the ocean currents before setting a course almost due west. After thirty-three days at sea, on June 24, Cabot sighted land ahead—the northern end of the clifflike, rocky coast of what we now call Newfoundland. By so doing, Cabot rediscovered North America—almost five hundred years after Leif Ericsson had discovered it.

Unfortunately, as we have seen, Cabot's logbooks have disappeared, so we do not know exactly where he first sighted land or what his reactions were. Some writers have said that perhaps Cabot landed farther south, maybe in Nova Scotia, at Cape Breton at the northern end of that island, or even farther south toward Cape Sable at the southern end. Cabot himself thought he had reached "the country of the great Khan," or China. The best analysis of the data indicates that Cape Dégrat at the northern end of Newfoundland was probably Cabot's first landfall.

Cabot turned south (presumably because he spotted ice to the north), looking for a harbor. When he found one, he landed and took possession of the new land in the name of King Henry VII of England. As was the custom at the time, he erected a cross and the banner of the king as a symbol of possession.

Then he took time to look around. He and his crew saw no Indians, but they found snares for game and fish nets, a sign that people had been there. They also found a stick painted red, with holes on both ends, presumably used in weaving fish nets. After filling their water casks, they reembarked on their ship, without making any attempt to find the natives for fear that they might be hostile.

They sailed south along the rocky coast of Newfoundland. Cabot and his crew saw tall trees suitable for providing masts for ships and fields of blueberry bushes. One of their most important discoveries was at sea—the abundant codfish in the cold waters off the mainland. They scooped up the fish by merely letting down baskets weighted with stones and drawing them up again.

On July 20, Cabot turned back toward England, making a speedy, uneventful trip home. The *Mathew* sailed up the Severn River on the morning tide of August 6, arriving in Bristol on the same day. After receiving a warm welcome from local residents, Cabot set out immediately on horseback to bring the news of his discovery to the king in London.

The king was delighted. He rewarded Cabot with a gift of ten pounds in money, a large sum for those times, and later granted him an annual pension of twenty pounds.

An Italian who lived in London wrote to his brother in Venice that Cabot was called "the Great Admiral" and received vast honors. Then he added one of the few human touches on record about John Cabot: "He goes dressed in silk and these English run after him like mad, and indeed he can enlist as many of them as he pleases, and a number of our rogues as well."

Most of what we know about Cabot, his voyage, and his return comes from two letters written at the time. In one of them, a friend of Cabot's, Raimondo de Soncino, who represented the Duke of Milan in London, wrote:

My most Illustrious and most Excellent Lord:
Perhaps amidst so many occupations of your Excellency it will not be unwelcome to learn how His Majesty here has acquired a portion of Asia without a stroke of his sword. In this kingdom there is a lower-class Venetian named Master Zoanne Caboto, of a fine mind, very expert in navigation, who seeing the most serene Kings, first of Portugal then of Spain, have occupied unknown islands, meditated the achievement of a similar acquisition for His Majesty aforesaid, and, having obtained royal grants securing to himself the profitable control of whatever he should discover, since the sovereignty was reserved to the Crown, with a small ship and 18 persons he committed himself to fortune, and set out from Bristol, a western port of this kingdom, and having passed Ireland, which is still farther to the west, and then shaped a northerly course, he began to navigate to the eastern parts, leaving (during several days) the North Star to the right. And having wandered about considerably, at length he fell in with terra firma, where he set up the royal standard, and having taken possession for this King and collecting several tokens, he came back again.

Soncino went on to say that Cabot, being a foreigner and a poor man, would not have been believed except that his crew, sturdy Englishmen from Bristol, testified that his tale of discovery was true.

The second letter was written by John Day, an English wine importer who traded in Spain, Portugal, and England. Shortly after Cabot's return, he wrote to Christopher Columbus:

He did not go ashore save at one place of terra firma, which is close to where they made the first landfall, in which place they went ashore with a crucifix and raised banners bearing the arms of the Holy Father and the arms of the King of England my lord, and they found big trees from which the masts of ships are made, and other trees beneath them, and the land was very rich with pasturage; in which place (as I have already told your Lordship) they found a very narrow way leading into the land, and saw a spot where someone had made a fire, and found dung of an animal, which they judge to be tame, and they found a stick of elbow length perforated at both ends and painted with brasil [red] and from the signs the land is judged to be inhabited; and as he found himself to be with few men, he dared not enter the land beyond a cross-bow shot, and he took on fresh water and returned to his ship and along the coast they found many fish of the kind that in Iceland are cured in the air and sell in England and other countries and which in England are called estoqfias [dried cod-fish].

As Cabot relished his triumphant return to London, he also began to make plans for a second and much larger voyage to the new-found lands. Using a globe, he demonstrated that if he sailed west to the land he had discovered and then south, he would reach Cipangu (Japan) and its riches quickly.

Impressed, King Henry granted Cabot authority to sail with six ships to "the land where he thinks grow all the spices of the world and also the precious stones." There Cabot expected to set up a trading depot to ship spices and jewels home, making England a major trading nation.

In the beginning of May 1498—the same month that Columbus left Seville on his third voyage of discovery—Cabot sailed with five ships, filled with coarse cloth, caps, laces, points, and other odds and ends that were believed to be useful in trading with natives. One ship ran into trouble at sea and put into an Irish port for repairs. The other four ships sailed on—and disappeared.

To this day, no one knows what happened to John Cabot—and he has not received the credit he deserves as the discoverer of North America. Part of the reason is confusion among some historians, who have attributed his discovery to his son Sebastian, a rogue who falsely claimed the credit at times. One biographer described Sebastian Cabot as "a man capable of disguising the truth, whenever it was to his interest to do so." Another historian called him "a genial and cheerful liar."

In his time, Sebastian Cabot served several kings of England and Spain as a maritime advisor, gained a reputation as a skilled cartographer, and made at least one voyage of discovery. Historians do not agree on when and where he was born. Some say Venice in 1482; others, in Bristol in 1474. They do agree that he died in London in 1557, when he was either seventy-five or eighty-three years old.

The first official mention of Sebastian is in his father's petition to the king in 1496 for a voyage to the Indies. It is not known whether he was one of the eighteen men who served as the crew of his father's ship, the *Mathew*. Whether or not he ever saw the coast of Newfoundland, he could tell amusing stories about it.

Peter Martyr, who wrote the first history of the New World, said that he had heard the following story from Sebastian himself. The codfish off the coast of Newfoundland were so numerous and hungry that they swam to the shore to feed on the leaves of tall trees that fell into the water. While the codfish were busy eating, bears rushed into the water, surrounding the fish. In the churning water, each bear grabbed a codfish for a meal.

Sebastian made his living as a mapmaker. In 1512, for example, King Henry VII of England paid him to make some maps. But

Sebastian apparently was not satisfied with his treatment in England, so he went off to Spain, where King Ferdinand hired him as a cartographer. He impressed the king, who appointed him to the posts of fleet captain, pilot to His Majesty, and a member of the council to oversee the New Indies.

When Ferdinand died, Sebastian returned to England briefly. By 1519, he was back in Spain as pilot major to King Charles V, employed in various maritime ventures there. During that period, he made his first documented voyage to the New World.

As captain-general of a fleet of four ships in 1526, he commanded an expedition with the objective of reaching "the Mollucas and Oriental China." Instead, he landed in South America, south of the bulge of Brazil. Although he and his men spent three years exploring the internal rivers that fed into the Rio de la Plata, which separates Uruguay and Argentina today, the expedition ended in disaster. Suffering from famine and attacked by Indians whenever they tried to fish or collect roots, Cabot and his men decided to return to Spain in 1529.

With little to show for his years in South America, Cabot was found guilty on charges of cruelty, mismanagement, and criminal abuse of his authority. His sentence: jail for a year and exile for two more years to Morocco. But King Charles, impressed by Sebastian's talk, cancelled the sentence and restored him to his office as pilot major of Spain.

Basking in the royal favor, he served as an examiner of pilots for the king and worked as a mapmaker. He made a famous map of the world in 1544, showing his father's discovery of Newfoundland and his own in South America. Only one copy of that map, about four feet by six feet, still exists (in the Bibliotheque Nationale in Paris), although some reproductions are available.

A few years later, in 1547 following the death of his Spanish wife and daughter, some of Sebastian's friends in England persuaded him to return there, where he took up residence in Bristol. An elderly man by that time, he received a yearly pension from the king. But his working career was not over. In 1551, he became the first governor of the Merchant Adventurers, a British combine interested in expanding trade. He commanded its first expedition in 1553, which touched on the coast of Russia.

Because his pension stopped in 1557, historians have concluded that he died in that year. They do not know where he was buried or any details about his will or family.

Copies of a portrait of Sebastian in his old age still exist, although the original was destroyed in a fire. They show a white-haired gentleman with a white, forked beard, holding a pair of dividers near a globe, illustrating his cartographic background. In the corner is this inscription, in Latin:

Sebastian Cabot, Englishman, son of John Cabot, Venetian knight, first discoverer of Newfoundland under Henry VII, King of England.

But there is no portrait remaining of John Cabot. He faded from memory fast because of his disappearance and the failure of England for many years to take advantage of his voyage. Except for the fish off Newfoundland, which attracted fishermen of all nations, little interest followed his discovery of North America. Like Columbus, he himself never learned the significance of his landing— that a new world had been discovered.

❧ 8 ❧

Last Voyages of Columbus

ALTHOUGH CHRISTOPHER COLUMBUS COULD HAVE RETIRED WITH HON-
ors and riches after completing his first two famous voyages of
discovery, he was not content. Now almost fifty years old, he
wondered why so many people had turned against him. Why were
they telling so many lies about him to the king and queen? Why
did they not see the importance of his discoveries? He came to
the conclusion that he had sinned against God by showing excessive
pride in his accomplishments and his rank as Admiral of the Ocean
Sea.

Thereafter, Columbus wore the simple brown robes of the Franciscan fathers and stayed in their austere quarters instead of accepting invitations to castles and palaces. He remained obsessed
with the idea that the islands he had discovered were the doorsteps
to the riches of the Indies. If he could make one more voyage,
perhaps a little to the south of where he had been, he could reach
the mainland of Asia.

Despite stories of mismanagement by discontented crew members, the king and queen received Columbus politely. They listened
courteously when he pleaded for more ships to conduct a third
voyage of discovery. They were not convinced until they heard

that the king of Portugal had approved a big overseas expedition under Vasco da Gama possibly to explore the same regions.

Then they quickly authorized Columbus to organize a new Spanish expedition, with three hundred colonists. Unfortunately, as it turned out, some of them were criminals released from jail on the promise that they would stay in Hispaniola for at least a year. As a sign that Spain intended to stay permanently in the New World, the colonists also included thirty women who were expected to marry on arrival.

In late May 1498, Columbus sailed once more from Spain, commanding a fleet of six ships. Three carried colonists and supplies for Hispaniola. The other three, directly under Columbus, sailed farther south in quest of the elusive lands where he thought gold would be plentiful.

With a fair and steady wind, the ships made a speedy and uneventful ocean crossing. At noon on July 31, a lookout spotted three hills on an island ahead. Because of those three hills, Columbus named the island Trinidad, a name it still bears. He landed on the south shore to refill his water casks, while the men washed in fresh water for the first time in weeks.

Then Columbus sailed between Trinidad and the north shore of South America into the Gulf of Paria, where the mighty Orinoco River pours fresh water into the sea. Still optimistic, Columbus hoped to meet some Chinese merchants, but all he encountered were more naked Indians. On August 5, 1498, he landed on the Paria peninsula, now part of the republic of Venezuela, and took formal possession of the land in the name of the Spanish king and queen. It was the first record of a European setting foot on the continent of South America.

Sailing around the northern tip of South America, Columbus stopped briefly at an island he called Margarita. There he met Indians who wore pearls on their arms. Columbus had discovered the rich Pearl Coast of South America, where pearls came from offshore beds of oysters attached to mangrove branches submerged in the water. But, obsessed with the idea of finding gold and impatient to sail on, he left before he could collect a goodly amount of that different kind of treasure.

By this time, Columbus began to suspect that he might be on the edge of a continent, not merely a group of islands. He wrote in his journal:

> I believe that this land may be a great continent that has remained unknown to this day. Reason bears this out because of the immense river and sea of fresh water formed at its mouth.

Despite those obvious facts, Columbus remained convinced that he was close to his objective, the riches of the Indies. He concluded that the vast new land was on the outer edge of Asia, close to the southern end of China.

He sailed on to Hispaniola, where two years before he had left his brother Bartholomew in charge with instructions to found a city on a good harbor. Bartholomew had done so, on the southern shore. Together, the two brothers named the new city Santo Domingo, after their father. Today that city is the capital of the Dominican Republic.

Columbus hoped to find peace and tranquility in Santo Domingo, a place to rest his aching body, racked by arthritis, rheumatism, and gout. Instead he found a revolt. Many of the new colonists, among them the criminals who had been given a second chance, refused to work. They preferred a life of ease with the Indians, instead of building a new colony for Spain.

In Spain, too, Columbus's position deteriorated. When Spaniards newly returned from Hispaniola spread more stories of discontent there, the king and queen listened. They came to the conclusion that Columbus was a good admiral but not a good administrator.

Modern historians agree. Columbus had been weak when he should have been strong. Not only had he failed to protect the Indians from exploitation, but he and his brothers had alienated most of the Spaniards.

As a result, the monarchs sent a representative, Francisco de Bobadilla, to take over the civil functions of the colony at Hispaniola. Bobadilla was a gentleman, a faithful servant of the king and queen, and a knight who considered Columbus an outsider, no matter how successful he had been.

Upon his arrival in Santo Domingo on August 24, 1500, the first thing Bobadilla saw was a gallows on which two Spaniards were hanging. They had been executed for revolting against the government. Five more Spaniards were scheduled for execution the next day.

Horrified, Bobadilla stepped in and took control of the government from Diego Columbus, in charge while his brother was on a trip inland. Without waiting to hear any explanations, Bobadilla threw Diego into jail. To quiet the population, he announced that everyone could keep as much gold as he wanted, which won the colonists to his side.

When Columbus returned to Santo Domingo, he, of course, protested. But Bobadilla, armed with royal power over people and possessions in Hispaniola, prevailed. When Columbus objected, Bobadilla arrested him. Worst of all, Bobadilla ordered him to be chained like a common criminal and sent him and his brothers, Diego and Bartholomew, back to Spain for trial.

In chains, Columbus left Santo Domingo in early October 1500. Once the ship left port, the captain offered to release Columbus, but he proudly refused. "I have been placed in chains by order of the sovereigns," he said, "and I shall wear them until the sovereigns themselves order them removed."

Thus humiliated, Columbus, still in chains, arrived back in Spain in late October. He sent a letter to a friend at the royal court, defending his conduct, complaining that he had been treated dishonorably, and mentioning that he had lost both his youth and his due honors in serving the king and queen. He ended with a reminder that "by divine will I have placed under the sovereignty of the King and Queen our lords an Other World, whereby Spain, which was reckoned poor, has become the richest of countries."

Several weeks passed before the king and queen ordered him

released from his chains and summoned to the royal court. As usual, they greeted him courteously. As he talked about his grievances, they saw no reason to alter their opinion that he had not been a successful governor and administrator.

Once again, Columbus, now fifty years old, could have retired with honor, riches, and even a new title. If he had been a sensible man, he would have been content, his place in history secure. But he was not a reasonable man. If he had been, he would not have pursued his dream of a westward voyage so persistently despite so many discouragements in the first place—and he would not have discovered America.

Even now, in the face of royal displeasure, Columbus drew up plans for a fourth voyage. By this time, in the year 1501, the oceans to the west of Europe were filled with ships of other "discoverers" following in the wake of Columbus. From both Spain and Portugal, new explorers sailed west in hopes of finding riches for themselves and their countries.

In examining the routes of these new explorers, Columbus noticed that none of them planned to venture into the oceanic area west of the islands he had discovered. Most of them aimed south of where he had been, a few to the north. Columbus believed that if he sailed west from Cuba into the unknown waters he would at last find a passage to the Indies.

Finally, in March 1502, the king and queen approved his trip. But they restricted his powers. No longer would he be the viceroy. The monarchs appointed Nicolas de Ovando as governor of the Indies, forbidding Columbus to stop at Santo Domingo and perhaps interfering with the new regime. Ovando sailed early in 1502, commanding a large fleet of thirty-two ships, with twenty-five hundred men aboard.

On May 11, 1502, Columbus sailed from Cádiz on his fourth and last voyage of discovery, with four small ships. With him was his son Diego, then twenty-two years old. After a speedy trip, Columbus arrived in the Lesser Antilles, familiar to him from his second voyage, on June 15. Two weeks later, he anchored off Santo Domingo, despite the royal orders to stay away.

He did so because of a threatening hurricane. Sending a messenger ashore asking permission to take refuge in the harbor, he warned the new governor to keep all his ships in safety until the storm passed. Ovando and his aides laughed at the ancient mariner who thought he could predict the winds. They ignored the warning.

Ovando sent a fleet of twenty-nine ships laden with gold back to Spain. As Columbus had predicted, the hurricane struck. Nineteen of the ships sank with all hands. Six others also sank, but some of their crews were rescued. Four battered ships survived, badly damaged. Among those lost at sea was Francisco de Bobadilla, the man who had put Columbus in chains two years earlier.

Columbus and his ships survived by finding a protected shore near Santo Domingo. When the storm passed, he sailed west across the Caribbean Sea. On July 27, a lookout spotted some islands off the coast of what is now Honduras. Columbus landed on Bonacca Island, the first man from Europe to step on the soil of Central America.

The Indians he encountered were more advanced than those he had met on the other Caribbean islands. They wore woven clothes, traveled at sea in large dugout canoes, melted copper, and made weapons with sharp edges of flint. Without knowing it, Columbus had made contact with an outpost of the Aztec empire of Mexico.

Impatient as always, Columbus decided to sail south to find a strait that would take him to the Indies. In stormy weather, he cruised parallel to the coast of what is today Nicaragua, Costa Rica, and Panama. The rain was so heavy that no one could see from ship to ship. Saturated with water, the galley stoves could not light, so the men ate rain-soaked biscuits. When the wind died down, hordes of mosquitoes from the mangrove swamps tormented the exhausted sailors.

Columbus persevered. He looked into every river opening, seeking the waterway to the Indies, but every channel ended in the jungle. His four ships stopped briefly at Limon Bay (now the Caribbean entrance to the Panama Canal), but Columbus found a better harbor farther south at Puerto Bello. He explored several other river channels before giving up his search for the passage to the Indies.

On New Year's Day, 1503, Columbus anchored in a harbor now called Cristobal, in the Panama Canal Zone. He did not know it, but he was very close to the Pacific Ocean on the other side of the mountains and jungles. Weary, Columbus sailed back north along the inhospitable coast of the land he called Veragua (present-day Panama), where the Indians displayed gold discs and jewelry.

At first the Indians were friendly. Columbus established a trading post there, Santa Maria de Belen, the first colony ever organized on the mainland of the Americas. It didn't last long. Everything went wrong for Columbus and his men.

Not only was gold difficult to mine in the mountains but the Spanish sailors found themselves in an area with one of the heaviest rainfalls in the world. Torrential rains swelled streams that swept ships from their moorings. Then came a dry spell in which the ships were marooned by low water, unable to get to sea. As the most devastating blow of all, the Indians turned hostile because of ill treatment of Indian women by the Spanish sailors.

The Indians attacked, killing many of the sailors on the ships and in the new settlement. The Spanish managed to get three ships to sea, abandoning one. Faced by the fierce enmity of the Indians, Columbus, suffering from malaria, decided to evacuate Santa Maria de Belen and leave the gold of Veragua. Ironically, despite the disaster there, Columbus's descendants were later given the title duke of Veragua.

On Easter Sunday, April 16, 1503, Columbus's three remaining ships, the *Capitana*, *Bermuda*, and *Vizcaina*, left Santa Maria de Belen behind. They proved to be scarcely seaworthy. During the long stay at Santa Maria, shipworms had so devastated the wooden hulls that water kept leaking in. Ferdinand Columbus described the efforts to save the ships: "The entire crew, using pumps, pots and other receptacles, was unable to remove all the water coming in through the holes made by the shipworms."

As the water reached almost to the deck level of the *Vizcaina*,

Columbus ordered her abandoned. With water pumps working full time, the two remaining worm-eaten ships slowly sailed across the Caribbean Sea to Jamaica, reaching the bay of Santa Gloria.

Ferdinand Columbus described what happened next:

> Once inside the bay, being no longer able to keep the ships afloat, we pushed them onto the shore and dragged them as far from the water as possible, beaching them one next to the other, side by side, and propping them up from each side to prevent them from listing. On the decks, and on top of the forecastles and the aftcastles, we built cabins to lodge the men, making them strong enough to serve as protection and shelter from the Indians.

Marooned in Jamaica, Columbus and his crew of 116 men knew that there was little chance of rescue by a passing ship. The immediate problem was food; the long-range problem was how to get back to Santo Domingo. They solved the first problem by bartering knickknacks with the Indians. But how would they get to Santo Domingo, about a hundred miles across the ocean to the north?

They would send a messenger, they decided. Columbus selected Diego Mendez, one of his most trusted aides, to make the trip. Using a canoe with a mast and sail, Mendez failed on his first attempt. Then, accompanied by a second canoe, Mendez tried again. Under a hot July sun, the Spanish and Indian men sailed and paddled slowly across the sea. Five days later, after their water and food had been exhausted, they sighted land ahead.

They made their way to Santo Domingo. But the governor, Ovando, hesitated about sending a rescue party. He dawdled for seven months—an incredibly long time—before permitting Mendez to organize a rescue mission.

Meanwhile the situation in Jamaica became worse for Columbus and his crew. Forty-eight men mutinied, seized ten canoes from the Indians, and tried to go to Santo Domingo by themselves. When they reached the open waters, they stopped and turned back.

The men who remained loyal to Columbus faced a different

problem: hunger. The Indians, who had little surplus food, began to refuse to trade it for beads and bells. They were beginning to tire of the demands of the strange white men.

At this critical moment, Columbus performed what seemed to be a miracle. With him he had an almanac, which predicted a total eclipse of the moon on the last night of February 1504. At sunset that night, Columbus summoned the Indian chiefs and notables on board one of the stranded ships.

The Christian God was angry, he told them, because of their failure to supply food for the white men. Look up to the sky, he went on. God would send a clear sign of his displeasure and of the punishment that would come unless the Indians changed their ways, he said.

The Indians laughed at him.

At midnight, as the moon rose, the earth's shadow began to black it out. As the blackened portion increased, the Indians flocked to the ship in fear, begging Columbus to stop the terrible spectacle.

Columbus retired to his cabin briefly. When he came out, he told the howling Indians that he had interceded with the Almighty. As the eclipse neared its end, Columbus told the Indians that God had consented to make the moon come back in return for their solemn promise to provide food for the white men.

The moon emerged from the shadows, pleasing the Indians. They kept their promise and the food shortage ended. But it was another four months before a rescue mission appeared, organized by Diego Mendez. On June 28, 1504, Columbus and his men finally sailed back to Hispaniola. They had been marooned on Jamaica for a year and five days.

In September, Columbus left for Spain, two and a half years after the start of his fourth and last voyage to the New World. Even though he was only fifty-three years old, he seemed like an old man. Suffering from gout and arthritis, he could hardly move out of the home he rented in Seville. He was sick in spirit, too, unhappy that his financial agreements with the king and queen were not being kept.

To add to his woes, he lost one of his major supporters. Queen Isabella died in November 1504, less than a month after Columbus arrived home. King Ferdinand did not consent to receive Columbus until months later, in May 1505.

Ferdinand was polite but cold. He suggested that an arbitrator be appointed to settle Columbus's claims against the crown. Columbus agreed. He did not receive all the monies that he thought were due him, but he did get enough to make him and his heirs rich. He also made sure that his son Diego would receive the hereditary position of governor of Hispaniola and the other titles that Columbus held.

As Columbus grew sicker, his arthritis worsened and he became confined to bed. He made his will, naming Diego as his heir. On May 20, 1506, Columbus died, at the age of fifty-five.

Today, five hundred years after his first voyage of discovery, Columbus stands out as one of the greatest explorers who ever lived—if not the greatest. It is no wonder that his birthday is still celebrated every year throughout the Americas, the land that he discovered.

❧ 9 ❧

The Discovery of Brazil

In the early 1400s, Portugal was a leading seapower of Europe. At a time when Spain, France, and England were wracked by internal disorder and war, bold Portuguese sailors roamed the North Atlantic Ocean fishing for cod. They also made frequent voyages to islands in the ocean and along the west coast of Africa.

A small nation, with a population of only one million, Portugal was ideally situated for maritime endeavors. Sitting on the westernmost edge of Europe, washed by the water of the Atlantic Ocean, Portugal became a seafaring nation.

The golden age of Portuguese maritime exploration began with a man who has come down in history as Prince Henry the Navigator. Born in 1394, he was the third son of King John I of Portugal and his wife, Philippa, the daughter of John of Gaunt, one of England's most powerful nobles.

As a young man, Henry took part in the Portuguese invasion of North Africa, helping to capture the Moroccan city of Ceuta. He spent three years as governor of Ceuta, listening to travelers bringing back tales of gold, ivory, and precious stones in the interior of the continent. When he returned to Portugal in 1418, he decided to seek ways to find those riches through exploration.

Henry set up a center for maritime learning at Sagres on Cape

St. Vincent, the southeasternmost point on the continent of Europe. Although he was not a sailor or a scholar himself, he brought to Sagres many learned men, collected maps and charts made by seamen, and encouraged sailors to venture out beyond the limits of the then-known world. He provided a focus for Portuguese exploration to Africa and India—and, incidentally, to the discovery of Brazil.

Step by step, Portuguese mariners opened up new worlds. In 1418, they reached the Madeira Islands, some four hundred miles southwest of Portugal. A few years later, they discovered the Azores, about seven hundred fifty miles to the west of Portugal. Slowly, under Prince Henry's guidance, they began to sail down the coast of western Africa.

Today it is difficult to conceive of how brave those ancient mariners were in facing the real and imagined perils of unknown seas. Their oceangoing ships were tiny and fragile. Propelled by sails, they depended on wind and ocean currents, and their masters could only use simple compasses and the sun to estimate where they were.

Sailors were superstitious, too. They believed, for example, that as they sailed toward the equator, the water would get so hot that it would boil and prevent any ship from passing through. It took a long time before the Portuguese mariners overcame their fears. The dangerous life at sea gave rise to the Portuguese proverb, "If you want to learn how to pray, go to sea."

It wasn't until 1434 that Gil Eanes, a Portuguese captain, sailed beyond Cape Bojador, on the northeast coast of Africa, and returned safely. Ten years later, Dinis Dias reached Cape Verde, the westernmost point of Africa, jutting out into the Atlantic Ocean.

Progress was slow, but ships continued to make exploratory trips south even after Prince Henry had died in 1460. As they touched on the coast of Africa, the Portuguese set up trading posts wherever they went. From these posts, large quantities of ivory, gold, and black slaves poured into Portugal, making it a major economic force in Europe.

It was many years later, in 1482, that Diogo Cão turned the bulge of Africa, crossing the equator for the first time. He sailed beyond the Congo River, thus proving that ships and men could survive the heat of the tropical seas. But it took one more voyage of discovery before the glittering prize of India and the islands around it seemed to be within reach.

Bartholomew Dias sailed from Portugal in August 1487 down the west coast to Africa, reaching Walvis Bay near present-day South Africa in December. A storm forced his ships south for thirteen days before he was able to turn east toward the coast. When he sighted land, it did not run north and south as expected, but east to west. He had turned the southern end of Africa and reached the Indian Ocean—the first European to do so.

Stopping for a few days to take on water and supplies (something every experienced sea captain did at every opportunity), Dias reached the Great Fish River on the east coast of South Africa before turning back. On May 16, 1488, he spotted a promontory facing south to the sea and named it the Cape of Good Hope. He arrived back in Lisbon in December 1488, where the crowd that greeted his return included Christopher Columbus, then in Portugal seeking support for his voyage to the west.

Even though it became clear that Dias had opened the way for sea voyages to India, it took nine years more before Portugal sent an expedition there. By that time, Columbus had already completed his famous voyage of discovery to America. Portugal delayed for various reasons, including the death of King John II. It wasn't until 1497 that his successor, King Manuel I, decided that he was ready to send a fleet to India.

To command the expedition, the king selected Vasco da Gama, a young man in his thirties, a gentleman of the royal household. Although he was not a sailor, he knew something about the sea and was "a discreet man, of good understanding and of great courage." An observer of the time described him as "an unmarried man of the right age to bear up under the strains of such a voyage."

Da Gama was born in Sines, a seaport on the Atlantic coast of Portugal, probably in 1460. His father was Estevan da Gama, a minor nobleman in the service of the king, but we know nothing about his mother. Nor do we know anything about da Gama's life before his great voyage.

With four ships and 170 men under his command, da Gama sailed from Lisbon on July 8, 1497. He had three objectives: to find India, to tap the spice market of the East, and to make treaties of peace and friendship with any Christian rulers he might meet. Getting there was the major problem, but he had some of the most experienced mariners in Portugal as the captains and pilots of his ships to help him.

Sailing in a vast ocean, da Gama somehow chose the best course possible for the long voyage. Instead of hugging the African coast, which might have seemed logical, he sailed far to the southwest, almost to South America, before turning east toward the Cape of Good Hope. By doing so, he took advantage of the prevailing winds and ocean currents. His trip was longer in miles but much shorter in time—and even today his course is used by modern mariners to make the trip around the cape.

After making several stops on the east coast of Africa, da Gama sailed across the unknown waters of the Indian Ocean. He reached his objective on May 22, 1498, ten months after he had left Portugal. After a series of misunderstandings, fights, and negotiations, da Gama was finally able to load the ships with cinnamon, cloves, ginger, pepper, and gems.

His voyage home was terrible, fighting head winds or becalmed by no winds at all. With fresh food and water scarce, men fell sick with scurvy; their teeth fell out, their bodies swelled. Sixty men died before a favorable wind carried them to the African shore, where they found food and water. Da Gama burned one of his ships because he did not have enough men to keep her sailing.

Despite the loss of men and ships, he finally made his way back to Portugal, arriving there in August or September of 1499. Da Gama spread his cargo of precious stones, porcelains, silks, and spices before the royal family. The king greeted him joyously, making him a nobleman of Portugal. For the king, the cargo was proof of the riches to be obtained in India and also of the opportunity to convert the heathens there to Christianity.

Within five months—an amazingly short time—Portugal had organized a second and more powerful fleet to go to India to show her power, to establish commerce on a regular basis, and to open diplomatic relations with the rulers of faraway countries. On February 15, 1500, Pedro Álvares Cabral was appointed to command the fleet of thirteen ships, with a crew of twelve hundred.

Like da Gama, Cabral was a trusted member of the royal court, with a fine presence and a sense of command. A young man thirty-two years old, he had gained the complete confidence of the king— perhaps the most important requirement for advancement at any royal court. One observer in Lisbon called him "a nobleman of good education and competent for the task."

He had been born in 1467 or 1469, the second of eleven children in a family of country nobility living in a castle in the small town of Belmonte. He attended a pages' school at the court of King John and later became a knight in the Order of Christ in the service of King Manuel. But there is no record that he ever went to sea or had any maritime experience.

Still, King Manuel had plenty of captains and pilots with long years of sea experience. Among those appointed to assist Cabral were some of the most experienced mariners of the day: Bartholomew Dias, who had been the first to reach the Indian Ocean; Bartholomew's brother Diogo Dias; and Nicolau Coelho, who had just returned with da Gama from India. Also aboard was Pedro Vaz de Caminha, described as a scrivener, to report on what happened during the voyage.

Cabral set sail on March 9, 1500, following a route recommended by da Gama: southwest to Madeira, south to the equator, and then southwest again, taking advantage of what we now call the Brazil current. Cabral hit the route just right to avoid the dangers of opposing winds and currents, but his ships were carried a little farther west than necessary.

On Wednesday of Easter week, April 22, 1500, a lookout

shouted, *"Terra!"* ("Land!"). Cabral had discovered the country that we now know as Brazil.

Ahead was a conical mountain, towering 1,758 feet in altitude. Although it is eighteen miles inland, it can still be seen from miles out at sea. Cabral named it Mount Pascal ("Easter Mountain"). The next day, he sent Captain Coelho ashore to talk to the natives, who appeared to be friendly.

After that, Cabral sailed forty miles north to find a good harbor. He found it at the mouth of the Santa Cruz River and called it Porto Seguro ("Safe Harbor"). There the Portuguese captured two natives, whom Cabral described as dark, rather reddish in color, with good faces and well-shaped noses. Another report described the natives as "between black and white and nude as they were born, without shame."

The Portuguese found it difficult to communicate with the natives, but they used sign language. They traded bells and other trifles for large, beautiful red parrots and caps and cloths of feathers woven together. One of Cabral's captains went inland and found that the Indians lived in longhouses and ate bread made from manioc or cassava roots, wild seeds, berries, and fish.

Some of the other sailors noticed the young and pretty girls ashore. Caminha, the scrivener, wrote: "One of the girls, all painted from head to foot, was so charming that many women of our land, seeing such attractions, would be ashamed that theirs were not like hers."

A delegation of Indians came aboard Cabral's flagship, where he received them wearing a colorful full-dress uniform adorned by a gold collar. By contrast, the Indians were naked as usual. They tasted the Portuguese food but apparently did not like it very much. After drinking some of the wine, the Indians stretched out on the deck to sleep.

Cabral's men fashioned a large wooden cross, carving on it the arms of Portugal, and erected it near the mouth of the Santa Cruz River. Cabral named the new discovery Terra da Vera Cruz ("Land of the True Cross"). The name was later changed to Brazil, after the wood that became its first profitable export.

Calling a council of captains, Cabral asked them if he should send news back to Portugal about the discovery before continuing the voyage to India. They decided to send a supply ship back, with a message by Caminha, who wrote:

And since Our Lord, who gave them [the Indians] fine bodies and good faces as to good men, brought us here, I believe it was not without purpose. And so Your Highness, who so much wishes to expand the Holy Catholic faith, should take measures for their salvation.

Cabral sailed from Brazil on May 2 and soon after ran into a storm. Four ships capsized and sank with all their crew members. After making extensive repairs, the remaining seven ships straggled into India on September 13. Cabral's stay in India was difficult, too. Because of opposition from Arab competitors, he loaded only a few of his ships.

Of the thirteen ships that left Lisbon in 1500, only seven returned in June and July of 1501. Six had been lost at sea. Two of the ships returned empty, but five carried cargoes of spices and other products of India. To the Portuguese, those five ships proved that the sea route to India was practical.

At that time Brazil, a country destined to surpass Portugal itself in area, wealth, and population, was considered valuable only as a place to replenish food, water, and wood on a passage to India. One historian has said, "Few voyages have been of greater importance to posterity, and few have been less appreciated in their time."

However, back in 1501, King Manuel of Portugal was very well satisfied. Despite his lack of experience and the disasters at sea, Cabral had proved himself to be a good leader of men. Unlike many other sea commanders, he was never toubled by insubordination or mutiny by members of his crew. The king appointed Cabral to command a third voyage to India, but he was superseded by da Gama, who was a senior officer, on that trip. Cabral never returned to Brazil nor to India.

Disappointed, he retired to a small country estate. He married a woman of royal lineage, Dona Isabel de Castro, one of the queen's ladies in waiting. They had six children. He died in 1530 and is buried in a small chapel of a church in Santarem.

His voyage of discovery tied together the trade of four continents: Europe, America, Africa, and Asia. It resulted in the immediate establishment of a huge Portuguese maritime empire from Africa to India and, more slowly, of a land empire in Brazil, which became one of the largest nations in the world.

Cabral is generally accepted as the discoverer of Brazil because its colonization followed immediately. But he may not have been the first explorer to catch sight of it. Three seamen under the Spanish flag, Vincente Yáñez Pinzón, Diego de Lepe, and Amerigo Vespucci, may have touched on the northern coast of Brazil before or in the same year as Cabral. Historians are still arguing about whether they did.

Pinzón, who was the captain of the *Nina* on Columbus's first voyage of discovery in 1492, sailed from Spain in November 1499. He crossed the Atlantic swiftly, sighting a cape that he called Santa Maria de la Consolacion on either January 20 or 26, 1500. Historians are still not sure about where in Brazil that landfall was, but they do agree that it was in Brazil.

Sailing north, Pinzón found something strange: water at sea that was fresh enough to drink. He had sailed just off the mouth of the mighty Amazon River, one of the longest rivers in the world. It pours so much fresh water into the salty ocean that for miles out to sea the water is good enough to drink.

Like Columbus, Pinzón thought he had reached the coast of Asia. He sailed about fifty miles up the Amazon, where he met some of the Indians who lived there, capturing some as slaves. Returning to sea, Pinzón sailed more than a thousand miles along the coast of Brazil and Guinea until he reached the familiar port of Santo Domingo. After suffering severe damage in a hurricane, Pinzón's ships returned to Spain in September 1500, with a cargo of logwood and twenty Indian slaves.

At about the same time, in late 1499, another Spanish sailor,

Diego de Lepe, sailed for the New World, too. Not much is known about de Lepe, except that he arrived somewhere on the northern coast of Brazil about a month later than Pinzón. Like Pinzón, de Lepe then sailed west along the coast until he reached the Gulf of Paria in April 1500 before returning home.

Portuguese historians question whether de Lepe actually touched the coast of Brazil before Cabral, but Brazilian historians accept his landing.

And then there is the story of Amerigo Vespucci, which is still cloaked in controversy five hundred years after his voyages to America. The tale of the man who gave his name to America is so complicated that it will be told in a separate chapter, which follows.

❧ 10 ❧

The Riddle of Amerigo Vespucci

WHY WEREN'T THE LANDS DISCOVERED BY CHRISTOPHER COLUMBUS named after him? Why were they called America?

For the answers, we have to turn to the life and letters of an unlikely explorer, a merchant from Florence named Amerigo Vespucci. Although two continents are named after him—North America and South America—his voyages of discovery remain among the most controversial in the history of exploration.

He made at least two trips to the New World, possibly three or four. Whether he made two, three, or four, we still do not know for sure. Then what did he accomplish that resulted in his enduring fame, and why are historians still debating it?

The evidence for what Vespucci did comes mainly from three sources: two of his letters that were published in his lifetime, manuscripts of other letters described as written by him that were discovered long after he died, and a few additional pieces of information from some of his contemporaries.

Some historians call the manuscripts forgeries and question their truth. To the doubters, Vespucci is an "imposter," a "liar," and a "fake discoverer." Others accept the documents as true accounts of Vespucci's voyages, attesting to his discovery of a new continent;

and maintaining that he was worthy of the honor of having it named after him.

If his discoveries are not well documented, his early life is, with a surprising amount of detail. Amerigo Vespucci was born on March 9, 1454, in Florence on the Arno River in northern Italy. His father was Nastagio Vespucci, a notary who was a member of a prominent Florentine family. Not much is known about his mother, Elizabetta, who had two sons before Amerigo was born and a son and a daughter after. The name Vespucci is derived from the Italian word *vespa*, meaning "wasps."

Amerigo grew up in the thriving city-state of Florence, ruled by the powerful Medici family. In those days of the Renaissance, Florence boomed in both trade and the arts. Amerigo's family included a banker, a bishop, and an ambassador, all in the service of the Medicis.

Among their neighbors was the Botticelli family. Young Sandro Botticelli painted one of Amerigo's cousins, Simonetta, who was considered the most beautiful woman in Florence, in his masterpiece, the *Birth of Venus*. Another distinguished artist, Domenico Ghirlandaio, painted Amerigo, Simonetta, and other members of the Vespucci family in his *Madonna della Misericordia* for a local church. It is the only known portrait of Amerigo Vespucci done in his lifetime.

Together with the sons of other prominent families, Amerigo went to a school at the Convent of San Marco, conducted by his uncle, Father Giorgio Antonio Vespucci. One of his schoolmates there was Piero Soderini, who rose to be the prime minister of the Florentine republic. It was to Soderini that Vespucci addressed one of his famous letters of discovery.

Giorgio Vespucci was a scholar, a collector of manuscripts, and the owner of a splendid library. At his school, Amerigo became skilled in mathematics, Latin, and the teachings of Aristotle and Ptolemy on astronomy, geography, and cosmography. The word *cosmography*, widely known in those days but little used today, meant the theoretical science dealing with everything in nature.

In contrast, geography was, and is, the practical science dealing with the countries of the world and their locations.

For Amerigo, studying maps was fun. He particularly liked large old parchment maps, brilliantly colored to show the world as Ptolemy knew it—faraway places with romantic names like India, the Nile, the Red Sea, the Spice Islands, Cathay, and the kingdom of Prester John. He pored over them, memorizing the strange places and their locations.

When his school days were over, Amerigo's father decided on a mercantile career for him. His eldest brother, Antonio, followed in his father's footsteps and became a notary. His second brother, Giralamo, went to the island of Rhodes in the Near East and joined a religious order that later became the Knights of Malta. Amerigo's youngest brother, Bernardo, entered the woolen business.

In his early twenties, Amerigo took his first step outside Florence as an aide to another uncle, Guido Antonio Vespucci, who was sent to Paris as the ambassador of the Medici. Acting as private secretary to his uncle, Amerigo became acquainted with the devious ways of kings and royal courts. He learned to be discreet, never brusque, and displayed a talent for making friends.

Shortly after his return to Florence, his father died. Amerigo, who had been trained to take care of the family's business affairs, soon faced a broader opportunity. In 1483, he became the manager of business and financial affairs for a branch of the Medici family.

For sixteen years, Vespucci acted on behalf of the family of Lorenzo di Pier Francesco de Medici. He dealt in fish, wine, cherries, mustard, cloth, seeds, tapestry, carpets, tablecloths, silver forks, knives, pigeons, poultry, damask, entertainments, banking, wheat, household affairs, the sale of crops, and investments. A confidant of the family, he himself prospered as they did.

With ample funds, he collected maps and books relating to geography and astronomy. He also made trips on Medici business to various cities in Italy and to Spain. The Medici had no branch in Seville or Barcelona, although they had agents there who supplied them with wool, dyes, almonds, horses, and mules while selling Florentine velvets, satins, damasks, and taffetas. In going over the accounts, Vespucci uncovered some irregularities. He and the Medicis decided that a trip to Spain was imperative.

On his first trip to Seville in 1489, Vespucci fell in love with the city. Although seventy miles from the sea, Seville had become a major port and trading center. It had the population, the harbor, access to the sea down the Guadalquivir River, and the financial organization needed to develop new trade.

More than that, for Vespucci, Seville was a handsome, congenial city, where he understood the language and made friends. In a setting bristling with commerce, Seville also reflected a Moorish heritage, with its mosques and bell towers. Vespucci liked the city, he liked the people, and he saw Seville as a land of opportunity, where he might work out a more independent life for himself.

He became friendly with Gianetto Berardi, an elderly member of an old Florentine family who had been working as a banker in Seville for years. One of Berardi's customers was Christopher Columbus, then in Spain seeking backing for a trip of exploration. There is no proof of a meeting between Vespucci and Columbus at that time, but it is possible.

Back in Florence, torn by discontent about the rule of the Medici family, Vespucci determined to change his life. In 1492, he left Florence on his own and returned to Seville. It was an epoch-making year in Spain: King Ferdinand and Queen Isabella finally drove the last Moors from Spain, they expelled the Jews from the country, and Christopher Columbus sailed on his famous voyage of discovery.

For Vespucci, it was also the year that started his transformation into an explorer. At the age of thirty-eight, an experienced merchant, a partner of a leading banker, a resident of a maritime area of Seville, he soon gained a growing reputation as an expert in charts, maps, and navigation.

Seville was at the heart of the new era of exploration—and Vespucci was at the right place at the right time. When Columbus returned from his first voyage of discovery in 1493, Vespucci listened with the others to his tales of the strange new lands. He and his partner, Berardi, helped raise funds for Columbus's second voyage, which started later that same year. After the death of Berardi in 1495, Vespucci financed several voyages by other mariners and helped outfit Columbus in 1498 for his third voyage.

His own desire to go and see for himself crystallized when Columbus left on his third voyage, still searching for the elusive passage to India. Vespucci wrote to his friend Piero Soderini in Florence:

> The reason for my coming to this Kingdom of Spain was to engage in trade, and during the four years I have pursued this purpose I had occasion to observe and experience the vicissitudes of fortune, which alters these perishable and transitory worldly goods. At one time fortune places a man at the top of the wheel, and at another casts him down and strips him of the possessions we may call borrowed. And so, knowing the unremitting effort man puts forth into securing such goods, suffering so many distresses and dangers, I decided to give up trade and devote myself to more praiseworthy things. I prepared myself to go and observe a part of the world and its wonders.

Even though some chroniclers put that first trip in 1497, most historians agree that it began two years later, in 1499. Vespucci, then forty-five years old, sailed on a Spanish expedition with Alonzo de Ojeda, who had served as a lieutenant on Columbus's second voyage, and Juan de La Cosa, a mariner and mapmaker who had sailed on the *Nina* with Columbus. Vespucci went along as an astronomer who knew something of navigation and as a merchant. But the lines of command were blurred. Ojeda commanded two ships with the help of La Cosa, but Vespucci, although he had no experience at sea, commanded two others.

They sailed from Spain on May 18, 1499, crossing the ocean in twenty-seven days. They parted company on approaching the shores of South America. Ojeda sailed northwest to the Gulf of Paria, collecting pearls that had been discovered there earlier by Columbus. Vespucci sailed south to Cape San Roque on the bulge of Brazil and then northwest along the coast, past the mouth of the Amazon River, to Paria.

Less interested in gold than almost all the other explorers, Vespucci devoted much of his time to observations of the stars, astronomical calculations, and attempts to calculate longitude. Like Columbus, he was interested in finding a passage to the Indies, and like his predecessor, he failed.

After nearly a year at sea, Vespucci's crew was ready to return. They had collected a few jewels to bring back to the king of Spain but little for themselves. Determined not to return empty-handed, they decided they could gain wealth by bringing back slaves. So they stopped at some islands, captured two hundred natives, and sailed back to Spain to sell them, arriving in June 1500.

In a letter to his former employer, the Medici, Vespucci wrote of the wonders he had seen: of cannibals who lived on human flesh, of wondrously colored parrots, of songbirds, and of trees "so beautiful that we thought we were in the Garden of Eden."

"We discovered a vast country and beheld an immense number of people, all naked and speaking various languages," he wrote. But not all were friendly. Many battles were fought with Indians, who tried to defend themselves against the strange newcomers. On one occasion, Vespucci's men tried to kidnap some beautiful young Indian women but were repelled by warriors with big clubs and bows and arrows.

King Ferdinand and Queen Isabella, pleased with the reports of Vespucci's trip, immediately made plans for another, offering him three ships to undertake further exploration. But these were the times when Spain and Portugal competed in the exploration of the unknown areas of the New World. Although by treaty the two nations had drawn a line on a map defining their territories, finding that line of division on land and sea sometimes gave rise to problems. Vespucci knew that he had landed and mapped Portuguese territory, even though he sailed for Spain. So did the king of Portugal.

Instead of being angry, King Manuel of Portugal invited Vespucci, who as a Florentine owed no allegiance to Spain, to come to Lisbon. Vespucci consented in the belief that he had to sail down the coast of the Portuguese territories in Brazil if he were ever to find a sea passage through the landmass.

"And when I presented myself before this king, he showed himself pleased at my coming, and asked me to accompany three ships he had ready to go to discover new lands," Vespucci wrote back to Florence. Vespucci went as scientific advisor to the captain-general of the fleet, Goncalo Coelho, a skilled mariner and a member of a prominent Portuguese family. Although Coelho was the commander, most history books overlook his contributions, focussing on his assistant, Vespucci.

They sailed from Lisbon on May 13, 1501. By coincidence, they met two ships of the Cabral expedition, returning from India, off the Cape Verde Islands. From them, they learned something of the coastline of Brazil. Battling storms, Coelho and Vespucci sailed on until, on August 15, they reached Brazil at about Cape San Roque.

They found a pleasing country, full of tall trees with sweet aromas, fields with herbs and flowers, and a multitude of wild animals—pumas, panthers, wolves, red deer, monkeys, wild hogs, wild goats, stags, and does. They also met the natives. "We found the whole land inhabited by people entirely naked, the men like the women without any covering of their shame," Vespucci wrote.

Those natives had one peculiar habit—they were cannibals. In one of his letters, written after the voyage was complete, Vespucci described a searing encounter with the natives:

And when we jumped ashore, the men of the land sent many of their women to talk with us. And seeing that they did not take courage, we decided to send to them one of our men who was a very agile and energetic youth; and we, to give them greater confidence, entered the boats. And he went among the women, and when he approached them they made a great circle around him; and touching and gazing at him, they displayed their wonder. Meanwhile we saw a woman approaching from the hill, and she carried a big club in her hand. And when she reached the place where our Christian stood, she came up behind him, and raising her club, struck him such a hard blow that she stretched him out dead on the ground. In a moment, the other women seized him by the feet and dragged him toward the hill; and the men sprange toward the beach and began to shoot at us with their bows. Our people, sitting in the boats which were made fast by anchors to the shore, were so demoralized by the shower of arrows that nobody thought of laying hand on his weapons. We fired four Lombard shots, but without hitting anyone. When the reports were heard, they all fled to the hill, where the women were already cutting up the Christian. And by a great fire which they had built, they were roasting him before our eyes, displaying pieces to us, and eating them.

The ships sailed away to the south and began a detailed examination of the coast of Brazil. It took them seven months to explore about thirty-three hundred miles, looking into many inlets and rivers—past the harbor of modern Rio de Janeiro and down to the Rio de la Plata, the mighty river that separates today's Uruguay and Argentina. Still they had not found the end of the land. Vespucci, who was mapping the trip, became convinced that they had found a new continent.

When he returned to Portugal in 1502, Vespucci wrote to his patron in Florence, Lorenzo di Pier Francesco de Medici, "We arrived at a new land which, for many reasons that are enumerated in what follows, we observed to be a continent." He cited the variety of the flowers and animals, the extent of the coastline, and the number and size of its rivers. But other explorers, including Columbus, had used similar phrases to describe their discoveries, which they believed to be part of Asia.

What made Vespucci's reports different? Why did they lead to naming America after him?

The major reason stems from two letters bearing his name that most historians now believe to be forgeries, or at best unauthorized expansions of his original letters. His earlier private letters to his friends in Florence were pirated, misquoted, embellished, and published presumably without his knowledge or consent in the days before there were any copyright laws. One historian has suggested that Vespucci himself wrote the expanded and lurid letters, but others have cited numerous errors of geography and fact in them to disprove that.

Both disputed letters contained a wealth of description of the sexual habits of the Indians—and became the bestsellers of their day. The first, called *Mundus Novus* ("New World") was published in August 1504. It went through at least forty editions in Latin, French, German, and Flemish. Shortly after, another letter, *Lettera al Soderine* ("Letter to Soderini") appeared. It gave details of four voyages to the New World, two more than Vespucci actually made.

His letters also contained much geographical information about the expanse of the land he had explored. They convinced some people that a new world had been found and that Amerigo Vespucci, although he may not have been its discoverer, was the first to identify and describe it as a continent.

The letters came to the attention of a well-known mapmaker, Martin Waldseemüller, a professor of geography at a college in the little town of Saint-Dié in Lorraine in France. At the time, Waldseemüller was busy preparing a new map of the world based on the work of the Greek cartographer Ptolemy.

Without consulting Vespucci, Waldseemüller used the name *America* for the first time on his map, published in 1507. He placed the word *AMERICA* on South America, at some distance north of Mount Pascal, the mountain discovered by Cabral in 1500.

Waldseemüller wrote: "Since another fourth part [of the world] has been discovered by Americus Vesputius . . . I do not see why anyone should object to its being called after Americus the discoverer, a man of natural wisdom, Land of Americus or America, since both Europe and Asia have derived their names from women."

That name sounded good, and it fit with the names of the other known continents—Europe, Asia, and Africa. As Waldseemüller's map circulated, other geographers, mariners, and mapmakers adopted the name for South America. In 1538, Gerard Mercator, in his large-scale map of the world, carried the idea one step further and divided the New World into North America and South America. Today, even though everyone now accepts the fact that Vespucci did not discover America, no one disputes the name *America* for both North and South America.

Vespucci himself knew nothing of Waldseemüller's map. After returning to Seville, he became a citizen of Spain and married a woman named Maria Cereso, about whom we know nothing. They had no children.

Pleased with his work, King Ferdinand named Vespucci the pilot major of Spain, a position equivalent today to the minister of marine, in charge of all overseas expeditions and training of navigators. That meant he had to stay at home while others went out on voyages of exploration. Remaining in that post for the rest of his life, he died in Seville on February 22, 1512, at the age of fifty-eight.

Today, every year, we celebrate the birthday of Christopher Columbus, who discovered America, but scarcely anyone remembers anything about Amerigo Vespucci, except his first name.

🞥 11 🞥

Balboa Discovers the
Pacific Ocean

IN ONE OF HIS FAMOUS POEMS, "ON FIRST LOOKING INTO CHAPMAN'S Homer," John Keats wrote:

> Much have I travell'd in the realms of gold
> And many goodly states and kingdoms seen;
> Round many western islands have I been
> Which bards in fealty to Apollo hold.
> Oft of one wide expanse had I been told
> That deep-brow'd Homer ruled as his demesne:
> Yet did I never breathe its pure serene
> Till I heard Chapman speak out loud and bold:
> Then felt I like some watcher of the skies
> When a new planet swims into his ken;
> Or like stout Cortez, when with his eagle eyes
> He star'd at the Pacific—and all his men
> Look'd at each other with a wild surmise—
> Silent, on a peak in Darien.

A great poet, Keats was, however, a poor historian. He confused Hernando Cortés, the man who conquered Mexico, with Vasco Núñez de Balboa, the first European to set eyes on the Pacific Ocean.

98

The story of Balboa's discovery started in 1475, when he was born in humble circumstances at Jerez de los Caballeros in Spain near the Portuguese border. His father, Don Nuno Arias de Balboa, was a poor nobleman, but nothing is known about his mother. In fact, little is known about Balboa—how he lived or what schools, if any, he went to. He had three brothers—Alvar, Gonzalo, and Juan—but we know nothing about them beyond their names.

As usual for the son of a poor nobleman, young Balboa went off to serve in the household of a nearby lord in the small port city of Moquer. There Balboa obviously heard tales of Christopher Columbus's voyages. As a young man, he also learned the martial arts, for later reports describe him as an excellent swordsman, skilled in duelling. One description that has survived is that he was a good-looking, fun-loving young man, attentive to women.

Balboa's name enters the historical record in the year 1500, when he was twenty-five years old. During that year, Rodrigo de Bastidas, a notary in Seville who was still in his twenties, decided that he wanted to sail off to the New World discovered by Columbus and make a fortune. He received permission from the king and queen of Spain, equipped two small ships, and hired Juan de La Cosa, who had been on the *Nina* with Columbus, as his pilot.

When Bastidas sailed from Seville in 1501, commanding the *Santa Maria* and the *San Anton* with a crew of about fifty, Balboa was somehow aboard. Obviously, like many poor young Spaniards of the day, Balboa saw an opportunity to get ahead, make a name for himself, and get rich in the New World.

The expedition sailed along the coast of present-day Colombia, trading cloth and beads for gold and pearls. In October 1501, the ships arrived at the Gulf of Uraba, at the western end of Colombia, where it borders Panama. There, in the Darien region of Panama, Balboa became interested in the Indians, trying to find out about how they lived. Bastidas traded for a little gold and a few pearls and then continued his voyage of exploration.

Bastidas soon faced one of the greatest dangers to seamen of the time—marine worms that ate the wooden hulls of the ships, making them porous and vulnerable to sinking. Somehow Bastidas and his men managed to sail across the Caribbean to the major Spanish colony in Hispaniola in 1502 before the ships sank. Bastidas returned to Spain, but Balboa remained behind.

Along with hundreds of other soldiers of fortune who had no place to go, Balboa scraped up a living in Hispaniola. He had a small plot of land, where he raised pigs. Like most Spanish gentlemen, he had no interest in farming. Bored with pastoral living, he borrowed money from his neighbors and went into debt.

While Balboa struggled on his farm, two other Spaniards received the king's permission to establish a colony along the coast that Bastidas had explored—in what is now western Colombia and southern Panama. Diego de Nicuesa was to colonize the Panama area and Alonzo de Ojeda the Colombia area. Both believed that they would find gold there and become rich. They sailed in 1509 and immediately ran into trouble with hostile natives who had poisoned arrows, an inhospitable climate, lack of food, and even a crocodile that ate one of the explorers' horses.

Ten months later a relief expedition, commanded by Martín de Enciso, sailed from Hispaniola with 150 new settlers. Hidden on the ship were two unauthorized recruits, Vasco Núñez de Balboa and his yellow-colored dog, Leoncico.

Barred by law from leaving because he owed money, Balboa decided that he would go secretly. With only the clothes he wore and a sword, he and his dog hid in a large empty flour cask on the deck. When the ship was well out to sea, he emerged from the cask and presented himself to Enciso.

Standing on the deck, with the officers and men watching, Balboa listened to an angry Enciso. The stowaway deserved the death penalty, Enciso warned, and would be left to die on a desert island. Some of the men spoke out for Balboa, citing his experience as a fighting man. Enciso yielded. But the seeds of distrust between himself and Balboa had been planted.

In early September, the relief expedition sighted the hills around the Gulf of Uraba. Enciso's flagship struck a rock in the water and broke up under the combined action of wind, waves, tide, and undertow. Most of the men swam ashore. All they could salvage from the ship was eighty swords, twelve barrels of damaged flour, a few cheeses, and some soggy hardtack. Ashore, they found hostile Indians.

Facing famine, fever, and fear of the poisoned arrows of the Indians, Enciso proved indecisive. His men watched him fumble the basic decisions that were needed for survival. Some thought it would be best to return to Hispaniola, giving up their expedition and quest for riches. In this time of trouble, Balboa stepped forward and spoke out: "I remember that years ago, when I came along this coast with Rodrigo de Bastidas, we entered this gulf, and on the western side, on the right hand, as it seems to me, we saw a village on the far side of a large river, and a land that was very cool and abundant with food. And the people there did not put poison on their arrows."

Enciso and his men decided to follow Balboa's advice. In their one remaining ship, the Spaniards sailed across the gulf to the land they called Darien. The Indians there were friendly at first, offering gold to the invaders. But they soon turned hostile because of the greed of the Spaniards. Enciso attacked, defeated the Indians, and took possession of their village. They named it Santa Maria del Antigua del Darien. It became the first European settlement on the North American continent.

In Darien, Balboa emerged as a leader. At that time, in 1510, he was thirty-five years old, fair in appearance, with reddish-golden hair and beard, graceful in his movements. One of the men described him as "very tall and well built, clean-limbed and strong, with the attractive bearing of a man of clear understanding, and capable of withstanding much hardship."

As a warrior, Balboa earned the respect of his fellow fighting men. Even more important, in the daily affairs of the colony, facing dangers from all around, he showed himself to be a man of common sense. It was a quality notably short in the faction-ridden outposts of Spain, where ambitious men plotted against one another to gain riches and fame.

Balboa provided a rallying point for the men who became angry at Enciso's high-handed methods. When Enciso issued an edict prohibiting them from trading for gold on their own under pain of death, their resentment boiled over. At a meeting to elect municipal officers, they ignored Enciso and chose Balboa and Martin de Zamudio as co-*alcaldes*, a position that was a combination of mayor and sheriff.

Enciso sailed back to Spain, where he spread stories to the royal court about what he called Balboa's disobedience to the orders of the king. At about the same time, in 1511, Diego de Nicuesa, who had been appointed governor of Panama, showed up after a series of disasters at sea. The men of Darien, having heard that Nicuesa was a tyrant, unstable, and incompetent, refused to allow him ashore. He sailed back, but his ship was lost at sea and he was never heard of again.

In Darien, Balboa sent his co-*alcalde*, Zamudio, back to Spain to report. That left Balboa in sole charge of the new colony. He knew that he had to keep his men busy, so he planned an expedition to the north. His objective was Careta, about twenty miles away by sea. Arriving there, Balboa showed that he was different from most of the other Spanish conquerors—he made a friend and ally of the local chief, Chima.

Chima offered a handsome gift of gold to the Spaniards, which pleased them. In addition, he made a pact with Balboa, whom he called Tiba, which means "great chief." In return for gold and food, Balboa would help him fight his enemies to the west, led by Chief Ponca. To seal the deal, Chima gave Balboa his young and beautiful daughter.

A few months later, Balboa and Chima attacked Ponca's village and burned it. That led Chima to ask Balboa to help him in his relations with a larger Indian tribe to the north, led by a chief called Comogre. Unlike the warlike expedition to the west, this was a peaceful mission. Balboa entered Comogre's village in friendly fashion.

After an exchange of gifts, the Spanish visitors admired some gold objects, clearly indicating their obsession with gold. As they weighed the gold, a violent quarrel broke out among the Spaniards.

Comogre's eldest son, Ponquiaco, watched the white men fighting over the golden objects that had just been presented to them as gifts.

Angrily sending the scales to the ground with a sweep of his hand, Ponquiaco addressed the newcomers.

What then is this, Christians, is it possible that you set such a high value on so little gold? Yet you destroy the artistic beauty of these necklaces, melting them into ingots. Why should you quarrel over such a trifle? If this gold is indeed so precious in your eyes that for it alone you abandon your homes, invade the peaceful land of others, and expose yourself to such sufferings and hardships, I will tell you of a region where you may gratify your wishes to the utmost.

He pointed to some towering mountains to the south. Beyond them, he said, there was a mighty sea, fed by streams abounding in gold. "Gold in fact is as plentiful among those people to the south as iron is among you Spaniards," he told his fascinated audience.

How could he get there? Balboa asked. Ponquiaco replied that they would have to go through a mountainous area inhabited by mighty kings who would try to bar the way. Balboa would need an army of at least a thousand men to fight his way through, but Ponquiaco said he would be glad to guide them. It was clearly a way to get the greedy Spaniards out of his territory.

From then on, the discovery of the sea beyond the mountains—and the gold there—obsessed Balboa. For the next two years he was occupied with fighting enemies, making friends with peaceful Indians, trying to grow enough food to keep alive, and coping with constant intrigue among ambitious Spaniards for command. In 1512, Balboa and his men faced their most dangerous threat—an alliance of Indians, five thousand strong, determined to wipe out the Spaniards.

The rebellion ended almost as it started, thanks to an Indian girl named Fulvia. She lived with Balboa, who had "so much esteem for her that it was as if she had been his legitimate wife."

Her brother warned her about the impending attack so that she could protect herself, but she, faithful to Balboa, told him. As a result, Balboa organized the Spaniards and surprised the hostile Indians before they were ready to attack, hanging the leaders of the conspiracy.

Obviously, Balboa was capable of savagery, as all the Spanish conquistadors were. But his displays of ferocity were calculated to win peace. He respected the native government and society, kept his promises to the Indians, and acted fairly toward them, winning their friendship. That was most unusual among the Spanish conquerors, who usually regarded the Indians as nonpeople, killing them without qualms.

One administrator reported back to the king that Balboa "had labored with very good skill to make peace with many *caciques* and principal lords of the Indians, by which he kept in peace about thirty *caciques* with all their Indians, and did so by not taking from them more than they were willing to give, and helping them resolve their quarrels, one with another, and thereby Vasco Núñez [Balboa] became so well-liked that he could go in security through a hundred leagues of Terra Firma. In all parts, the Indians willingly gave him much gold and also their sisters and daughters to take with him to be used as he wished. By these means was peace spread and the revenue of your highness increased."

Inevitably, Balboa's success brought him enemies, who were jealous and eager to take his place as the leader in Darien—and to take over the gold they saw there. When Balboa heard from Spain that he might be called back to answer charges made by Enciso, whom he had displaced as the leader in Darien, he decided he had to make a great discovery to keep his position—he would cross the mountains and find the great sea beyond.

On September 1, 1513, Balboa set out on the first leg of his trip. With him were 190 armed men and a number of bloodhounds. The Spaniards had found that ferocious dogs were valuable allies in fighting Indians, who were terrified of them.

Among the dogs was Leoncico, Balboa's constant companion. An immensely strong animal, Leoncico was a veteran in battle, his body bearing the scars of many wounds. Balboa thought so highly of Leoncico that the dog received the same share of loot as armed soldiers did. That, of course, went to Balboa, his master.

In the village of a friendly *cacique*, Balboa's men were furnished guides for their trek through the mountains. After leaving half his men behind at a base camp, Balboa and the other men, although heavily weighed down by armor, slowly climbed the rugged, thickly forested mountains inland. They came to a hostile village, where six hundred Indian warriors, armed with bows and arrows, blocked the trails. Although they fought to halt the white strangers, the Indians were defeated by the guns of the invaders.

After resting briefly, Balboa, with sixty-seven men, climbed the last mountain to the west. Before he reached the top, he ordered his men to halt, while he himself climbed to the peak. On reaching the summit, he looked out to the south. Beyond the rocks and forest below, he saw the open waters of the ocean. Because the Isthmus of Darien at that point runs east and west, Balboa, facing south, named the ocean Mar del Sur, "the Southern Sea"—now called the Pacific Ocean. The date was September 27, 1513.

With his dog, Leoncico, at his side, Balboa knelt to the ground and gave thanks to God for allowing him to be the first European to see the great ocean. He called to his troops to come up and look at the distant waters, too. And he was anything but "silent, on a peak in Darien," as Keats described the scene.

An historian of the era reported:

And he told the people with him to kneel also, to give the same thanks to God and to beg Him fervently to allow them to see and discover the great secrets of that sea and coast for the greater glory and increase of the Christian faith, for the conversion of the Indians, native of those southern regions, and for the fame and prosperity of the royal throne of Castile and its sovereigns present and to come.

Balboa had actually discovered an inlet of the Pacific Ocean, which he named the Gulf of Saint Michael. Two days later, he and his men descended to the shores of the gulf and found that the water was low, exposing a mud flat. They waited patiently for the tide to come in. When it did, Balboa held up a banner with a picture of the Virgin Mary and another of the royal arms of Castile and León. This is what happened next:

> With his drawn sword in his hand and his shield on his arm, he waded into the salt sea up to his knees, and paced back and forth, reciting, "Long live the most high and most mighty monarchs, Don Fernando and Dona Juana, sovereigns of Castile and Aragon and Navarre, etc. in whose name I now take possession, in fact and in law, of these southern seas, lands, coasts, harbors and islands, with all territories, kingdoms and provinces which belong to them or may be acquired, in whatever manner, for whatever reason, by whatever title, ancient or modern, past, present or future, without let or hindrance."

The Spaniards tasted the water to make sure it was salty and therefore oceanic. It was. A scribe wrote down the names of the men who were present. Balboa, of course, led the list. The others included Andrew de Vera, a priest, and Francisco Pizarro, who was later to become famous in his own right.

Balboa remained on the borders of the ocean for two months, exploring the coastline and collecting gold. He returned over the mountains by a different route, arriving back in Darien on January 19, 1514. He immediately wrote to the king, reporting his discovery. But bad news awaited him. The king, troubled by the tales of Enciso and other jealous men, had dispatched a new governor for the territory before he received news of the discovery of the great ocean.

The new governor was Pedro Arias de Avila, generally called Pedrarias, whose wife was close to the throne. Pedrarias had some credentials. In his youth he had gained the nickname the Jouster because of his ability in tournaments; later he was called the Gallant because of the magnificence of his dress. He had fought with distinction in Africa. More important, he had a powerful friend,

Bishop Juan Rodriguez de Fonseca, the king's advisor on affairs in the Americas.

Taking his wife with him, Pedrarias sailed from Spain in April 1514, with fifteen hundred men. His instructions were to depose Balboa and to call upon him to justify his expulsion of Enciso. Pedrarias arrived in Darien at the end of June and found a thriving city, with a population of about five hundred Europeans, all men, and about fifteen hundred Indian men and women.

Balboa yielded his command graciously and explained his actions satisfactorily. His spirits rose when another ship arrived from Spain bearing news that the king, in honor of his discovery, had named him *adelantado*, or governor, of the South Sea, as well as governor of the province of Panama, but still subordinate to the general command of Pedrarias.

Relations between the popular Balboa and the jealous Pedrarias soon deteriorated, though, despite a remarkable development. A priest in Darien suggested that Pedrarias arrange a marriage between one of his daughters and Balboa to encourage the two leaders to cooperate in the future. Both men agreed that Balboa would marry Pedrarias's oldest daughter as soon as she arrived from Spain.

Unhappily, when Balboa departed on another expedition to prepare for an exploration of the western ocean, Pedrarias became convinced that a plot was being hatched against him. He ordered a band of armed men, led by Francisco Pizarro, to arrest Balboa and four of his companions. Bound in irons, Balboa and the others returned to Darien. By that time, feelings were so strong in Darien for and against Balboa that one of his enemies even poisoned his faithful dog, Leoncico.

Balboa's trial was a farce. He was accused of many crimes— that he had mistreated Indians, that he had betrayed the trust of the king and the governor, and that he had treacherously plotted a revolt against the authority of the governor and the king. He denied the charges and made an obvious defense: Why would he have returned voluntarily if he were guilty? Pedrarias would not listen. He demanded the death of the man who might have been his son-in-law, and his subordinates obliged by finding Balboa guilty.

On January 21, 1519, a town crier walked in front of Balboa and his four lieutenants, leading them to the public square for execution. The crier proclaimed, "This is the punishment inflicted by command of the king and his lieutenant, Don Pedro Arias de Avila, on this man, as a traitor and a usurper of the territories of the crown."

"It is false," Balboa cried out indignantly. "Never did such a crime enter my head. I have served my king with truth and loyalty and have sought to augment his dominions."

But he knew it was no use. He walked to the execution block and put his head upon it. The executioner swung his ax, severing Balboa's head from his body. When his companions were executed, too, their bodies were thrown to the vultures. Thus at the age of forty-four, Balboa, the discoverer of the Pacific Ocean, died, the victim of a jealous rival.

𝒞12𝒟

The Fountain of Youth

JUAN PONCE DE LEÓN SET OUT TO FIND THE LEGENDARY FOUNTAIN of youth, a magical stream of water that would transform old people into young ones. Instead he discovered Florida. Today, although Florida does not contain water that rejuvenates people, it does have a warm climate that attracts millions of senior citizens to enjoy a more relaxed way of life—perhaps an equivalent of the legendary fountain of youth. Who was Ponce and how did he come to discover Florida?

He was born in 1474 in Tervas de San Campos in Spain. His father, Luis Ponce de León, a minor nobleman, had married a cousin, Francesca, who bore the same last name. She was the daughter of Don Rodrigo Ponce de León, a noted warrior. Young Juan resembled his grandfather, not only because of his red hair but also because of his strong personality.

Like most young noblemen who were not rich, Juan served as a page for a powerful lord for many years. From an early age, he had been schooled in warfare, taking part in the many campaigns waged by the Spaniards, under the leadership of King Ferdinand and Queen Isabella, to expel the Moors from Spain.

Ponce's first contact with the Americas came in 1493, when, at the age of nineteen, he volunteered to accompany Christopher

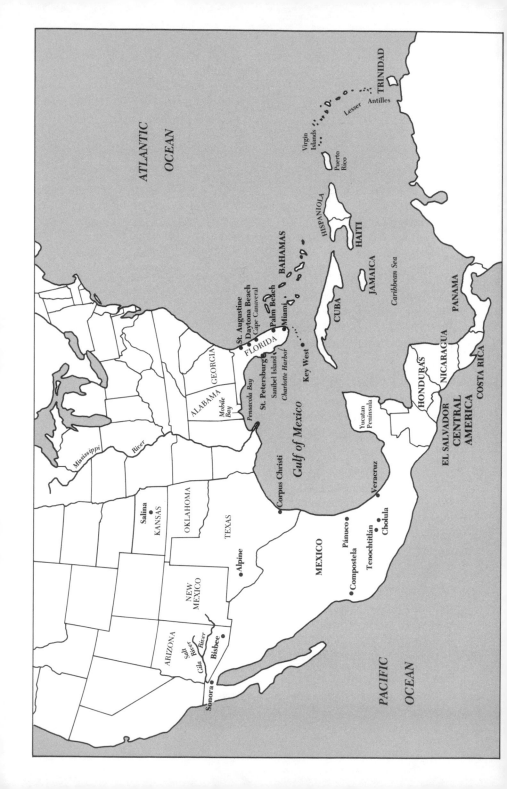

Columbus on his second voyage to the New World. During that voyage (see chapter 6), Columbus and his men sailed through the island chain of the Lesser Antilles, stopping at Puerto Rico, which was later to play an important role in Ponce de León's life, and also visiting Hispaniola and Cuba.

Not much is known about how Ponce spent the next few years, except that he served as a soldier, distinguishing himself for his bravery. In Hispaniola, he acted as second in command in a battle against the Indians at Higuey, on the eastern end of the island, in what is now the Dominican Republic. His reward was an appointment as commander of the province.

Impatient with the details of governing, Ponce looked for new worlds to conquer. He found his opportunity across the water to the east on the beautiful island of Borinquen (later to be called Puerto Rico). Various Spanish ships had touched on the island, but their crews had never penetrated into the interior.

Yet the Indians of the two islands frequently visited each other. After one of those visits, Ponce heard that a native of Borinquen had brought a big nugget of gold with him. Like most Spaniards of his day, Ponce was attracted by the possibility of becoming rich quickly from gold deposits. He obtained permission from the governor of Hispaniola to explore Borinquen.

In 1506, when he was thirty-two years old, he landed in Borinquen on a peaceful scouting mission. He met the principal *cacique*, Aguaybana, who greeted him cordially. When Ponce asked the chief to show him the treasures of the island, Aguaybana took him to groves of trees bursting with fruit and streams of cool, clear water.

Not interested in the riches of nature, Ponce demanded whether the island produced any gold. Aguaybana took him to two inland rivers, where grains of gold shone through the pebbles. When Ponce returned to Hispaniola with some gold, he received permission to conquer Borinquen.

The Indians once again welcomed Ponce in a most hospitable way on his next trip. When he received an appointment as governor of the island in 1509, he set up a capital in a town called Caparra, about three miles from the sea. In front of it was a port called Rico, from which the entire island later became known as Puerto Rico.

The friendly Indians soon learned the difference between receiving the Spaniards as guests and as masters. Under Ponce's rule, the Indians were driven to despair by the heavy tasks forced upon them. Ponce used "the labors, blood and sufferings" of the Indians, as one contemporary put it, to grow rich. The Indians finally organized an island-wide rebellion and attacked the Spaniards, killing many and burning their settlements.

Under attack, Ponce showed his skill as a military leader. First, he remained on the defensive, killing many Indians as they attacked his fortified positions. Then, armored in steel, his men surprised an Indian stronghold, killing the Indian chief in battle.

Among Ponce's surprise weapons were ferocious dogs, commonly used by the Spanish against the naked Indians. Trained to attack natives as though they were wild boars or fleet deer, the dogs soon terrorized the Indians, who were not accustomed to the powerful animals.

One of Ponce's most efficient warriors was his own dog, Berezillo, medium in size, reddish in color, with black eyes, and of unknown breed. At the time, it was said that Berezillo could distinguish allied Indians from hostile ones by using his sense of smell. Ponce valued his dog's prowess so much that he awarded him the pay, allowance, and share of the booty assigned to a soldier, which he collected himself.

Berezillo was renowned throughout the Caribbean for his ferocity, courage, and strength. Several years after the Puerto Rican adventure, he was killed by a poisoned arrow while swimming in the sea in pursuit of a Carib Indian. He left behind many offspring, including Leoncico, the faithful dog of Vasco Núñez de Balboa (see chapter 11), who looked like him and performed warlike exploits as well.

With Puerto Rico conquered, Ponce resigned as governor in 1512. During the following three years, he made a fortune by dealing in gold, slaves, and land. It was then that he first heard the legend of the fountain of youth told by some old Indians.

Far to the north, the Indians said, there existed a land that possessed a river of such miraculous powers that anyone who bathed in it would be restored to youth. Years ago, before the Spaniards arrived, they went on, a large party of natives had gone northward in search of the river of life. Since they had never returned, the Indians concluded, they must have found the promised land and must be living there in perennial youth.

Ponce was a hard-bitten soldier, now thirty-eight years old, skilled in warfare and in the political rivalries in Hispaniola. How could a man of his years and experience believe such a tale? Yet he did, and he received permission from the king to discover and conquer Bimini, the island of the magical fountain of youth.

Using his own money, for he had become rich in Puerto Rico, Ponce outfitted three ships and recruited a number of sailors and gentlemen to accompany him. He sailed from Puerto Rico on March 1, 1513, on a northwest course that took him alongside the Bahama Islands. Landing on many of the islands, he drank the water he found, but without any magical effects.

Not discouraged, he continued to sail northwest until he sighted what he thought to be a large island. He landed on April 3 at an inlet a little above what is today Daytona Beach, about fifty miles south of St. Augustine. It was the height of spring, with flowers blooming everywhere. Because of the many flowers he saw, Ponce called the new land La Florida.

Ponce took possession of Florida in the name of the Spanish king. With his landing, Ponce became the first Spaniard to touch the shores of what is today the United States.

Unfortunately, the Indians of Florida were hostile. Everywhere Ponce landed, he found an implacable resistance by the local residents. Disappointed at not finding any gold or rivers or fountains that possessed special qualities, he decided to explore further.

Off Florida, Ponce made another discovery: the Gulf Stream. Trying to sail south, he met a head current so strong that it drove his ships back, even though they had a fair wind behind them. The discovery of the mighty Gulf Stream, which always flows south to north, was almost as important as the discovery of Florida. One historian has said that Florida was originally valued as a base for sending ships north from the Caribbean Sea and using the power of the Gulf Stream before making the Atlantic crossing from America to Europe.

But Ponce did find a small southward current along the edge of land and sailed south, passing Cape Canaveral and the future sites of Palm Beach and Miami before reaching Key West. He turned the cape of Florida and sailed north until about halfway up the west coast, near today's Charlotte Harbor. Stopping to fill water casks and cut firewood, he and his men invariably met hostile Indians. Moreover, none of the Indians they encountered had ever heard of a fountain of youth.

Disappointed, Ponce started his voyage home in June. He sailed south, discovering a group of islands covered with sea birds and mammals. One night there, his men captured one hundred sixty turtles, fourteen seals, and a large number of pelicans and other birds. He named the islands the Tortugas ("Turtles").

Sailing southwest across the Gulf of Mexico, Ponce landed on the Yucatan Peninsula on June 26, thus discovering Mexico, near what is Merida today. He thought it was an island and named it Bimini, even though it, like Florida, did not have any water that resembled a fountain of youth.

Giving up his search for the elusive magical waters, Ponce returned to Puerto Rico in October. Shortly thereafter, he went back to Spain to report to the king. Even though he could not claim success in his quest for the fountain of youth, he did bring back gold and news of the discovery of Florida as presents to the king. In return, he was named *adelantado* of Bimini and Florida.

He also received command of a fleet of three ships and orders to free the Caribbean of the fierce Carib Indians, who were interfering with Spanish trade and shipping. In 1515 he sailed from Spain, but he met with disaster on his first landing—on the island of Guadeloupe. As usual, he sent a party ashore to fill water casks and gather firewood. But they were surprised by the Caribs, who killed some of the Spanish sailors and made prisoners of others.

Discouraged, Ponce returned to Puerto Rico, where he was still the governor. He moved the capital to the waterfront and founded the city that is now San Juan. A soldier at heart, he did not enjoy the peaceful pursuits of government. When he heard of the exploits of Hernando Cortés in Mexico (see chapter 13), he decided to make one more expedition—to explore and colonize the land he had discovered earlier, Florida.

He sailed from Puerto Rico on February 15, 1521, in two ships carrying two hundred men, fifty horses, other domestic animals, seeds, and roots—obviously with the intention of establishing a permanent colony. Although his precise landing point is not known, it is believed to have been near today's Sanibel Island, not far from Tampa Bay.

But the local Indians resisted. One chronicler described them as "rough, and very savage and bellicose and ferocious and not accustomed to peace." The Indians fought fiercely to defend their shores against the white invaders. Even though they had only bows and arrows against the Spanish guns, they killed many of the Spaniards and wounded many more.

Ponce himself was wounded by an arrow in the thigh. Unable to lead his men, he was carried to his ship, disabled. He ordered a withdrawal. His crew sailed to Havana, the nearest Spanish port in Cuba. His wound became infected, and Ponce died there in July 1521, at the age of forty-seven.

Today, almost five hundred years later, his name lives on in Florida, where the words Ponce de León are visible everywhere—on streets, hotels, restaurants, and even taverns. But Juan Ponce de León should also be remembered because he was the first European to set foot in the lands that are today Mexico and the United States—the "discoverer" of both those countries—as well as of Florida.

∽13∾

The Conquest of Mexico

THE FIRST DISCOVERERS OF MEXICO WERE, OF COURSE, THE FIRST
Indians who wandered down into Central America from the north
(see chapters 2 and 3). They were followed by successive tribes,
the last of which were the Aztecs, who settled in what is now
central Mexico in the early 1300s. Two hundred years later, the
Aztecs ruled a mighty empire, controlling ten million people
throughout Mexico, from the Atlantic to the Pacific Ocean.

High in the mountains, seventy-four hundred feet above sea
level, the Aztecs built the city of Tenochtitlán ("Place of the Prickly
Pear Cactus") in the middle of a lake, connected to the shores by
long, narrow causeways. More than sixty thousand people could
fit into its central marketplace. Into the market flowed crops grown
on raised fields in the nearby valley of Mexico and the products
of the empire—maize, gold, paper, chocolate, pottery, jewels,
spears, feathers, cotton, rubber, tobacco pipes, and incense.

The Aztecs were ruled by an elected monarch, supported by
nobles, soldiers, and priests. Montezuma ("the Courageous
Lord"), a man then in his thirties, who had been both a general
and a high priest, assumed the throne in 1502. At first, the new
king was attentive to the concerns of his kingdom. For example,
he would walk the streets in disguise to see if citizens were abused.

Later he became arrogant, imposing huge taxes on neighboring peoples to support a lavish court. This, of course, made many enemies for both him and the Aztecs.

During his reign, he embodied the role of religion in the daily life of the Aztecs. To them, humankind was at the mercy of unseen powers, which had to be placated often by human blood and human hearts, torn from a person's living body, fresh, hot, and still beating. With the object of capturing prisoners who would be sacrificed, they waged perpetual war on their neighbors.

Linking their life and prosperity to the gods, the Aztecs built many huge temples in their honor. Their major god of the sun was called Huitzilopotchli, or "the Humming Bird of the Left," because, as seen in its images, the bird had feathers on its left foot. The Aztecs believed that unless they presented sacrifices to him, he would not rise the next day, bringing his life-giving rays. He also had another aspect as Tezcatlipoca, or "the Mirror That Smokes," associated with the night skies.

Another principal god was Quetzalcoatl, or "the Feathered Serpent," sometimes referred to as a great teacher who opposed human sacrifice. In Aztec legend, Quetzalcoatl—a god with white skin and a black beard—had been defeated and driven into exile by Tezcatlipoca, leaving Mexico's gulf shore on a raft. Before he went, though, he warned: "I will return . . . and reestablish my rule. It will be a time of great tribulation for the people." Montezuma and his priests expected that sooner or later Quetzalcoatl would return from the sea, and they worried about his revenge.

That feeling intensified in the early 1500s. An earthquake, a fire in a temple, three comets in the sky, a mysterious wailing in the air—all seemed to be omens that Quetzalcoatl would soon be back. With his own hands, Montezuma sacrificed some human victims at the altar of Quetzalcoatl, hoping for a signal from the god. Then he sent watchers to the gulf coast to await the god's return.

Twice before, Montezuma had heard about strange white men landing on the shores of Mexico. In 1517, an expedition led by Hernandez de Cordova had landed north of the Yucatan Peninsula, but had been driven off by hostile Indians. Cordova took back some gold ornaments to Cuba, however, and that impelled the Spanish governor to send another expedition in 1518.

In that year, Juan de Grijalva led 240 men back to Mexico. He landed near what is now Veracruz and found an astonishing sight— three well-dressed chiefs politely offering corn bread, pineapples, and other fruit. He did not know it, but they were emissaries of Montezuma, awaiting Quetzalcoatl. Grijalva exchanged some glass beads for gold and then returned to Cuba, while the envoys went back to report to Montezuma.

When the governor of Cuba, Diego Velasquez, heard how rich the new lands were, he ordered a new and larger expedition to be dispatched there. As captain-general, he appointed Hernando Cortés, then thirty-four years old, an ambitious planter whose background was not very distinguished.

Cortés had been born in Medellin in Spain in 1485 to Martin Cortés de Monroy, a captain of infantry, and his wife, Dona Catalina Pizarro Altamirano. At the age of fourteen, he went to the University of Salamanca to study law, but he showed little interest in books. Idle and adventuresome, he sailed to the New World in 1504. When he arrived in Hispaniola, he told the governor, "I came to get gold, not to till the soil like a peasant," an attitude almost all Spanish gentlemen shared.

Nevertheless, Cortés did accept a grant of land to farm, became a notary because of his legal training, and often went out on military expeditions to quell native revolts. In that way, he became familiar with the tactics of both the Spanish soldiers and the natives. After taking part in the conquest of Cuba, Cortés became the *alcalde*, or mayor, of Santiago.

One of those who accompanied him to Mexico, Bernal Diaz del Castillo, later wrote one of the great eyewitness accounts of history in the making. He described Cortés on the eve of the conquest of Mexico:

He was of good height and strongly made, with a somewhat pale complexion and serious expression. If his features lacked something, it was because they were too small, his eyes mild and grave. His beard and hair were black and thin. His chest and shoulders were broad. His legs were bowed and he was an excellent horseman. I have heard that when he was young he was wild about women. A scar that appeared through his beard came from one of those affairs.

Already deeply in debt for fine clothes he had bought for himself and his new wife, Catalina Suarez, Cortés borrowed more to outfit his ships and men. When he was almost ready, Velasquez, the governor, who was envious of the possible riches in Mexico, changed his mind about the young captain-general and sent messengers to arrest him. Warned of the attempt to stop him, Cortés set sail from Cuba on February 10, 1519, before the new orders reached him.

His expedition consisted of eleven small ships carrying 508 soldiers armed with swords, 100 sailors, 32 crossbowmen, 11 musketeers, 10 brass cannon, 4 small cannon, 16 horses, and a number of dogs.

Disembarking in a strange land where the natives spoke strange languages, Cortés showed that he possessed the major attribute of a successful conqueror—luck. During his first landing, he picked up a Spanish prisoner of the Indians, Jerónimo de Aguilar, who spoke Mayan as well as Spanish.

At a second landing, at Tabasco, hostile Indians attacked, but were routed by the armed men on horses, which they had never seen before. The defeated Indians brought many gifts to the conquering Spaniards, including gold and twenty women. Among the women was a chief's daughter, who was christened Dona Marina. She spoke Mayan and Nahuatl, the language of the Aztecs (some commonly used words today of Nahuatl origin are *chocolate*, *tomato*, *chicle*, *chili*, *cacao*, and *coyote*).

Thus on April 21, when Cortés landed a bit farther north, near the site of the present city of Veracruz, he had a translation team ready. When a group of Indians came bearing gifts and speaking

Nahuatl, Dona Marina translated into Mayan and Aguilar into Spanish. After an exchange of gifts, the Indians returned to Tenochtitlán to report to Montezuma.

As soon as Montezuma heard a description of the newcomers and their weapons, he became convinced that Cortés was indeed the god Quetzalcoatl returned. As the high priest of the Aztecs, Montezuma felt that he had to bow to the will of Quetzalcoatl. As the head of state, though, perhaps he could persuade the angry god to leave by showering him with gifts.

The more gifts he sent, though, the more Cortés and his men became anxious to see the fabulous city that had produced them. First, however, Cortés had an internal problem to deal with. Some of Velasquez's friends wanted to take the gold they had already received and return to Cuba. Cortés knew that to do so would be a personal disaster for him—he might even be arrested for treason for disobeying Velasquez's orders.

With his knowledge of Spanish law, Cortés found a way to outmaneuver his opponents. Under the law, any group of Spanish subjects could set up a municipality and elect its officers if they obtained the king's permission. Cortés's supporters immediately organized a new town called Villa Rica de la Vera Cruz ("the Rich Town of the True Cross"), elected Cortés as their leader, and sent word, together with a handsome gift of gold, to the king in Spain. Now Cortés legally reported to the king, not to Velasquez in Cuba.

He took one other bold, even rash, action. To prevent anyone from returning to Cuba, he wrecked his eleven ships so that there could be no retreat to safety for anyone. For Cortés, it was either victory and glory in conquering Mexico or death—and in his mind there was no doubt that he would succeed.

In front of him lay two hundred fifty miles of high mountains, some ten thousand feet in altitude, narrow valleys, volcanoes, rapid rivers, jungles of scrubby growth and cactus plants, a desolate plateau forty miles wide—and hostile natives. The march to Tenochtitlán was of immense danger and difficulty, but Cortés did not hesitate, even though his army totaled only about four hundred men.

On August 15, 1519, Cortés, riding a chestnut horse, led his small band toward Tenochtitlán. In back of him came his captains in their armor, soldiers with muskets, lances and crossbows, Dona Marina and the other women, and forty porters carrying cannon and ammunition. Slowly they climbed the winding paths toward the plateau of Mexico.

Their first major obstacle came near Tlascalan, where six thousand Indians awaited. The Spaniards formed a square, advancing foot by foot toward the enemy. In a furious battle, many of the Indian captains were killed, causing them to retreat. But the remaining Tlascalan army numbered fifty thousand. Bernal Diaz recalled the scene:

> We saw the fields filled with warriors, wearing feathered crests and various devices, and making a din with their trumpets and horns. The whole plain was swarming with them, with ourselves in the middle, some four hundred soldiers. We knew for certain that this time they were coming with the idea of leaving none of us alive except for a few to be sacrificed to their idols.

But the Tlascalan commanders were divided and did not coordinate their attack. Faced with an overwhelming number of Indians, the Spanish fought bravely and repelled them. Cortés thanked God for his success. The Tlascalans attributed their defeat to the gods, too, accepting Cortés himself as a god. After several uncertain days, the Tlascalans opened peace talks.

They said they had attacked because they believed the strangers were allies of Montezuma. Never conquered by the Aztecs, the Tlascalans hated their neighbors, who raided their lands and carried off their young men to be sacrificed to the gods. Cortés seized the opportunity to make an alliance with the Tlascalans. More important, he had found the key to the conquest of Mexico: using Indian tribes to conquer other Indians. It wasn't that the Tlascalans welcomed the Spaniards, but that they hated the Aztecs more.

One more barrier stood between Cortés and Tenochtitlán—the city of Cholula, allied with the Aztecs. Fearing that the Cholulans would attack him, Cortés struck first. He seized their chiefs and, with the help of six thousand Tlascalan soldiers, the Spanish invaders massacred at least three thousand men in the city.

For Montezuma, the massacre at Cholula was another sign of the anger of the avenging god. To placate him, Montezuma sent six of his lords carrying a large amount of gold, jewels, and rich cloth, together with assurances of his friendship. As Cortés continued to advance, Montezuma sent more presents, begging him not to come any farther toward Tenochtitlán. Cortés, of course, had no intention of going back.

He knew that he could not fight his way into the Aztec stronghold, protected by narrow causeways over the lake. He would have to enter peacefully. Although Cortés did not realize that Montezuma had already concluded that he could not resist the Spaniards, he deduced that he could enter the city only by advancing confidently in a nonbelligerent way. And so his tiny army marched on.

To reach Tenochtitlán, his men climbed over a pass twelve thousand feet high, between the volcanoes of Popocatepetl ("the Mountain That Smokes") and Iztaccihuatl ("the White Woman"), two of the highest mountains in North America. At the top of the pass, they could see the city many miles away, in the center of a large lake some fifty miles long. As they neared the city, several sets of emissaries from Montezuma greeted them, still offering gold if Cortés would turn back. But Cortés was confident now that a ruler who offered such gifts was already defeated.

On November 8, 1519, a memorable day in the history of Mexico, Cortés entered the capital of the Aztec empire, the first European to do so—the discoverer of the heartland of Mexico. First he was greeted by many of the Aztec chiefs, dressed in richly decorated mantles, adorned with gold. Then Montezuma himself came to welcome him.

Here is how Bernal Diaz, the eyewitness, described the first meeting between Montezuma and Cortés:

Montezuma descended from his litter while these great chiefs supported him with their arms beneath a rich canopy of green feathers worked with gold and silver, pearls . . . he was richly dressed and wore shoes like sandals, with soles of gold covered with precious stones. . . . When Cortés saw the great Montezuma approaching, he jumped from his horse and they showed great respect toward each other. Montezuma welcomed him, and through Dona Marina, Cortés replied that he hoped Montezuma was in good health. It seemed to me Cortés offered his right hand, and that Montezuma did not take it, but he did give his hand to Cortés.

After an exchange of gifts, Cortés and his men were shown to their quarters, close to Montezuma's own palace. Soon thereafter, Montezuma came to visit the Spaniards, assuring them of his friendship. "For the kings, my ancestors, told me that you would appear, that you would return to sit on your mat, your stool," he told them. For Montezuma, Cortés's appearance fulfilled the prophecy of the priests.

For a week, Cortés and his men wandered around the fabulous city of the Aztecs, marveling at its architecture, its size, and its wealth. A thousand persons watered and swept the streets daily. An immense aviary housed thousands of birds of splendid plumage, alongside a menagerie of fierce animals. Extensive gardens of fragrant shrubs and flowers, with fountains throwing up towers of water, surrounded the palaces of the king and the nobles and the many temples. The numerous canals with their small boats reminded the Spaniards of Venice.

Cortés worried that his small force was in danger from the overwhelming numbers of Aztecs around them. Even though Montezuma displayed only friendship and lavished gold and presents on the Spaniards, as military men they knew that they were surrounded by forces that could turn hostile at any moment.

Cortés decided to seize Montezuma and hold him as a hostage against any attack. Montezuma bowed to his fate and established his court in the palace occupied by Cortés. But he was a prisoner and he knew it.

Now Cortés asked Montezuma to pay tribute to the king of Spain. Montezuma opened his treasure rooms to the Spaniards and ordered his vassals to bring gold, silver, and jewels to Cortés, which they did. It was an immense treasure, larger than that possessed by any monarch in Europe.

One-fifth was set aside for the king of Spain, as was the law, and one-fifth for Cortés, which would make him wealthy. After making deductions for expenses, the remaining amount was divided among his officers and men.

After capturing Tenochtitlán without firing a shot and assembling the treasure, Cortés faced mounting troubles. His Spanish rival in Cuba, Diego Velasquez, not only denounced Cortés to the king but sent an army of thirteen hundred men in eighteen ships to Mexico under the command of Panfilo de Narvaez to capture Cortés and bring him back for trial. Cortés, of course, had no intention of surrendering.

Instead, he divided his forces in two, leaving a contingent in Tenochtitlán. First he sent messengers with gold to some of the new Spanish soldiers to show them how rich they could become if they joined him. Then, on a rainy night, he made a lightning surprise attack on the sleepy Narvaez forces across a river.

Narvaez, after losing an eye to a pike attack, surrendered. His soldiers, who outnumbered Cortés's force, also surrendered when he called upon them to yield in the name of the king. Lured by the promise of gold, the soldiers joined Cortés's army.

Then came the bad news. The Aztecs had revolted. They had been provoked by an attack on an Aztec religious ceremonial dance by the commander of the small garrison Cortés had left behind in Tenochtitlán, Pedro de Alvarado. Help was urgently needed to save the Spanish soldiers, surrounded by angry mobs of Aztecs. Cortés, with a reinforced army of thirteen hundred men and ninety-six horses, turned around immediately and marched to the Aztec capital.

He walked into a trap. First the Aztecs cut the water and food supply to the Spanish garrison. Then they attacked. On the fifth day of the battle, Cortés asked Montezuma to ask the attacking

Aztecs for a truce so that he could leave Tenochtitlán. Reluctantly, Montezuma climbed to the roof of the building and began to speak. The angry Aztecs would not listen. They told him that they had replaced him with another lord. Then, according to Bernal Diaz, the eyewitness, this is what happened:

> They had hardly finished this speech when there was such a shower of stones and javelins that Montezuma was hit by three stones, one on the head, another on the arm, and the third on the leg, for our men who were shielding him neglected to do so for a moment, because they saw that the attack had stopped while he was speaking with his chiefs. They begged him to be doctored and to eat something, speaking very kindly to him, but he wouldn't, and when we least expected it, they came to say that he had died.

Thus death came in June 1520 to the tragic sovereign of the Aztecs. Cortés wept for him, as did many of his soldiers. They had seen Montezuma as a good and kindly man, generous and understanding. As a king-priest, however, he had been made ineffective by his firmly held belief that he could not oppose Cortés, whom he regarded as the god Quetzalcoatl returned to take revenge on the Aztecs.

Cortés decided that he had to fight his way out of the city. Under cover of darkness, he used a portable bridge to cross gaps in a causeway that had been severed by the Aztecs. The Aztecs cut his line of retreat when only half of the Spanish had crossed.

Cortés faced two problems: whether to go back to try and save half his army and how he himself would get out safely. He reluctantly concluded that there was no way to save the trapped soldiers, and so he fought his way out of the city with his remaining troops. He left behind all his guns, all his golden treasures, most of his horses, and half his force of thirteen hundred men.

"It was a miracle that any of us escaped," he wrote. Afterward, the Spaniards called it *el noche triste* ("the sad night").

After fighting his way through another large army of Aztecs, Cortés finally reached the borders of the friendly Tlascalan Indians.

His army had dwindled to four hundred forty men, with twenty horses, twelve crossbows, and seven muskets. Undaunted, Cortés, ever a bold soldier, immediately started making plans to return to the Aztec capital.

Several things helped him. First, the Tlascalans responded to his pleas and furnished thousands of troops. Second, several Spanish ships landed at Veracruz, and their crews and supplies were immediately seized by Cortés to reinforce his army. Finally, a European disease, smallpox, made the Aztecs helpless. An epidemic broke out among the Aztecs, killing thousands of them, including Montezuma's successor.

Even though the Aztecs were weakened, Cortés knew he could not fight his way back into Tenochtitlán. Nor could he enter in peace, as he had the first time. So he changed his tactics. He ordered a fleet of sloops built to carry his troops into the heart of Tenochtitlán and across its lakes, without fighting his way up the narrow causeways. After capturing all the cities on the lakeshore, so that the capital was surrounded, he cut its water supply.

From January to May 1521, Cortés besieged Tenochtitlán. The Aztecs fought bravely, led by their new monarch, Guatemozin ("Lord Falling Eagle"), the nephew of Montezuma, and their priests. Battles were fought, thousands of men were killed, and Cortés was almost captured twice. But Guatemozin failed to concentrate his forces and make a united, determined assault on the Spaniards.

Almost daily the Aztecs furiously attacked the Spanish forces. They captured many Spaniards. One day Bernal Diaz and his companions heard the dismal booming of a drum on top of the great pyramidal temple in the city square.

We all looked toward the lofty temple where they were being sounded and saw that our comrades whom they had captured when they defeated Cortés were being carried by force up the steps. They were taking them to be sacrificed. When they got them to the platform before the shrine, we saw them stick plumes to the heads of many of them. They made them dance before the

Humming Bird with what looked like fans in their hands. After they danced they were immediately placed on their backs on the sacrificial stones and with stone knives they sawed open their chests, drew out their palpitating hearts, and offered them to the idols. They kicked the bodies down the steps.

Despite that horror, the determination of Cortés and the fighting ability of his men finally prevailed. As Cortés slowly fought his way into the heart of the city, Guatemozin fled in three large canoes with his wife and some of his attendants. One of Cortés's fast sloops captured the fleeing monarch.

In a letter to King Charles of Spain, Cortés wrote: "This lord having been made prisoner, the war immediately ceased, which God Our Lord was pleased to bring to its end on this day, the 13th of August, 1521, seventy-five days after we first laid siege to the city."

That day in August 1521 marked the end of the Aztec empire. More than one hundred twenty thousand Aztecs had been killed in the gory battle. Relatively few of the Spaniards had been killed, but tens of thousands of their Indian allies died. Bernal Diaz described the scene at the end of the battle:

I swear that all the houses on the lake were full of heads and corpses. I have read of the destruction of Jerusalem, but I cannot believe that the massacre was greater than that of Mexico, although I cannot say for certain. The streets, squares, houses, and courts were filled with bodies so that it was almost impossible to pass.

Even Cortés was sick from the stink in his nostrils. But he began a systematic destruction of the temples and other buildings of the Aztecs, a task that was to take four years. Streets were widened, canals were filled in, and a cathedral devoted to St. Francis arose on the site of the temple of the Aztec war god.

In 1522, Cortés finally received official recognition from King Charles of Spain, with the titles of governor and captain-general of New Spain.

After a series of expeditions in Central America, Cortés returned to Spain in 1528. The king raised him to the nobility with the title of marquess of the Valley of Oaxaca, awarding him a large grant of land and feudal powers over twenty-three thousand Indians who lived there. But the king, following the Spanish tradition, refused to confirm him as governor of the conquered empire; that role was reserved for a civil administrator, not the triumphant military man.

In Spain, Cortés made a second marriage, to Dona Juana de Zuñiga, a niece of the duke of Bejar. They had a son and four daughters. Despite his new connection to the noble Bejar family and honors at the royal court, Cortés the soldier felt out of place in the civilization of Spain.

A rich man, he went back to Mexico in 1530. He lived in luxury on his huge estate and occasionally left on a trip of exploration. Once more, in 1540, he returned to Spain.

By now, though, other conquests in the New World, like that of Peru, eclipsed his accomplishments, and Cortés became a minor figure on the Spanish scene. The famous conquistador lived quietly in Seville, where he died on December 2, 1547, at the age of sixty-two.

∽14∾

Magellan Discovers the Way

"The most remarkable voyage in recorded history"
—*Samuel Eliot Morison*

"The greatest human achievement on the sea"
—*Edward G. Bourne*

THAT IS HOW MODERN HISTORIANS DESCRIBE FERDINAND MAGELLAN'S three-year voyage around the world in the years 1519 to 1522. Not only is he credited with being the first man to circumnavigate the globe, but he was also the first to find the elusive westward passage between the Atlantic and Pacific oceans and the first to discover the immensity of the Pacific Ocean.

What about Columbus's discovery of America? Isn't that what all Americans, indeed almost all people of the world, consider the most important geographical discovery in history?

No, according to many scholars. They say that the first navigation of the Strait of Magellan was a far more difficult problem of seamanship than crossing the Atlantic. Columbus's voyage was completed in thirty-five days, but Magellan's took a year. And Magellan weathered an icy winter before the second part of his voyage began—over a trackless expanse of water—that took three times as long as the first crossing of the Atlantic.

Although most people today recognize Magellan's name, nobody celebrates his birthday, as we do Columbus's. Indeed, we still do not know exactly when Magellan was born. Sometime in 1480 is the best that historians have been able to determine. And although we call him Ferdinand Magellan, that is the anglicized version of his name. He signed himself Fernão de Magãlhaes, reflecting his Portuguese birth.

His parents, Rui de Magãlhaes and Alda de Mesquita, lived in the mountainous area of northern Portugal. Ferdinand, the youngest of three children, had a sister, Isabel, and a brother, Diogo. They lived in a farmhouse, which years before had been a small castle. That reflected their station in life as poor but respected members of a noble family.

When Ferdinand was twelve years old, his father obtained an appointment for him as a page in the court of Queen Leonora in Lisbon. He and his cousin Francisco Serrão joined his older brother, Diogo, who was already serving there.

The job of a page was to act as a messenger and an usher at court events, but pages also attended school. They learned manners, music, dancing, horsemanship, hunting, the use of lances and swords, and how to conduct themselves in a royal establishment.

As Portugal emerged into a major seapower during the late 1400s, the pages were required to study mapmaking, astronomy, and navigation as well. Duke Manuel, the queen's brother, was in charge of these studies. Unfortunately for Ferdinand, Duke Manuel disliked him. No one knows the reason, but everyone at court recognized the duke's feeling. It became an important factor in Ferdinand's future when Duke Manuel became King Manuel of Portugal in 1495.

The three pages, Ferdinand, Diogo, and Francisco, grew up in an exciting time in Portugal, with far-off places beckoning to ambitious young men. Vasco da Gama pointed the way to glamorous India on his return to Lisbon in 1499 after his epoch-making voyage around the Cape of Good Hope. When in the following year Pedro

Álvares Cabral left for India, young Ferdinand tried to go along but was refused permission.

In those formative years, Ferdinand, his brother, and his cousin worked as clerks in the king's new maritime department. Instead of seeking their fortunes amid the riches of the Indies, they helped to outfit ships for others. For almost ten years, Magellan worked in obscurity before he and his two companions got their chance to sail abroad.

Ironically, it was their knowledge of the details of supplying ships, not of seamanship, that gave them the opportunity. Their clerical talents were needed in the huge fleet organized by Francisco de Almeida, the newly appointed viceroy of India, who had received orders to establish trading bases on the east coast of Africa and the west coast of India.

Almeida sailed on March 25, 1505, in twenty-two ships, carrying fifteen hundred soldiers, four hundred artillerymen, and a small group of civil servants. Among them was Ferdinand Magellan, then almost twenty-five years old.

After four stormy months at sea, Almeida's fleet turned the Cape of Good Hope and sailed up the east coast of Africa into an area dominated by Arab traders. Almeida captured the port city of Kilwa (in the present country of Tanzania) and built a fort there. He continued north along the African coast to the Arab city-state of Mombasa (in the present country of Kenya), capturing and burning that port. Magellan served for twenty-seven months in Africa, helping to pacify rebellious local forces before going on to India in October 1507. His transformation from a clerk to a fighting man had begun.

Portugal's undeclared war aimed to break the monopoly of Arab traders, backed by Venice, in the lucrative spice markets of the Indies. Before the Portuguese found the new sea route around the southern tip of Africa, the normal transportation of spices from the East had followed a complicated route: by small boats to Malacca on the Malay Peninsula, by Indian boats to the west coast of India, by Arab ships across the Arabian Sea to Abyssinia, on camelback (with fifty camels fastened head to tail by chains, plodding along at about two miles an hour) to Alexandria, then by Venetian ships to the markets of Europe.

For four years, a naval war raged in the Arabian Sea, with Portuguese vessels fighting combined Egyptian-Venetian forces. In the last great battle, on February 2, 1509, the Portuguese boarded the Egyptian flagship, defended by hundreds of armored soldiers. In five hours of desperate hand-to-hand fighting, the Portuguese prevailed. When the battle was over, Ferdinand Magellan lay on the deck, wounded almost to death.

That battle established Portuguese supremacy on the west coast of India. For Magellan, it meant a long period of recuperation. By now he was almost thirty years old, with a reputation as a first-class fighting man, experienced in handling ships and men. When he recovered, he took part in a new expedition, east toward the Spice Islands themselves.

He and his Portuguese companions landed on the southern tip of Malacca (now Malaysia), a bustling port filled with Chinese junks, in late 1509. In an action there, Magellan again distinguished himself by his bravery and common sense. When he returned to India, he was promoted to captain.

Once more he demonstrated his leadership abilities following the wreck of a ship in 1510. After hitting a shoal near the Maldive Islands at night, the ship broke up, leaving its sailors clinging to the wreckage. At dawn they made their way to a small nearby island. When a small boat left to seek help, Magellan, unlike the other officers, remained behind with the shipwrecked mariners. For three weeks, he rallied the men, supervising the fair rationing of short supplies and protecting whatever was left of the cargo, until they were rescued.

Magellan returned to the Spice Islands in 1511, as commander of one of three ships. Their first step was the capture of Malacca, where Magellan received his reward—a thirteen-year-old Malay slave boy whom he named Enrique de Malacca. Enrique remained with him for the rest of his life.

Magellan's cousin Francisco Serrão continued on to Ternate,

one of the major Spice Islands, east of Borneo, but Magellan apparently remained for the most part in and around the Strait of Singapore. He made one voyage farther east, possibly to the Philippines or to other Spice Islands near Ternate. That unauthorized trip got him into trouble. His superiors relieved him of his command and sent him back to Portugal.

After eight years in the Far East, Magellan returned to Lisbon in 1513 and found himself a forgotten man. Even though he was thirty-three years old and a veteran sailor and soldier with the rank of captain, the only employment he could get at the royal court was that of usher. He volunteered to serve in a Portuguese army in Morocco, where he received a leg wound that made him lame for life.

Back in Lisbon, Magellan appeared in court, on his knees as was the custom. He appealed to King Manuel for an increase in pay and rank, citing his experience in battle. The king, who had detested Magellan ever since his days as a page, refused. Magellan persisted, asking for the command of a ship. Annoyed, the king replied that he had no opening at all for Magellan.

Could he then enter the service of another lord? Magellan asked.

Exasperated, the king shouted that he did not care what Magellan did or where he went.

Thus humiliated, Magellan left the court of the Portuguese king. But Magellan had some friends, among them Rui Faleiro, a former fellow page who was now a leading astronomer and mapmaker, and John of Lisbon, a navigator who had been named chief pilot in Portugal. Together they studied maps and came to the conclusion that there was a shorter way to the Indies—by sailing west instead of around the Cape of Good Hope.

At the age of thirty-seven, Magellan left Portugal for Spain, the other leading seapower of the day. He arrived in 1517, a year in which his fortunes changed for the better. Not only was he befriended by Duarte Barbosa, an important Portuguese pilot in the service of the king of Spain, but he was introduced to Barbosa's uncle, Diogo, a Spanish official. They liked the penniless Portuguese exile so much that they approved his engagement to Beatriz Barbosa, Diogo's daughter, an aristocratic, rich young woman. They were married in December 1517.

Together, Magellan, the Barbosas, and Faleiro planned a voyage across the Atlantic, via an unknown strait through the landmass of the Americas to eastern waters and the Indies. Their map studies had convinced them that the Spice Islands were on the Spanish side of the line drawn by the Treaty of Tordesillas (see chapter 6), which divided the world into Spanish and Portuguese spheres of influence. But receiving permission from the Spanish king for such a voyage was not easy.

Even getting to see the king was difficult. The Spanish court was a labyrinth of intrigue, dominated by Juan de Fonseca, bishop of Burgos, a greedy man who controlled all Spanish voyages of exploration. He had his own plan to tap the wealth of the Spice Islands.

When that plan failed, Fonseca turned to Magellan and arranged an interview with King Charles of Spain. Bishop Bartolomé de Las Casas, who was there, described Magellan as rather short, but broad in body, and strong and agile despite his slight limp. Dark in complexion, he had a full black beard and mustache. Las Casas described the interview:

Magellan brought with him a well-painted globe showing the entire world, and thereon traced the course he proposed to take, save that the Strait was purposely left blank so that nobody could anticipate him. . . . Magellan was perfectly certain to find the Strait because he had seen on a nautical chart made by one Martin of Bohemia, a great pilot and cosmographer, in the treasury of the King of Portugal the Strait depicted just as he found it.

And, because the Strait was on the coast of land and sea within the boundaries of the sovereigns of Castile, he [Magellan] therefore had to move and offer his services to the king of Castile to discover a new route to the said islands of the Moluccas and the rest.

The young king was enchanted not only by Magellan and his plan but by what seems to have been a theatrical performance by Magellan's slave, Enrique de Malacca, and his wife, a slave girl from Sumatra, dressed in her native costume. The king approved Magellan's proposal to sail to the Spice Islands. Still, it took two years of preparation before he was ready to leave.

In that time, in 1518, his son Rodrigo was born. The king raised Magellan to the rank of knight commander of the military Order of Santiago, a high honor. But Magellan had some troubles, too. His partner, Rui Faleiro, grew irrational in his demands and had to be replaced. Bishop Fonseca took the opportunity to appoint Juan de Cartagena, a relative, to replace Faleiro and to name other supporters to key positions in the armada, loyal to him and not to Magellan.

Unknown to Magellan at that time, the Portuguese plotted to make his expedition fail. They did so by bribing suppliers to provision the ships with much less food than Magellan paid for. The basic rations included ship's biscuits, salt beef, salt pork, dried codfish, pickled anchovies, dried beans, raisins, honey, olives, figs, nuts, and a goodly supply of wine. Magellan thought he had ample supplies, but he found out differently later.

Magellan's fleet consisted of five ships—the *Trinidad*, his flagship, the *San Antonio*, the *Concepcion*, the *Victoria*, and the *Santiago*. His crew numbered two hundred forty officers and men. Among them was a gentleman volunteer, Antonio Pigafetta, of Vincenza in Italy, who kept notes and later wrote one of the most famous sea narratives of his time.

On September 20, 1519, Magellan sailed from Spain down the coast of Africa and headed west. As the trip began, the first of his troubles with Fonseca's men began, too. Cartagena, who commanded one of the ships, refused to obey orders. But men loyal to Magellan seized him and Cartagena was relieved of his command.

Two months later, the fleet landed in Brazil and then sailed south along the coast of South America, looking for a passage to the west. In January 1520, they reached the Rio de la Plata. Magellan spotted a large mountain and shouted, *"Monte video!"* ("I see the mountain!") Today the city of Montevideo is the capital of Uruguay.

Magellan continued along the coast of Patagonia, searching for the elusive passage. As winter came, he decided he would have to camp on the shore until better weather came. He anchored his ships at an inlet he called Port San Julien, far down the coast of present-day Argentina.

With food running low, the sailors began to grumble. More important, some of Magellan's captains argued that they should turn back. Magellan refused. That brought on a mutiny, led by Cartagena, whose followers took possession of three of Magellan's five ships. They sent a message to Magellan, saying they would follow his lead only if he returned to Spain.

Outnumbered by the rebels, Magellan acted decisively. He sent a letter to Luis de Mendoza, captain of the *Victoria*, ordering him to return to duty. After reading the letter, Mendoza threw it away, laughing. One of Magellan's faithful followers grasped Mendoza's beard and cut his throat, killing him.

Magellan fired a broadside of cannonballs onto the decks of the *Concepcion*, causing its captain, Gaspar de Quesada, to surrender. With his supporters defeated, Cartagena surrendered, too. Magellan, a tough survivor, punished the leaders of the revolt after a court-martial found them guilty. Quesada was beheaded and Cartagena marooned on a desolate shore. Magellan was more merciful to the mutinous ordinary sailors. He put them in chains while they worked during the rest of the winter.

When spring came, Magellan sailed south with only four ships; the *Santiago* had been wrecked on a sandbar on an exploratory trip. On October 21, 1520, Magellan discovered an inlet that looked promising. To the south, he saw signal fires of the natives. He named that land Tierra del Fuego ("Land of the Fires"). Then he sent two of his ships into the inlet to explore it before committing his entire fleet.

A week later, the two ships, flying every flag and standard they had, returned. As his ship came alongside Magellan's, Captain Álvaro de Mezquita reported: "I have the honor to report the discovery of the paso. It is a deep, narrow strait, with a heavy tidal flow, and we penetrated a hundred miles before we turned back."

Despite the good news, his captains felt that the fleet should not enter the unknown strait but go to the Indies the known way, in the opposite direction around the Cape of Good Hope. They cited a lack of supplies for a long voyage into the unknown. But Magellan spoke forcefully: "Even if we have to eat the leather wrappings on the masts and the yards, I will still go on to discover what I have promised Our Lord the King, and I trust that God will aid us and give us good fortune."

At dawn, the fleet of four ships sailed into the waterway, which has ever since been known as the Strait of Magellan. From beginning to end, the strait was not simply a long, straight passageway between one ocean and the other. Unknown to Magellan at the time, it was, and is, 334 nautical miles long, twisting and turning, with many narrow passageways leading to dead ends.

Facing many choices of water courses to follow, Magellan sent his ships out separately to explore them. One ship, the *San Antonio*, never came back. While she was searching the passageways, Esteban Gomez, an experienced pilot, organized a successful mutiny and took over the ship. Gomez, who had hoped to be commander of the expedition, hated Magellan, according to members of the crew, and decided to return to Spain without even telling his superior.

After looking in vain for the *San Antonio*, which they considered to be lost and wrecked, Magellan called a meeting of his remaining officers. Down to only three ships now, they were shocked to find their food stores dangerously low. Corrupt suppliers in Seville had loaded provisions for only six months instead of the year and a half as specified.

Still, Magellan felt he had little alternative but to continue. He knew that if he returned to Spain, he would fall into the hands of Bishop Fonseca and certain punishment. So he sailed on.

For days, the *Trinidad*, the *Concepcion*, and the *Victoria* sailed slowly westward, discovering new islands, mountains, and water passages, stopping only to catch fish for food. The men landed on the shore occasionally to hunt prairie hens, rabbits, and birds for additional food supplies.

Thirty-eight days after entering the Atlantic opening of the strait, Magellan's ships completed their passage on November 28, 1520. In front of him, Magellan saw a limitless blue ocean—one of the great moments in the history of maritime discovery.

Magellan had not discovered the Pacific Ocean, of course; seven years earlier, Balboa had stood upon that peak in Darien, the first European to gaze upon the ocean (see chapter 11). But Magellan had discovered what many bold captains had sought for years: a westward passage between the oceans to the Indies.

Magellan ordered a ceremony for the momentous day. With sea birds flying overhead almost in an aerial salute, the officers and men knelt in prayer. After the three ships displayed their most colorful flags, their guns thundered a salvo to salute the discovery.

Magellan turned to his officers. "Gentlemen," he said, "we are now steering into waters where no ship has sailed before. May we always find them as peaceful as they are this morning. In this hope, I shall name this sea the Mar Pacifico." And to this day it is still called the Pacific Ocean.

Like other mariners of his era, Magellan believed it would only be a short journey to the Indies. He was wrong. He sailed briefly north and then west on what seemed to be an endless body of water—and ran out of food. Pigafetta told the story:

> We were three months and twenty days without getting any kind of fresh food. We ate biscuit, which was no longer biscuit, but powder of biscuit swarming with worms, for they had eaten the good. It stank strongly of the urine of rats. We drank yellow water that had been putrid for days. We also ate some ox hides that covered the top of the mainyard to prevent the yard from chafing the shrouds. We left them in the sea for four or five days and then placed them for a few moments on top of the embers

and so ate them; and often we ate sawdust from the boards. Rats were sold for one-half ducado, and even then we could not get them. The gums of both the upper and lower teeth of some of our men swelled, so that they could not eat under any circumstances and therefore died. Nineteen men died from that sickness.

After two months of sailing across the boundless ocean, they finally sighted land, an uninhabited island east of Tahiti, on January 24, 1521. They gorged themselves on sea birds, turtle eggs, crabs, and fish they caught on the reefs. But sailing west, they ran out of food once more. By March 5, there was absolutely nothing left to eat on the ships.

The very next morning, a lookout in the crow's nest in the masthead cried out, "Praise God, praise God, land, land, land, land!" He had sighted the island of Guam, rich with coconut palms and occupied by a handsome, fearless people. They swarmed aboard the Spanish ships, picking up everything that was not nailed down—iron, crockery, pins, hatchets, and even a longboat on the deck of one of the ships. Magellan named the island and its neighbor, Rota, the Islas de Ladrones ("Isles of Thieves").

Depite the mischief of the natives, Magellan replenished his supplies there. In a few days, he sailed on to the Philippine Islands, sighting Samar on March 15. He anchored in a sheltered bay at the island of Homonhon in Leyte Gulf, where he and his men found food plentiful. After a week of recuperation, they sailed to the nearby island of Limasawa in the Surigao Strait.

When a boatload of Filipinos approached, Enrique de Malacca, Magellan's slave, spoke to them in his native Malaysian language. To Magellan's pleasant surprise, they answered in the same language. For Magellan and his men it was all the proof they needed that they had reached the Indies by sailing west.

With friendly relations established, gifts were exchanged, and the weary, hungry Spanish sailors for the first time began to live a life of ease. The Rajah Colambu, the ruler of the island, visited the ship, and the sailors went ashore to relax among the very friendly Filipino women. On Easter Sunday, after a solemn Mass was celebrated on shore, Magellan took possession of the islands in the name of King Charles of Spain.

He learned from Rajah Colambu that the island of Cebu, the richest and most populous of the area, was only a short distance away. He sailed there, entering its harbor on April 7, 1521. The Sultan Humabon, its ruler, greeted Magellan courteously and even consented to become baptized as a Christian.

Intrepid in the face of adversity, Magellan was surrounded by friendly natives, an ample supply of food, newly converted Christians, and a lively trade. Almost as if he were unable to cope with a life of ease, Magellan now made the first major mistake of his voyage—a mistake that was to prove fatal.

He decided to support Sultan Humabon in forcing a chief on the nearby island of Mactan to accept the sultan's rule. Despite the advice of his captains, Magellan agreed to lead the attack himself. At dawn on April 27, he and forty-eight men waded ashore on Mactan. This is what happened, according to Pigafetta, who went with him:

We found the islanders, 1,500 in number, formed into three battalions [which] showered on us such clouds of bamboo lances, staves hardened in fire, stones, and even dirt, that it was with difficulty that we defended ourselves. . . . A poisoned arrow struck the Captain on the leg, who on this ordered a retreat in slow and regular order, but the majority of our men took to flight precipitately, so that only seven or eight remained about the Captain. . . . We retreated gradually still continuing to fight and were now at a bow shot from the islanders, and in the water up to our knees, when they renewed their attack with fury, throwing at us the same lance five or six times over as they advanced. As they knew our Captain, they chiefly aimed at him, so that his helmet was twice struck from his head. . . . An islander, at length, succeeded in thrusting the end of his lance through the bars of [Magellan's] helmet, and wounding the Captain in the forehead, who, irritated on the occasion, ran the assailant through the body with his lance, the lance remaining in the wound. He now attempted to draw his sword, but was unable, owing to his right arm being grievously wounded. The Indians, who perceived this, pressed in crowds upon him, and one of them having given him a violent cut with a sword on the left leg, he fell on his face. On this, they immediately fell upon him. Thus perished our guide, our light, and our support.

Magellan died on April 27, 1521, at the age of forty-one. Leaving his body behind, the survivors fled back to Cebu. But their troubles were not yet over. Sultan Humabon became convinced that the Spaniards were plotting against him after listening to Enrique de Malacca, Magellan's former slave, who considered himself to be a free man following his owner's death. Angry at what he considered bad treatment by Magellan's successors, Enrique suggested that Humabon invite the Spaniards to a banquet. When they arrived, the Filipinos attacked them, killing most of the thirty-eight who came and capturing the others, selling them into slavery.

Reduced in number to 110 men, the Spaniards decided to scrap the *Concepcion*, which was riddled with ship worms. Under the command of Joao Lopes Caravalho, the remaining two ships, the *Trinidad* and the *Victoria*, meandered in the Sulu and South China seas before he was replaced as incompetent. The officers elected Gonzalo Gomez de Espinosa as captain-general. Their wanderings ended on November 8, 1521, when they landed in the Spice Islands, their destination.

Loaded with spices, the *Victoria* sailed from the Indies on December 21, 1521, commanded by Juan Sebastian de Elcaño, with Pigafetta, the writer, as one of the crew. Because she needed repairs, the *Trinidad* stayed behind (and was later captured by the Portuguese). It was a long voyage home for the *Victoria*, around the Cape of Good Hope. She arrived back in Seville on September 8, 1522.

Only eighteen emaciated survivors of the two hundred forty men who had started, including de Elcaño and Pigafetta, completed the circumnavigation of the globe for the first time. They marched barefoot, carrying lighted candles, through the streets of Seville to give thanks at a church.

King Charles greeted de Elcaño warmly and rewarded him handsomely with an annual pension and an appropriate coat of arms, showing a castle, two crossed cinnamon sticks, three nutmegs, and twelve cloves, and above them a globe bearing the motto in Latin, *Primus circumdedisti me* ("Thou first circumnavigated me").

Today de Elcaño and the others have been forgotten. But the name of Magellan lives on. Even though he did not complete the first voyage around the world, he is given credit for it. First, he had reached the Philippine Islands twice, once from the west and once from the east, thus circling the world. More important, his voyage of 1519–1522 demonstrated that the world was round and that all its oceans were connected, opened up a passageway between the Atlantic and Pacific oceans, and disclosed the vast dimensions of the Pacific Ocean.

๛15๛

The Discovery of Canada

WHEN JACQUES CARTIER SAILED UP THE ST. LAWRENCE RIVER IN 1535, he stopped in the area of what is now Quebec City. In French and in sign language, he asked the natives what they called the land. They replied, *kanata*, referring to their village. From that misunderstanding, the world's second-largest country got its name, Canada.

Cartier was not the first European to set foot in Canada, of course. More than five hundred years before, Leif Ericsson had touched the shores of Newfoundland (see chapter 3). And in 1497, John Cabot had landed in Newfoundland, too (see chapter 7). Morever, fishermen from many nations, including some from Cartier's native village of St. Malo, came to the rich fishing grounds off Canada every year. Undoubtedly some of them stopped off on the rocky coast. But Cartier did discover the St. Lawrence River, opening up Canada for exploration and settlement.

He was born in 1491 in St. Malo, on the northern seacoast of Brittany in France. The ancient town was the home port of fleets of hardy seamen who ventured out into the sometimes stormy Atlantic Ocean as fishermen. Nothing is known about his early life or his education, nor is there any painting made in his time

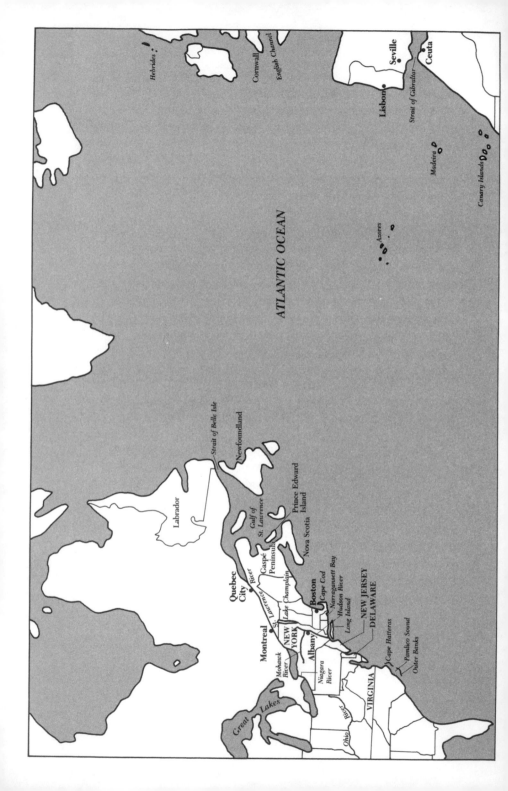

that still exists, although there are some portraits indicating what he might have looked like.

Like many of his neighbors, he obviously went to sea, because when he got married in 1519 at the age of twenty-eight, he was known as a master mariner. The marriage register of St. Malo on May 2 records: "The nuptial benediction was received by Jacques Cartier, master pilot of the port of St. Malo, son of Jamet Cartier and of Gaseline Jansart, and Marie Katherine des Granches, daughter of Messire Honore Granches, chevalier of our lord the king, and constable of the town and city of St. Malo."

With that marriage, Cartier entered the upper echelons of St. Malo society, becoming one of the most respected members of the community. Although he and his wife had no children themselves, he served as godfather to children of friends and relatives no less than twenty-seven times.

After his marriage, Cartier continued his life at sea. Although there are no records, historians have concluded that he sailed to the shores of Brazil and possibly to Newfoundland. He enters the pages of history in 1533, when he was forty-two years old, an experienced mariner.

In that year, King Francis I of France began to take an interest in the New World, where Spain and Portugal were already carving out empires. Like the other monarchs of Europe, King Francis sought a waterway to the riches of the Indies through the barrier of America. Since Spain and Portugal had already laid claim to most of Central and South America, the only way open to the French was in the north.

With the help of Philippe de Chabot, the high admiral of France, Cartier convinced the king that the long-sought route to the Indies could be found in one of the many openings in the coast of Newfoundland. The king approved an expedition under the command of Cartier, described in the royal documents as "captain and pilot for the king."

Like Columbus, Cartier found out that royal commands are not obeyed promptly in far-off ports. Despite the king's order, the merchants of St. Malo, afraid that supplying men and material for

Cartier's ships might deplete their own resources, delayed. It wasn't until orders were received barring other vessels from leaving port that Cartier was able to get his ships manned.

Cartier sailed on his first expedition to the New World on April 20, 1534, in two small ships, with a crew of sixty-one men. With a favorable wind, he made a rapid Atlantic crossing in twenty days, arriving on the east coast of Newfoundland on May 10. After repairing his ships, he sailed north to Cape Dégrat (coincidentally, the point of John Cabot's landfall in Newfoundland thirty-seven years earlier) and across a narrow channel to Labrador.

Everywhere Cartier sailed he found exciting things: birds of every color and kind, icebergs, polar bears, fresh duck eggs, rocky shores, a sandy beach. On the south shore of Labrador, he had his first encounter with the natives. Cartier and the other French explorers never called them Indians, as Columbus did. They called them *sauvages* ("savages") or sometimes *peaux-rouges* ("redskins") or *indigenes* ("natives"). This is how Cartier described the first savages he met:

> The men are well enough formed but untamed and savage. They wear their hair bound on top of their heads like a fistful of twisted hay, sticking into it a pin or something and adding birds' feathers. They are clothed in peltry, men and women alike, but women shape theirs more to their figures and gird their waists. They paint themselves with tan colors. They have boats in which they go to sea made of birch bark, and from which they catch a great quantity of seal. Since seeing them, I have ascertained they are not natives of this place, but come from warmer regions to take seal and other things to eat.

Cartier sailed into the Gulf of St. Lawrence, discovering and naming new islands, capes, and inlets. In late June, he sailed to the north end of Prince Edward Island, describing it as "the most temperate land that one could ask for." In July, he reached the Gaspé Peninsula, where two fleets of natives circled the sailing ships, yelling and holding up animal skins to trade—an indication that European vessels had been there before. Not trusting them, Cartier fired cannonballs over their heads to disperse them.

Nine canoes appeared the next day, again displaying pelts for sale. "We made them signs that we wished them no harm and sent two men ashore to deal with them, bringing knives and other cutlery, and a red cap to give their chief," Cartier later wrote.

Cartier anchored in Gaspé Harbor, where he encountered a party of about two hundred Hurons in about forty canoes, who had come from the interior on a fishing trip. The meeting was friendly, with the French giving the natives the usual beads, knives, and combs. A problem arose, though, when Cartier erected a cross thirty feet tall, inscribed *Vive Le Roy de France* ("Long Live the King of France") as a token of possession.

Even though he could not read the foreign language, the Huron chief, Donnaconna, gathered what was happening and didn't like it. Dressed in an old bearskin, he came aboard Cartier's ship, accompanied by his two teenage sons. Shaking his head from side to side vigorously to indicate his displeasure, Donnaconna conveyed his message: This land is our land, not yours.

Cartier managed to convince Donnaconna that the cross had no significance. With gifts, he quieted the angry chief. Cartier decided that it would be a good idea to take the two native boys, named Domagaya and Taignoaguy, back to France with him so that they could learn the language and be interpreters for his next trip. Somehow, perhaps by a display of arms, he convinced their father, promising that he and they would return.

Cartier sailed north from Gaspé in late July and sighted the large island of Anticosti, which meant "the place where you hunt bear" in the Indian language of the area. He found the tidal currents so strong there, at the mouth of the St. Lawrence River, that he could not continue west. After consulting with his officers, Cartier decided to return to France. He left the Gulf of St. Lawrence on August 2 and arrived back in St. Malo on September 5, 1534.

His glowing accounts of the new lands were received with enthusiasm at the French court. Before the end of October, he received a new commission to return to the Gulf of St. Lawrence with these instructions:

By royal command, to conduct, lead and employ three ships equipped and victualed for fifteen months, for the perfection of the navigation of the lands by you already begun, to discover beyond les Terres Neuves [Newfoundland]; and on this voyage to do and accomplish that which it has pleased the said Lord King to command and order you to do.

Clearly his mission was to explore beyond Newfoundland and to discover faraway countries, like the Indies, for the greater glory and wealth of France. For that purpose, he became captain-general of a fleet of three ships from the French Royal Navy—the *Grande Hermine*, a large vessel that became his flagship, the *Petite Hermine*, and the *Emerillon*. His crew numbered one hundred ten men and the two native boys who had been taken from Canada to learn French.

On May 19, 1535, Cartier sailed into the Atlantic Ocean. Despite stormy seas, he arrived at the coast of Canada in June, and the three ships gathered in July off the south coast of Labrador. A month later, the ships arrived back in the strait between Anticosti Island, the farthest point reached on the first trip, and the coast of what is now the province of Quebec.

He entered a harbor on August 10, the day honoring Saint Lawrence in the Roman Catholic calendar of feast days. Cartier named the harbor the Bay of St. Lawrence. His successors gave the same name to the gulf that Cartier had explored and the mighty river that he was just about to enter.

A few days later, Cartier sailed into the river that his two young captives called "the grand river of Hochelaga" and that we know as the St. Lawrence River. They told Cartier that the river "always narrowing, leads to Canada, where one finds fresh water in said river, which comes from such a distance that no man has been to the end, so far as they heard say; and no other passage was there except for boats."

On September 1, Cartier reached the mouth of the Saguenay River, with its towering cliffs, noting in his log with amazement that spruce trees seemed to be growing out of the bare rocks. A week later, his ships approached what is now the site of the city of Quebec, about eight hundred miles west of the Atlantic Ocean. On September 8, Donnaconna, the lord of Canada, came aboard the *Grande Hermine*, accompanied by sixteen warriors.

After talking to his two sons, whom he had not seen for more than a year, Donnaconna learned that they had been treated well in France. He asked Cartier to put out his bare arms and kissed them, an Indian way of greeting. In return, Cartier treated the Indians with bread and wine.

Cartier anchored his ships under the Great Rock of Quebec, near where the St. Charles River flows into the St. Lawrence. At its foot stood the small village of Stadaconé, one of the most important settlements of the Huron-Iroquois of the St. Lawrence Valley. Surrounded by beautiful elm, ash, maple, and birch trees, the village was the winter home of the tribe.

At first the Indians were most friendly, bringing corn, pumpkins, and fish to the French visitors. When Cartier tried to get their help in sailing up the river to Hochelaga, though, Donnaconna tried to persuade him not to go. He said it was dangerous, that there was too much ice and snow there, that they would die. Cartier concluded that Donnaconna did not want the rival chief at Hochelaga to receive any of the French presents or guns.

In his smallest ship, the *Emerillon*, Cartier and about fifty of his men sailed upstream on September 19. As the river got shallower, he moored the ship and proceeded in longboats, each rowed by six oarsmen. On October 2, they arrived below Hochelaga, the site of the present city of Montreal. More than one thousand Indians greeted him, bearing gifts of corn bread that they threw into the boats.

The next morning, Cartier, dressed in his finest cloak, marched with some of his gentlemen and twenty sailors armed with pikes toward Hochelaga. As they passed throught fields of ripening corn, one of the chiefs met and welcomed him. Cartier himself described the scene:

> In the midst of these fields is the city of Hochelaga, placed near and, as it were, joined to a very great mountain, that is tilled about, very fertile, on the top of which you may see very far. We named it Mount Royal. The city of Hochelaga is round compassed about with timber, with three courses of [stockades] one within another, framed like a sharp spire, but laid across. . . . There are in the town about fifty houses, about fifty paces long, with twelve or fifteen broad, covered over with the bark of wood as broad as any board, very finely and cunningly joined together. Within the said houses there are many rooms, lodgings, and chambers.

Cartier and his men climbed to the top of Mount Royal. To the north they could see the Laurentian Mountains, to the south the Adirondacks, and below them the St. Lawrence River from east to west. In the distance to the southwest, he could see the foaming waters of the Lachine rapids, an effective barrier to further exploration by boat.

From the natives, Cartier learned of another river, the Ottawa, that led to the land of Saguenay, a country rich in precious metals but occupied by "bad people." As the Indians pointed to the Ottawa, they touched Cartier's silver whistle and a sailor's metal knife handle to show that silver and gold came from Saguenay.

After a few days at Hochelaga, Cartier and his men went downriver back to Stadaconé. There his sailors had built a fort of vertical logs, mounted with guns from the ship. Since it was so late in the year, Cartier decided to spend the winter in Canada. From mid-November to mid-April, his ships were frozen solid in the ice of the river, while snow four feet deep covered with ground.

The greatest menace came not from the cold, though, but from scurvy, the dread disease of all sailors on long voyages. Today we know that scurvy is a result of a lack of vitamin C, but in those days it was looked on as a plague without known cause. Both the Indians and the Frenchmen came down with the unmistakable signs of the disease—teeth falling out, gums rotting, swollen limbs, and acute pain. By mid-February, most of the Frenchmen were affected; twenty-five died. Only ten were healthy enough to help the others.

On one of those frigid February days, Cartier met Domagaya, the young interpreter. He appeared healthy, although only a few days before he, too, had showed signs of the disease. When Cartier asked how he had been cured, he replied that he had drunk a beverage made from the branches and bark of a tree, probably a white pine. Two native women helped Cartier collect branches with pine needles, which were then boiled to make a drink.

"If all the doctors of Lorraine and Montpellier had been there with all the drugs of Alexandria, they could not have done as much in a year as the said tree did in six days," Cartier wrote in his log.

The Frenchmen recovered and made plans to return to France when the ice broke in the spring. Cartier abandoned one ship because he did not have enough men to handle all three. But he did not want to go back without a visible sign of his achievements. So he decided to kidnap Donnaconna, who had told him tall tales about the wealth of the mythical kingdom of the Saguenay to the west, and bring him to France to tell the king in person about the riches that lay in the wilderness of Canada.

On May 3, 1536, Cartier planted a tall wooden cross on the river bank at Stadaconé, bearing the arms of France and a scroll that read, in Latin: "Francis I, by the Grace of God King of the French, is Sovereign." After the ceremony, the French sailors seized Donnaconna, his two sons, two little girls, two little boys, and three adults and took them aboard the ships.

On shore, the war cries and howls of the Indians echoed through the night, but Cartier was not moved. Donnaconna appeared on deck in the morning, apparently appeased by Cartier's promise to return in "ten or twelve moons." Cartier also distributed gifts to the Indians, who swarmed around his ship in canoes, in an attempt to show his friendship for them.

A few days later, on May 6, Cartier and his captives sailed for France in the *Grande Hermine* and the *Emerillon*. He arrived back in St. Malo on July 15, ending his second voyage to the New World. It was his most successful, too, opening up a great waterway for penetrating North America and preparing the way for the settlement of French Canada. The only stain on his honor was the betrayal of the chief Donnaconna and the other nine kidnapped at Stadaconé. Not one of them lived to return to Canada.

King Francis was fascinated by Donnaconna's tales of one-legged people who inhabited Saguenay, where men had wings instead of arms and flew from tree to tree like bats. The chief also made up stories about the wonderful things that Saguenay produced, like cloves, nutmeg, and pepper, as well as gold and silver. So even though it was quite clear by this time that the St. Lawrence would not lead to the riches of China, the French believed it was the path to riches in Canada.

Despite that, King Francis had a more pressing problem to deal with first—war with Spain. While Cartier waited for approval of another expedition to Canada, he lived in his house in St. Malo and his nearby farm. It wasn't until 1538, after a truce was declared in the war with Spain, that the king approved a third expedition to Canada.

He issued a commission to "our dear and good friend Jacques Cartier, who having discovered the great country of the lands of Canada and Hochelaga, constituting a westward point of Asia to return to Saguenay if he can find it . . . to mingle with their people and live among them, the better to fulfill our aforesaid intention to do something agreeable to God."

Although Cartier had the title of captain-general and master pilot of all the ships, the king appointed a nobleman, Jean-François de La Roque, sieur de Roberval, as commander in chief, viceroy, and lieutenant-governor of Canada and all the lands to be discovered. It took a long time to prepare the new expedition, which was much larger than the previous two.

Cartier sailed from St. Malo on May 23, 1541, in five ships, with colonists, including some convicts, animals, and food and supplies for two years, as well as a large crew. While Roberval stayed behind, still gathering ammunition and other supplies, Cartier arrived back at Stadaconé on August 23.

The Indians flocked to the ships to greet their returning chief, Donnaconna. When Cartier reported that Donnaconna had died, the new chief, Agouhanna, did not seem too sad. It meant, of course, that he remained as chief.

Cartier built a fort about eight miles upstream from Stadaconé at Cap Rouge as a base for exploring the kingdom of Saguenay. In several longboats, propelled by oars, he went farther upriver above Hochelaga to the Lachine rapids, a formidable barrier in which the river falls forty-two feet in two miles. He never got closer to Saguenay than that.

Discouraged by that failure and signs that the friendly Indians were turning hostile, Cartier gave up. By now the natives in Canada had learned that contact with the strange white men meant almost certain death for them and their culture. If they accepted the invaders, the Europeans took over the land, hunting the game, tilling the soil, and making it almost impossible for the natives to remain. If they fought, the Europeans always came back with more ships, more guns, disease, and death.

Cartier concluded that without Roberval's support he could not protect his base and also search for Saguenay. After spending the winter at Cap Rouge, he set sail for France in June 1542. In the harbor of St. John's, Newfoundland, he found Roberval in his three ships, just arrived from France. The two men disagreed on plans for the future.

Roberval ordered Cartier to return to Canada. Cartier refused. Cartier tried to convince Roberval that it was difficult, perhaps impossible, to defend the French fort at Cap Rouge. Roberval refused to listen. As a result, Roberval sailed up the St. Lawrence and Cartier sailed back to France.

When Cartier returned to St. Malo in October 1534, his reputation did not suffer. His government and his fellow citizens continued to regard him as a master mariner. Never had he lost a ship at sea or faced a revolt or mutiny from his men, as other sea captains of that era did. He spent the rest of his life in St. Malo, one of its most prominent citizens. He died there on September 1, 1557, at the age of sixty-six.

As for Roberval, he sailed up the St. Lawrence to Cap Rouge and attempted to set up a colony there. He ran into the same problems that Cartier had faced—shortages of food, scurvy, which killed at least fifty Frenchmen, Indian hostility, and the inability to pass through the Lachine rapids. He returned to France in September 1543, his mission unaccomplished.

For fifty years, Canada was left to the natives before the next round of French exploration began.

✑16✑

The Discovery of New York

TODAY, THE LONGEST SUSPENSION BRIDGE IN THE WORLD, 4,260 FEET long, stretches across the entrance to New York harbor. It is called the Verrazzano-Narrows Bridge, named after Giovanni da Verrazzano, the first man to enter the magnificent waterway that later made New York City the leading seaport and the biggest city in the world.

But Verrazzano tarried there only briefly in 1524, without exploring the land around the harbor. It wasn't until almost a hundred years later, in 1609, that another explorer, Samuel de Champlain, paddled down from Canada into Lake Champlain from the north. In that same year of 1609, Henry Hudson sailed into the harbor and up the river that now bears his name.

Those three men—Verrazzano, an Italian; Champlain, a Frenchman; and Hudson, an Englishman—discovered New York. It was an early sign of the diverse city and state that New York later became.

• I •

Giovanni da Verrazzano

Giovanni da Verrazzano was a gentleman of Florence, one of the richest cities in the world at the time, the center of the spice trade, powerful in finance, and the home of some of the world's most famous artists. We know a lot about his famous voyage to America in 1524 because his official report has survived. But the circumstances of both his birth and his death remain a mystery.

Verrazzano always referred to himself as a Florentine, but no one to this date has been able to find any document showing when or where he was born. However, the Verrazzanos were an important family in Tuscany, where the Castello Verrazzano still stands some thirty miles south of Florence. One of his first biographers described him as "born of a great and wealthy family, related to the principal men of the city."

Some other biographers say that he may have been born in Lyons, France, the center of the silk trade, where many Florentine bankers and merchants had settled. The records show that Giovanna, daughter of Simon Guadagni, was married there in 1480 to Alesandro di Bartolomeo da Verrazzano. Just as in Florence, though, there are no birth records for him nor for his brother, Gerolamo, in Lyons.

Historians agree, however, that Giovanni was born in 1485 and, whether born in Italy or France, went to Florence for his education, like any other proper Florentine boy of the upper class. His later letters showed that he had a good knowledge of the classics and of mathematics, proving that he must have been well schooled.

Very little is known about his early years. There are indications that he moved to Dieppe, France, in 1506 to pursue a maritime career. A Jean Verason, perhaps Giovanni da Verrazzano in the French translation, sailed on a ship to Newfoundland in 1508. Some records suggest that he may have gone to the Middle East and that he may have accompanied Ferdinand Magellan from Portugal to Spain in 1517, but there is no documentary proof. Historians accept those travels as probable because Verrazzano later proved to be an experienced and competent ship captain.

By 1522, when he arrived in France, Verrazzano had impressive maritime credentials. Although there are no existing portraits of him that were painted during his lifetime, copies of one show him with strong features, black or dark brown hair, with a heavy beard and mustache, and a prominent Roman nose. At the age of thirty-seven, he was "a thoroughly attractive and impressive figure," said one historian.

At that time, a group of Italian bankers and merchants in Lyons became interested in seeking a sea passage to the Indies through the new-found lands in America. Such a discovery would reduce the costs of shipping raw silk from China to the processing factories in Lyons, thus increasing their profits. They interested Francis I, the king of France, in their venture. And they had one of their own—Giovanni da Verrazzano—with the proper credentials to command such an expedition.

With the help of Jean Ango, a leading French shipper and merchant in Dieppe and Rouen, Verrazzano outfitted his expedition. The only other members of the crew that we know by name are his brother, Gerolamo, a mapmaker, and Antoine de Conflans, the pilot. In a letter to the king, Verrazzano outlined the objective of the trip: "My intention on this voyage [is] to reach Cathay and the extreme eastern coast of Asia."

In a small ship, the *Dauphine*, Verrazzano sailed from France on January 1, 1524, south to the Madeira Islands and then due west. He sailed north of the route chosen by Columbus and other explorers to avoid trouble with Spanish authorities, who considered the Caribbean area as theirs. On March 1, Verrazzano sighted land—Cape Fear in what is now North Carolina.

Unlike Columbus, Verrazzano was certain that he had not reached Asia. He described it as a "new land which had never before been seen by any man, either ancient or modern." He was wrong, of course, because, like other early European discoverers, he did not consider the natives to be "people." Verrazzano was a keen observer, though, one of the first to write detailed descriptions of the appearance, life, customs, and character of the native tribes in what is now the United States between the Carolinas and Maine.

After going ashore on the sand dunes of Cape Fear, he described the natives:

> They go completely naked except that around their loins they wear skins of small animals like martens, with a narrow belt of grass around the body, to which they tie various tails of other animals which hang down to the knees; the rest of the body is bare, and so is the head. Some of them wear garlands of birds' feathers. They are dark in color, not unlike the Ethiopians, with thick black hair, not very long, tied behind the head like a small tail. As for the physique of these men, they are well-proportioned, of medium height, a little taller than we are. They have broad chests, strong arms, and the legs and other parts of the body are well composed. . . . They have big black eyes, and an attentive open look. They are not very strong, but they have a sharp cunning and are agile and swift runners. From what we could tell from observation, in the last two respects they resemble the Orientals.

Verrazzano sailed north along the Outer Banks to Cape Hatteras. Beyond the sand dunes, he saw the open waters of what is now Pamlico Sound. He thought it might be the Pacific Ocean, with China just beyond. Continuing north, he looked for a passageway into the waters but could not find one. As he sailed, he gave French names, which have not survived, to many of the capes and inlets he passed in present-day North Carolina, Virginia, Delaware, and New Jersey.

On April 17, 1524, the *Dauphine* sailed into "a very agreeable place between two small but prominent hills." One of the hills rose in what is now Staten Island, the other in Brooklyn. Verrazzano had sailed into the Narrows, the entrance to New York harbor, the waterway that is now spanned by the Verrazzano-Narrows Bridge. Between the hills, Verrazzano noted a very wide deep river that flowed into the sea. "With the help of the tide, which rises eight feet, any laden ship could pass from the sea into the river estuary," he wrote.

Here is his description of what he saw and did:

Since we were anchored off the coast and well sheltered, we did not want to run any risks without knowing anything about the river mouth. So we took the small boat up this river [the Narrows] to land which we found to be densely populated. The people were about the same as the others, dressed in birds' feathers of various colors, and they came toward us joyfully, uttering loud cries of wonderment, and showing us the safest place to beach the boat. We went up this river for about half a league, where we saw that it formed a beautiful lake [the Upper Bay of New York] about three leagues in diameter. About thirty of their small boats ran to and fro across the lake with innumerable people aboard who were crossing from one side to the other to see us. Suddenly, as often happens in sailing, an unfavorable wind blew in from the sea, and we were forced to return to the ship, leaving the land with much regret on account of its favorable conditions and beauty; we think it was not without some properties of value, since all the hills showed signs of minerals.

He named the area Angoulême after the principality in France that Francis I ruled before he became king. And he named the bay Santa Margarita in honor of the king's sister, Marguerite, the duchess of d'Alençon, describing her as a woman "who surpasses all other matrons in modesty and intellect." Neither name lasted very long.

Sailing northwest along the Atlantic coast of Long Island, Verrazzano reached a sheltered harbor that he named Refugio and that we now call Narragansett Bay in Rhode Island. For fifteen days in May, he and his crew explored the land, which he found "as pleasant as I can possibly describe," inhabited by friendly Indians.

Every day the native people came to visit the French crew on their ship, exchanging copper and food for little bells, blue crystals, and other trinkets. Verrazzano had one complaint: "When they come aboard and stay a long time, they make the women wait in the boats; and however many entreaties we made or offers of various gifts, we could not persuade them to let the women come aboard ship."

From Rhode Island, Verrazzano sailed northeast again, to the coast of Maine. Instead of friendly Indians, he found them "so barbarous that we could never make any communication with them, however many signs we made to them." Whenever the crew tried to go ashore, the Indians attacked them with arrows. The reason for the hostility may be that other Europeans had landed there before and had acted badly.

But the Indians did trade with a French crew in a boat, taking knives, fishhooks, and cutting tools for "what it pleased them to give us," presumably food. Verrazzano called the area Terra Onde di Mala Gente ("The Land of the Bad People").

Verrazzano continued along the coast to Newfoundland. There, he said, "Having spent all our naval stores, and having discovered 700 leagues and more of the new country, we topped off with water and wood and decided to return to France." He arrived back in Dieppe on July 8, 1524. He had not found the passage to China, as he had hoped, but he had closed the last significant gap in the knowledge of the time of the coast of America between Patagonia and Labrador.

After he returned to France, Verrazzano proposed another voyage, this one to the Spice Islands. His backers included Jean Ango of Dieppe once more and Philippe de Chabot, the high admiral of France. Following in the sea wake of Magellan, Verrazzano planned to sail through the Strait of Magellan to the Indies.

Things went wrong from the start following his departure in 1526, commanding a fleet of four ships. One ship became separated in a gale and another turned east and sailed around the Cape of Good Hope in Africa to the Indies. With the two other ships, Verrazzano sailed to the coast of Brazil, never reaching the Strait of Magellan. He loaded his ships with Brazil wood, in great demand as the source of dyes for the cloth merchants of France, and returned to France in September 1527.

Still determined to find a passageway through the Americas, Verrazzano organized a third voyage. He sailed from Dieppe in the spring of 1528, arriving off the coast of Florida. Then he turned south to the Bahama Islands and west toward Darien on the Isthmus of Panama, stopping at one of the islands of the Lesser Antilles. This is what happened, in the words of an Italian poet several years later, which many historians accept:

> He turned his ship around and, sailing to the south, he decided to go to Darien, a very beautiful place on land. Sailing and always seeking with his intelligence to discover more places, with six of his men he disembarked on a deserted island, which seemed all covered with trees.
>
> They were taken by cruel people who suddenly attacked them. They were killed, laid on the ground, cut into pieces and eaten to the smallest bone by those people. And there was also Verrazzano's brother who saw the ground red with his brother's blood, but could give no help, being aboard the ship.
>
> He saw everything and, having later come to Rome, one day he told us, in tears about this bitter event. Such a sad death had the seeker of new lands.

Giovanni da Verrazzano died in 1528 at the age of forty-three, eaten by cannibals.

· II ·
Samuel de Champlain

The first European to set foot on the soil of what is today's New York State was Samuel de Champlain, who is better known as "the father of New France," or Canada. Back in July 1609, he came down from Canada by canoe on the Richelieu River to Lake Champlain, landing at its southern edge. That was two months before Henry Hudson sailed up the Hudson River.

A man who loved the sea, Champlain was born in 1567 in Brouage, a small fishing village in France not far from the Atlantic Ocean. His father was Antoine Champlain, who rose to the rank of sea captain; his mother was Marguerite Le Roy, about whom we know nothing. There are no records of any formal education, but Champlain, either in school or by himself, learned to write a good, serviceable French and enough mathematics to become an expert navigator.

He himself wrote later that his education came on ships at sea, possibly serving under his father: "From my childhood, the art of navigation won my love, and has impelled me to expose myself nearly all my life to the impetuous waves of the ocean." He also served in the French army of King Henry of Navarre from 1593 to 1598, fighting in many campaigns against the Spanish.

When the war was over, Champlain was thirty-one years old and, like many veterans of wars everywhere, unemployed. "I resolved, not to remain idle, to find some means of making a voyage to Spain and, being there, to make and cultivate acquaintances, so that by their influence and intercession I might ship in one of their vessels that the King of Spain sends every year to the West Indies," he wrote in one of his books.

He went to Spain later in 1598 and sailed the next year on a French ship chartered by the Spanish. He visited Puerto Rico, Cuba, and Mexico, taking notes and making sketches of everything he saw to bring back to the king of France. When he was on the Isthmus of Panama, for example, he wrote that it would be comparatively easy to cut through the narrow land to make a canal that would connect the Atlantic and the Pacific oceans.

Champlain returned to France in 1601, unemployed once more but with powerful friends. The king granted him a pension, and he became an officer on an expedition to Canada under the command of François Gravé, usually called Pontgravé. Arriving in Canada in May of 1603, they sailed up the St. Lawrence to Tadoussac, at the junction of the Saguenay River.

While Pontgravé's other men collected furs, Champlain went farther up the St. Lawrence, to the heights where Quebec now stands, and to the island that is now Montreal. He found that the Huron town of Hochelaga, described by Cartier (see chapter 15), had disappeared. Champlain questioned the Indians of the area about what lay beyond and heard tales of great lakes and waterfalls in the distance.

In August 1603, he and Pontgravé sailed home, their ships filled with furs to be sold in France. Champlain prepared maps of the region and wrote a book, *Des Sauvages* ("About the Savages"), published in 1604. The king named him a captain in the navy and geographer for a new expedition preparing to colonize Canada.

To command the new expedition, the king appointed Pierre du Gua, sieur de Monts, an old companion in arms, naming him lieutenant general of Canada as well. With four ships, Monts sailed in 1604 and made his first settlement on the island of Sainte Croix in Passamaquoddy Bay, now on the border of Canada and the United States.

While a fort was being built there, Champlain left on the first of a series of voyages of exploration to the south along the coast of Maine and Massachusetts. He discovered and named Mount Desert Island and later passed Cape Ann, entering Plymouth harbor years before the Pilgrims landed there. He also sailed past Boston harbor and circled Cape Cod.

In that time, the French found that Sainte Croix Island was not a good place to stay, mainly because of the cold winds that swept down on it. De Monts dispatched Champlain and Pontgravé to find a better place. They sailed across the Bay of Fundy to the sheltered western coast of Nova Scotia and established a settlement there called Port Royal. It is now a Canadian national historic park.

Back in France in 1607, Champlain was then forty years old, an experienced soldier, sailor, and explorer. No original portrait of him exists. The one that is reproduced most often was probably mistakenly copied from that of another man of the French court. One of his biographers has deduced that Champlain was a small, wiry man, because he kept pace with Indian braves on long marches.

Uncomfortable in civilized Paris, Champlain longed to return to the wilderness in Canada. He believed that the settlement on Nova Scotia was a mistake because it had no economic base. The thing to do, he concluded, was to return to the St. Lawrence River, the channel of the beaver trade, and establish a permanent colony there.

He and de Monts convinced the king that such a colony would bring wealth to France. It would also furnish a base for further exploration for Champlain. Like the Spanish explorers of the time, Champlain had two objectives: to find a passage to the Indies and to bring Christianity to the natives of the New World.

Champlain sailed from France on April 5, arriving in the St. Lawrence on June 3. Exactly a month later, on July 3, 1608, he began to build what became the city of Quebec, the first permanent French colony in America. Tormented by flies by day and mosquitoes at night, Champlain and his men erected three wooden buildings two stories high, surrounded by a moat with a drawbridge, just like a castle in France.

When winter came, with its snow and the cold, the nearby Indians became thin and emaciated. Always friendly to the natives, Champlain supplied food for them. But he had a problem learning their complicated language. Luckily, among his men were two bright fifteen-year-old boys, Étienne Brûlé and Nicholas Marsolet, who picked up the strange Indian languages easily.

Every one of the Frenchmen came down with scurvy. Unlike the Indians who had told Cartier about boiling pine needles to cure scurvy, their successors, the Montagnais, did not know how to do it. As a result, when the snow melted, only eight of the twenty-four Frenchmen, including Champlain himself, had survived.

In the spring, after Champlain had recovered, he traveled up the St. Lawrence toward the land of the beaver. He met a large party of Hurons and Algonquins, who were at perpetual war with the Iroquois. The Hurons proposed that the French join them in fighting the Iroquois, who lived in the area south of the St. Lawrence River.

Why did Champlain consent? The best answer seems to be that he did not see how he could remain neutral. The French needed the Hurons to remain in the beaver trade. In addition, Champlain saw himself as a leader of the tribes of Canada, which could help him open the way to discoveries farther to the west. By allying the French with the Hurons, Champlain did indeed cement a friendship, but he also made implacable enemies of the Iroquois, the ablest warriors of all the tribes.

By boat and canoe, Champlain, two other Frenchmen, and about sixty Hurons made their way up the Richelieu River to the foot of a long lake that stretched south into what is the United States today. Far to their left rose the ridges of the Green Mountains of Vermont and to their right the Adirondack Mountains of New York. By day, the warriors rested under the trees; at night, they silently paddled south. On the night of July 29, they hid on the western shore of the lake.

They looked out into the darkness and saw a flotilla of Iroquois canoes approaching. The Iroquois sent two canoes out to meet the Hurons to learn if they wanted to fight. According to the Indian custom, they held a parley to decide the rules of battle—and agreed to wait until dawn so that they could see each other better. Both sides spent the night dancing, singing, and shouting insults at one another.

As dawn approached, Champlain and the two other Frenchmen put on breastplates of armor and plumed iron helmets. In one hand, Champlain held a sword, in the other his arquebus, a primitive sort of rifle. He stood hidden behind the Hurons, armed with their traditional bows and arrows. In front of them, two hundred Iroquois, also armed with bows and arrows, filed out of their barricade to face them.

This is what happened, according to Champlain's own account:

Our men began to call me with loud cries; and, to give me a passageway, they divided into two parts and put me at their head, where I marched about twenty paces in front of them, until I was about thirty paces from the enemy. They at once saw me and halted, looking at me, and I at them. When I saw them making a move to shoot at us, I rested my arquebus against my cheek and aimed directly at one of the three chiefs. With the same shot two of them fell to the ground, and one of their companions, who was wounded and afterward died. I put four balls into my arquebus. When our men heard this shot so favorable to them, they began to make cries so loud one could not have heard it thunder.

Astonished at the deadly impact of the French firearm, the Iroquois fled. That defeat had a dramatic impact on the future of France in America. Champlain had made enemies of the powerful Iroquois confederation, which became allied to the British later in the struggle for mastery of the American continent.

On that day in July 1609, though, the Hurons and Champlain celebrated their victory. Champlain won the respect of the Hurons as a man of valor, who kept his promise to help them. He named the lake on which the battle was fought for himself, and we still know it today as Lake Champlain.

In 1610, Champlain began what was the first student-exchange program. He sent Étienne Brûlé, then seventeen years old, to live with the Algonquins to learn their language and took a young Huron named Savignon back to France to learn French.

When the Algonquins left to return to their home territory, Brûlé went with them. In that year of 1610, he became the first European to travel up the Ottawa River, to stand on the shores of Lake Nipissing, and to see the vast Lake Huron—which became the well-traveled route of the French fur traders. Later, Brûlé also became the first white man to gaze upon the waters of Lakes Ontario and Superior—and he may be called the discoverer of the Great Lakes.

Champlain returned to France with presents for the king, setting a pattern of yearly trips to bring back supplies for the colony at Quebec. In France, Champlain, now forty-three years old, decided it was time to get married. His choice of a bride was surprising— a twelve-year-old girl named Hélène Boullé, the daughter of an official in the French court. Marriages of girls so young were not uncommon in France in those days, but they usually did not live as wives until they were a few years older.

When Champlain returned to Canada, he left his young bride with her parents in Paris. With Savignon as a companion, he once more sailed up the St. Lawrence River past Quebec to Montreal, where he thought another colony could be established. After inspecting a little island in midstream, he named it Ile Sainte Hélène, after the patron saint of his wife. It still bears that name.

In June of 1611, a party of about two hundred Hurons and Algonquins arrived from the west, bringing with them Brûlé, who had learned their language very well. Over a campfire conference one night, the Indians told Champlain that they objected to many of the lawless French fur traders but that they trusted him and would follow him.

Later that year, Champlain once more sailed back to France, where he tried to organize a more orderly control of the lucrative fur trade. His objective was to maintain peace in the colony so that he could make further explorations.

In 1612, the king appointed the prince of Condé as viceroy of New France. Champlain, in turn, was appointed Condé's lieutenant, with full power to rule in New France—to convert the Indians to Christianity, to seek gold, to make war if necessary, and to find an easy route to China and the Indies. Armed with those sweeping powers, Champlain sailed back to Canada.

He made one attempt to travel far to the west that year, but it proved unsuccessful and he returned to Paris. There, in 1613, he published his second book, *The Voyages of Champlain*, with many illustrations, maps, and descriptions of Indian customs. After gaining a renewal of a monopoly in the fur trade, Champlain sailed once more for New France in 1615, accompanied by four Recollect monks to bring the word of Christ to the wilderness.

He found his Huron friends eager for his help to carry their ongoing war into the home territory of the Iroquois. With Brûlé, one other Frenchman, and ten Indians in two canoes, Champlain paddled up the Ottawa River, portaging to Lake Nippissing and stopping at the site of the present city of North Bay. From there,

he and his companions canoed into what he called the Fresh Sea—
Lake Huron, the center of the homeland of the Hurons. It was a
most beautiful area, with corn, squash, sunflowers, plums, straw-
berries, and nuts growing everywhere.

After a conference with the chiefs, a war party of about five
hundred—and Champlain—left by canoe to invade the Iroquois
stronghold. They canoed east to Lake Simcoe, south to the shores
of Lake Ontario, crossed the eastern end of Lake Ontario, and
landed on the southeastern shore near the Salmon River. Marching
silently in single file, with each man stepping in the footsteps of
another, they headed south to the fortified Iroquois village near
the present city of Syracuse.

Champlain and the Hurons attacked on October 10, 1615, but
made no headway against the Iroquois fortifications. Champlain
ordered a tower built so that his men could shoot arrows over the
barricades, but the Iroquois held firm. Champlain himself was
wounded in the leg by Iroquois arrows. Discouraged after five days
of failing to break the Iroquois defenses, the Huron attackers
retreated.

Unable to walk, Champlain was carried back on the shoulders
of a Huron warrior. He spent the winter in Huron country, re-
covering before returning to Quebec in 1616. It marked the end
of Champlain's personal explorations of New York and the Great
Lakes. From then on, he devoted himself to building the colony
of New France, making frequent trips between it and France.

Appointed governor of Canada, Champlain made his last trip
there in 1633. He learned of the horrible death the year before of
his protégé, Étienne Brûlé, who lived among the Hurons almost
as if he were one of them—before they turned on him. Here is
how one of his biographers described what happened:

In 1632, he was barbarously and treacherously murdered—
clubbed to death—by those in whom he had always placed the
utmost confidence as his faithful protectors. What cause he gave
them—whether fancied or real—for their bloodthirsty and most

cruel act is unknown. But their savageness did not stop with his death. In their wild and horrible ferocity to take revenge on their victim, they feasted on his lifeless remains.

Champlain died peacefully on Christmas Day, 1635, at the age of sixty-eight and was buried in Quebec, the city that he founded.

• III •
Henry Hudson

The story of Henry Hudson is remarkably similar to that of Verrazzano. Little is known about his early life, but his famous voyage of discovery is well documented. And, like Verrazzano, he came to a tragic end.

Diligent research by historians has failed to uncover any evidence of when or where he was born, except that he was an Englishman, probably a native of London. One researcher concluded that Henry Hudson, the discoverer, was the descendant, probably the grandson, of a Henry Hudson who died in 1555 while holding the office of alderman of the City of London.

Young Henry became an apprentice in an organization of English merchants who called themselves The Merchants Adventurers of England for the Discovery of Lands, Territories, Isles, Dominions and Seignories Unknown—commonly know as the Moscovy Company. Its purpose was to discover new markets for English woolens in Asia—and make a handsome profit, of course—by finding a short sea route there.

Among the founders of the company were some of Henry Hudson's ancestors, possibly his grandfather. Over the years, Henry obviously performed satisfactorily, because he rose to command rank as a captain in the maritime services. He also acquired a wife, Katherine, and three sons, Oliver, John, and Richard.

The first record bearing Henry Hudson's name is that of a communion service in the St. Ethelburga's Church on Bishopsgate Street in London on April 19, 1607. On that day, Hudson, ten members of a crew of a ship under his command, and his second son, John, attended a religious service, just before putting out to sea.

After many unsuccessful attempts by English sea captains to find a northwest passage from the Atlantic to the Pacific oceans, Hudson had proposed to the Moscovy Company a voyage across the North Pole to China and Japan. Not only would it be the shortest route, but he and some others argued that the barrier of ice in the North Atlantic might disappear farther north. Wasn't it clear that there might be open water in the land of the Midnight Sun?

On May 1, 1607, Hudson left England on the *Hopewell*, a small ship of about eighty tons. He sailed almost straight north, past the Faroe Islands and across the Arctic Circle, until he reached the northeast coast of Greenland. Looking for open water to the north, he sailed to the east to Spitsbergen, one of the northernmost islands in the world. All he found was snow, mist, fog, and ice.

He returned to England in September. Although he had not succeeded in finding the northern route to the Indies, the Moscovy Company decided to try once more. In April 1608, Hudson sailed north in the *Hopewell* along the coast of Norway, rounding North Cape into the frigid waters of the Arctic Ocean. He reached Novaya Zemlya, a large island north of Russia, but once again found an ice barrier.

Having sailed farther north than any mariner before him, Hudson had nevertheless failed to find an open sea passage to Asia. On his return to England in August 1608, the Moscovy Company decided to give up the search. But the Dutch East India Company in Holland invited Hudson to Amsterdam to talk about further exploration in the northern waters.

As a result of those talks, a contract was signed in January 1609, under which Hudson was to search for a sea passage to the north, once more near the island of Novaya Zemlya. One interesting fact in that contract is that Hudson's name is written in plain English as Henry Hudson, despite later American references to him as Hendrik Hudson.

Hudson sailed on his third voyage of discovery in April 1609 on the *Half Moon*, a small ship with a mixed crew of English and Dutch sailors. The crew included Robert Juet, an elderly sailor who had sailed as first mate with Hudson on the previous voyage to Novaya Zemlya. Juet kept a journal of the voyage, which is a remarkable first-hand account of Hudson's discoveries.

Following his instructions, Hudson sailed to North Cape at the tip of Norway, preparing once again to seek an opening through the ice barrier. But the Dutch sailors, who had experience in ships in the tropical East Indies, rebelled at sailing farther into the cold and snow of the Arctic. A peaceful man, Hudson yielded, perhaps because of his two previous failures to penetrate the northern ice.

Instead of returning to Amsterdam to face the merchants who had paid for the voyage, Hudson decided to sail west to look for a passage to Asia through America. Driven by stormy winds, the *Half Moon* arrived off the coast of Maine in July 1609. "So we came to anchor, the sea being very smooth and little wind, at nine of the clock at night," Juet wrote in his journal. "After supper, we tried for fish, and I caught fifteen cods, some the greatest I have ever seen."

A few days later, the *Half Moon* sailed south, reaching Cape Cod, which had been discovered in 1602 by Captain Bartholomew Gosnold. During the month of August, Hudson continued sailing south along the coast, sighting land in New Jersey, Delaware, and Virginia but not entering any of the rivers or bays because of shallow water. Hudson turned around and sailed back up along the coast.

On September 2, Hudson arrived at the entrance to New York harbor. After anchoring, Hudson noticed high hills far to the north. Juet wrote his first impression of New York: "This is a very good land to fall with, and a pleasant land to see."

The next day, Hudson sailed into the Lower Bay of New York harbor, the first European to do so since Giovanni da Verrazzano had discovered it eight-five years earlier. Juet wrote:

This day the people of the country came aboard of us, seeming very glad of our coming, and brought green tobacco, and gave some of it for knives and beads. They go in deerskins loose, well dressed. They have yellow copper. They desire clothes, and are very civil. They have a great store of maize or Indian wheat, whereof they make good bread. The country is full of great and tall oaks.

Hudson sailed through the Narrows into the Upper Bay of New York and then slowly up the Hudson River. The ship floated upriver with the tide, anchoring when the tide ran back to the sea. Hudson anchored off what is now Forty-second Street and looked out on an island covered with green, where wildflowers were so numerous that one observer noted the sweet smell of perfume.

On September 13, the *Half Moon* reached what would later become Yonkers, where the crew bought oysters from the Indians. The next day, Hudson sailed through the highlands area near West Point, where his crew noticed a great number of striped bass and other fish in the river. Near the present city of Hudson, Hudson went ashore to visit some Indians in a house "well-constructed of oak bark and circular in shape," with an arched roof. After eating a meal of maize, pigeons, and dog meat, Hudson reported in his journal:

> The land is the finest for cultivation that I have ever in my life set foot upon, and it also abounds in trees of every description. The natives are a very good people, for when they saw that I would not remain, they supposed I was afraid of their bows, and taking their arrows, they broke them in pieces, and threw them into the fire.

Day by day they sailed up the pleasant river, meeting friendly Indians who brought them grapes, pumpkins, tobacco, beaver skins, and otter skins, which they exchanged for beads, knives, and hatchets. On September 19, the *Half Moon* anchored off what was to become the city of Albany. Hudson sent a small boat north to check the river for further sailing. Near where the Mohawk River flows into the Hudson, the crew found that they could not go on—the river was getting narrower and more shallow. That ended Hudson's hope of finding a passage through the landmass of America.

So he turned downriver on September 23 and sailed back to the ocean. On November 7, the *Half Moon* returned to Europe, landing first at Dartmouth in England. Hudson sent word to Holland reporting his discovery of a great river. But the English forbade Hudson from leaving the country because they felt that the discovery of one of their nationals should not be used for the benefit of a commerical rival.

Without Hudson, the *Half Moon* returned to Holland in 1610. In England, though, some independent merchants decided to back Hudson in another attempt to find a passage to the Pacific Ocean. And so on April 17, 1610, Hudson sailed from London on his fourth voyage on a ship called the *Discovery*. His crew numbered nineteen, among them his son John, with Robert Juet once more as mate.

This time Hudson sailed farther north, past Iceland and Greenland, arriving off the coast of Labrador. He entered the narrow body of water now called Hudson Strait in July but his crew, disturbed by the ice and apparent danger, wanted to turn back. A reasonable man, not a stern commander, Hudson convinced his men to continue. He sailed south in a great body of water that is now named Hudson Bay.

He could not find a way through it. His crew, led by Juet, began to grumble and complain. Hudson accused Juet of disloyalty and removed him as mate. As winter approached, Hudson went into winter quarters at the base of James Bay, with the *Discovery* frozen into the ice. During the bitterly cold Arctic winter, Hudson's crew grew restless.

When the ice melted in mid-June 1611, the *Discovery* set sail once more. With food running short, some of the men thought Hudson was dividing their rations unfairly. A small group, led by the dissident mate Juet, mutinied. Seizing Hudson on the morning of June 23 as he came up on the deck, they threw him, his son John, and eight other sailors into a small boat and set it adrift.

Only nine members of the mutinous crew survived. Somehow

they sailed the *Discovery* back to England, where they reported to the British authorities. Several years later, they were put on trial for mutiny and acquitted.

No trace was ever found of Hudson and the men in the boat left behind in the icy waters of the Arctic. Presumably they starved and froze to death. But the name of Hudson lives on—in the river, strait, and bay that bear his name.

༄17༄

The Conquest of Peru

Francisco Pizarro was a late bloomer, very late. His rise to fame began after his fiftieth birthday, at a time when most Europeans of his age were considered to be old men.

Like many of the other early conquistadors, he came from a poor area of Spain, where living was very difficult. He was born in the village of Truxillo in the mountainous Estremadura region of Spain, probably in 1471. His birth and its exact date do not appear in the village records because his parents were not married. His father, Gonzalo Pizarro, was a colonel in the Spanish army, who apparently took little interest in his son. Not much is known about his mother, Francisca Gonzalez, except that she had several other children as well.

As a poor boy, Francisco grew up without any formal education and never learned to read or write. In that poor farming region of Spain, he worked as a swineherd, taking care of pigs. When he was in his early twenties, he, like all other young Spaniards, heard about the great discoveries of Christopher Columbus far off to the west. Breaking out of the poverty around him, Pizarro somehow made his way to Seville and then to the New World.

He arrived in Santo Domingo in 1502, when he was thirty-one years old. His name is first mentioned eight years later, in 1510, when he took part in an expedition led by Alonzo de Ojeda to establish a colony on the Caribbean coast of Colombia. More interested in quick riches than settlement, Ojeda began to raid the surrounding country for gold, food, and slaves.

The Indians fought back fiercely, driving the Spaniards into a makeshift fort, where they held on for their lives. Ojeda went back to Hispaniola for reinforcements, leaving Pizarro in command. Obviously, by this time Pizarro had made a name for himself as a competent soldier and able leader. He held out for two months before returning to Hispaniola with the tattered remnants of Ojeda's colonizers.

After that, Pizarro became associated with Vasco Núñez de Balboa in Panama. In 1513, Pizarro accompanied Balboa as he crossed Panama to discover the Pacific Ocean. Pizarro also served as a lieutenant under Pedrarias, the governor of Panama, for many years. In that capacity, acting under orders from his superior, Pizarro arrested Balboa, who was unjustly executed as a traitor in 1519 (see chapter 11).

From the time of Balboa on, Spanish officers had heard about an Indian kingdom rich in gold far to the south. Little was done to reach it until Pizarro, a reluctant settler in Panama, seized the opportunity. As an aide to Pedrarias, he had served on several military expeditions to extend Spanish rule in Central America, thus gaining the experience he needed to command a large force. But he had no money.

He found the necessary funds in an agreement with two partners, also looking for a way to get rich. One was Diego de Almagro, a soldier of fortune like himself, and the other, Hernando de Luque, a priest with political connections. Luque furnished the money, Almagro equipped two small ships, and Pizarro took command of the expedition, the first of three he led, seeking the gold of Peru.

With about a hundred men, Pizarro sailed south from Panama in November 1524. After landing in a jungle on the west coast of Colombia at the height of the rainy season, he became bogged down in a hot, sticky swamp. Dependent on the land for food,

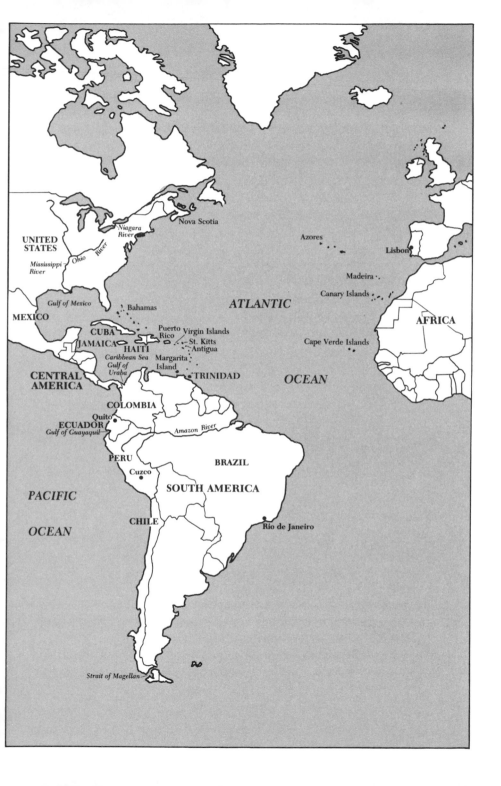

UNITED
STATES

Niagara
River

Nova Scotia

Ohio River

Mississippi
River

Gulf of Mexico

Bahamas

MEXICO

CUBA

JAMAICA

HAITI

Puerto
Rico

Virgin Islands

St. Kitts

Antigua

ATLANTIC

Azores

Lisbon

Madeira

Canary Islands

AFRICA

Caribbean Sea
Gulf of
Uraba

Margarita
Island

TRINIDAD

Cape Verde Islands

CENTRAL
AMERICA

OCEAN

COLOMBIA

Quito

ECUADOR

Gulf of Guayaquil

Amazon River

PERU

BRAZIL

Cuzco

SOUTH AMERICA

PACIFIC

CHILE

OCEAN

Rio de Janeiro

Strait of Magellan

which was not available in the jungle, the men grew hungry and cursed their leader for bringing them to such a dismal place.

Faced with a possible mutiny, Pizarro persisted. He showed his leadership abilities by convincing his men that they could not return to Panama as failures. With lack of food his most pressing problem, Pizarro divided his force in two, sending half back with a trusted officer to get supplies from the nearest Spanish settlement.

When the ship left, Pizarro explored the countryside to see if there were any Indian settlements nearby. He found none. His hungry men scoured the shoreline for shellfish, and they ate the berries and herbs that grew wild in the woods. Some of the berries proved poisonous. Twenty-five of the fifty men left behind in the jungle died before the supply ship returned six weeks later. As they sailed away to the south, Pizarro named the land Puerto de la Hambre ("Port of Famine").

Pizarro sailed along the coastline, landing once more in a densely wooded country. This time he came across a large native town. Unfortunately for the Spaniards, the Indians immediately attacked them. The Indians singled out Pizarro as the chief of the invaders and concentrated their attack on him. Despite his armor, he was wounded seven times before he was able to rally his men and retreat.

Meanwhile, his partner Almagro followed Pizarro down the coast of South America, finding hostile Indians, too, but also a few trinkets of gold in the native villages. When Pizarro returned to Panama in 1526, the three partners signed a contract to share equally in the wealth they were sure they would find in Peru. Pizarro, Almagro, and Luque would each receive a third of the riches.

In the second expedition south, Pizarro landed at an Indian village where he found a considerable number of gold ornaments. These, he felt, would convince the authorities in Panama to support the venture with more money and men. Almagro was dispatched back to Panama with the treasure.

Pizarro and his men marched inland, looking for a pleasant country described by the natives. Instead, they found a frightening jungle, hot and humid. Monkeys chattered overhead, alligators lurked in the streams, and boa constrictors threatened anyone who came near. Food was difficult to find, too. Occasionally, they uncovered a wild potato or found a cocoa nut, but hunger was their constant companion.

They were rescued by Almagro, who arrived in a ship loaded with supplies and reinforcements. Together, Pizarro and Almagro sailed south to the island of Gallo, off the coast of northern Ecuador, and then a little farther south to the port of Tacamez. Instead of a jungle, the Spaniards saw in front of them a town of two thousand houses or more, laid out in streets. The native men and women displayed many ornaments of gold and jewels.

As usual, though, the natives were hostile toward the newcomers. An army, estimated by the Spaniards at about ten thousand, gathered on the shore, ready to attack as Pizarro with a small number of mounted men landed. The Indians charged forward. Their warlike yells startled one of the horses, which reared and threw off its rider.

The Indians, who had never seen mounted men on horses before, were so stunned to see the strange animal divided into two living parts—the man on the ground and the horse nearby—that they fell back in astonishment. That permitted Pizarro and his men to regain their ships in safety.

It became clear to the two captains that they could not prevail against the more numerous natives. Once again, they decided that Almagro would return to Panama with additional evidence of the gold and jewels, while Pizarro remained.

One of the soldiers, angry at being left behind in the hostile jungle where so many companions had died, sent a hidden message back to the governor. It read:

> Look out, Señor Governor,
> For the drover while he's near,
> Since he goes home to get the sheep,
> For the butcher who stays here.

When Almagro arrived in Panama, he found a new governor, Pedro de los Rios. Angry at the loss of life as a result of the expedition, Rios was adamant against sending additional aid. Instead, he dispatched an officer to bring back all the Spaniards still alive. When that officer arrived, the soldiers greeted him enthusiastically—it meant they could get back to the safety of Panama.

For Pizarro, it was a turning point. He knew that if he returned, it meant the end of his dream of riches. He rose to the occasion, demonstrating not only his courage but his faith in himself and the future. Standing on the sandy beach, he drew his sword and traced a line on the sand from east to west. He said:

Friend and comrades, on that side are toil, hunger, nakedness, the drenching storm, desertion, and death; on this side ease and pleasure. There lies Peru and its riches; here Panama and poverty. Choose, each man, what best becomes a brave Castilian. For my part, I go to the south.

With those words, he stepped across the line. One by one, thirteen of the two hundred men present followed him. The others returned north to Panama, where the governor at first was angry at Pizarro's disobedience.

Little by little, Luque and Almagro convinced him that Pizarro, despite his rash decision, was acting to bring riches for the crown. Finally, the governor sent a small ship to search for the marooned men, giving Pizarro six months to return with a report on what he had found.

During that time, Pizarro sailed south into the beautiful Gulf of Guayaquil in southern Ecuador and came to anchor off Tumbez at the northern tip of Peru. The natives gazed with amazement at the Spanish ship, a sight they had never seen before. By chance, an Inca nobleman was also in Tumbez at the time. He came aboard Pizarro's ship to inspect the strangers, the first Europeans to arrive in Peru—the discoverers of Peru.

On the very next day, Pizarro sent some of his aides to look over the city. They came back with reports of temple walls covered with plates of gold and silver. Everywhere Pizarro went he heard accounts of a powerful monarch who held his court in a city to the south that blazed with gold and silver. The Spaniards were delighted by the news—at last they had reached the realm that would make them rich.

Returning to Panama to get the reinforcements he needed to conquer Peru, Pizarro found that the governor was not impressed by what he called "the cheap display of gold and silver" and a few Indian llamas. So the partners decided to appeal for help to the king in Spain. In the spring of 1528, Pizarro sailed back to Spain, carrying with him some vases of gold and silver, two or three llamas, and fabrics made of llama wool as vouchers for his tale of the riches of Peru.

Unlike the disappointed governor of Panama, King Charles of Spain examined Pizarro's gifts with fascination. He listened eagerly to Pizarro's story of the jungle and of how his men survived hunger, thirst, and disease in their efforts to reach Peru. Although he was not tutored in the protocol of the court, Pizarro made a most favorable impression on the king.

Tall and well-proportioned in stature, Pizarro, like many of his countrymen, dressed simply. Instead of the fancy clothes of the courtiers around the king, he wore a simple black cloak with a white hat. Despite his lack of education, he spoke simply but eloquently. He convinced the monarch, as he had the soldiers in the field, that Peru was there for the taking.

On July 25, 1529, the crown signed a paper granting Pizarro the power to conquer Peru, or New Castile, as it was then called. In recognition of his accomplishments, Pizarro received the titles of governor and captain-general of Peru, but his partners got lesser positions. Almagro became commander of the fortress of Tumbez and Luque the bishop of Tumbez and "Protector of the Indians of Peru."

Before Pizarro sailed from Spain in January 1530, he returned to his birthplace and recruited his four brothers, Hernando, Gonzalo, Martin, and Juan. When he arrived in Panama and told his partners in Panama about their new titles, both Almagro and

Luque were bitterly angry at their lesser roles in the enterprise. They accused Pizarro of deceit, but he replied that the king had insisted on one overall commander.

In January 1531, Pizarro, at the age of sixty, sailed on his third and last expedition to Peru. His force consisted of one hundred eighty men and twenty-seven horses for the cavalry. He landed on the coast and marched south, establishing a base on the island of Puna at the mouth of the Guayaquil River.

Attacked by the natives there, Pizarro received welcome reinforcements under the command of Hernando de Soto (see chapter 20). With those new recruits, numbering about a hundred men, he crossed to the mainland to Tumbez, only to find it in ruins. The Indians told him it had been destroyed in local warfare.

Unknown to Pizarro at the time, he had arrived in Peru at a critical period in its history. It was split by internal war between two brothers contending for power. The legitimate heir to the throne, Huascar, a prince of generous and easy nature, ruled in Cuzco. His half brother, Atahuallpa, who ruled in Quito, was warlike, ambitious, daring, and eager to extend his kingdom.

A few months before Pizarro landed in Peru, Atahuallpa had launched an army south to make himself the undisputed Inca, or king, of all Peru. He had defeated the army of Huascar on the plains in front of Cuzco in a bloody battle that lasted from sunrise to sunset.

Soon afterward, Atahuallpa invited the surviving Inca nobles to meet with him in Cuzco. His soldiers butchered them all to prevent anyone from contesting his claim to the throne. Then, in the presence of Huascar, he put to death all the females of the royal family—his aunts, nieces, and cousins—in an attempt to prevent the birth of a rival for the throne. Huascar was kept a prisoner.

At the age of thirty, Atahuallpa became the Inca of Peru, a kingdom that stretched along the Andes Mountains from Chile in the south to Ecuador in the north, from the Pacific Ocean to the eastern slopes of the Andes. Its center was the holy city of Cuzco, with a great stone temple to the sun.

The far-flung kingdom was connected by roads of stone. Its cities were imposing, with buildings and temples of stone, too. Peru was a prosperous nation, displaying its wealth in gold, silver, and jewels in its temples and public buildings.

As Inca, Atahuallpa ruled over a kingdom of perhaps ten million people. He was an absolute monarch—he raised armies, imposed taxes, made laws, and appointed judges. As the representative of the sun, he was also head of the priesthood, presiding at all important religious festivals (see chapter 2).

Despite the cruelty with which Atahuallpa eliminated his rivals, he inherited a government of benevolent despotism. When the Incas conquered a new land, they admitted the people to all the rights and privileges of the Peruvians. Although everybody had to contribute goods and labor to the government, no family suffered from want of food or clothing.

The noted historian William H. Prescott wrote that life for ordinary people under the Incas was surprisingly good. "Under their rule," he wrote, "the meanest of people enjoyed a far greater degree of personal comfort, at least, a greater exemption from physical suffering, than was possessed by similar classes in other nations on the American continent—greater, probably, than was possessed by these classes in most countries of feudal Europe."

Atahuallpa became the Inca on the eve of the Spanish invasion. That started on September 24, 1532, when Pizarro boldly marched out at the head of his small body of soldiers into the heart of the powerful Peruvian empire, leaving some behind to protect his base.

Five days into the jungle, Pizarro called a meeting. He announced that any soldier who did not want to continue could turn back without penalty, but that he would continue on no matter how many stayed with him. Nine men chose to return, leaving him with one hundred sixty-eight men—they could scarcely be called an army—for the conquest of Peru.

Pizarro dispatched Hernando de Soto and a small party to scout out the land ahead. Thus it was de Soto who made the first contact with representatives of the Inca. He returned with an envoy of the Inca himself, bringing greetings and gifts. But Pizarro's scouts also reported that Atahuallpa was camped with a large army, estimated at fifty thousand men, south of Caxamalca (now Caxamarca in Peru), in a valley behind the rugged Andes peaks.

In front of them lay high mountains with narrow passes, difficult to traverse. If Atahuallpa chose to defend those passes, he could ambush the Spaniards easily. Pizarro, always a bold soldier, advanced warily, with his small group of men, over the steep and narrow mountain paths. Soon he met a messenger from the Inca with the welcome news that the road was clear of enemy soldiers ahead.

After seven days of difficult climbing, late in the afternoon of November 15, 1532, Pizarro entered Caxamalca. He sent his brother Hernando and de Soto ahead. They became the first Europeans to see the Inca of Peru.

In a courtyard, surrounded by nobles and women of the royal household, Atahuallpa sat on a cushion. The only sign of his royal status was the crimson *borla*, or fringe, that hung on his head down to his eyebrows, the symbol of the Inca.

Without dismounting from his horse, Hernando Pizarro informed the Inca, through an interpreter, that he came as an ambassador from his brother, the commander of the white men, who were the subjects of a mighty king across the water. Their object, he said, was to impart to him the doctrines of the true faith that they professed.

Atahuallpa remained silent, his eyes fastened on the ground. One of his nobles broke the silence by saying, "It is well." Hernando Pizarro persisted, requesting the Inca to speak himself.

With a smile, Atahuallpa replied, "Tell your captain that I am keeping a fast, which will end tomorrow morning. I will then visit him with my chieftains. In the meantime, let him occupy the public buildings on the square, and no other, till I come, and I will order what shall be done."

De Soto, noticing that Atahuallpa looked with some interest at his horse, decided to put on a show. Striking his heel into the horse's side, de Soto dashed around the plain, displaying the beautiful movements of his charger. Suddenly he reined the horse to a stop directly in front of the Inca, so that it reared up on its hind legs, with foam splattering on the Inca himself.

Atahuallpa retained his calm composure, but a few of his soldiers flinched. Some of the Spaniards reported later that the Inca put them to death for betraying such an unworthy weakness in front of strangers.

That evening, Pizarro called a meeting of his officers. It was clear that they could not overcome the large numbers of Peruvian soldiers. To retreat was impossible; it would be a sign of weakness, leading to their certain destruction in the mountain passes leading north. To stay as guests of the Inca was equally perilous; sooner or later the Peruvians would turn on them.

Pizarro saw only one way out: to seize Atahuallpa and make him a prisoner, thus not only securing their own safety but taking control of the Incan empire. Clearly, Pizarro had in mind the tactic used by Cortés against the Aztecs, when he seized Montezuma and became the master of Mexico (see chapter 13).

The next day, November 16, 1532, changed the course of Peruvian history. A parade of natives led the way to the square where Pizarro had spent the night, followed by Atahuallpa, carried on a throne of gold. Around Atahuallpa's neck was a collar of emeralds. His hair was decorated with gold ornaments above the crimson *borla* that encircled his temples. With him came several thousand of his people.

Pizarro's chaplain, Vincente de Valverde, stepped forward, with a Bible in one hand and a crucifix in the other. After telling the story of Jesus Christ, the friar called upon the Inca to give up the errors of his own religion, to embrace Christianity, and to acknowledge King Charles of Spain as his master.

"I will be no man's tributary," replied Atahuallpa angrily.

He went on: "For my faith, I will not change it. Your own God, as you say, was put to death by the very men whom he created. But mine"—he stopped for a moment and pointed to the sun—"my God still lives and looks down on his children."

He threw the Bible to the ground.

The friar picked it up and ran to Pizarro. "Did you not see that, while we stand here wasting our breath talking with this dog, full of pride as he is, the fields are filling with Indians? Set on, at once, I absolve you."

Pizarro waved a white scarf in the air, a signal for the attack. Shouting "Saint James and at them!" Pizarro led a charge of the Spaniards, some of them mounted, on the unarmed Indians surrounding Atahuallpa. Nobles and commoners alike were trampled underfoot or cut down by the armed invaders. The fighting was fierce around the royal litter, but Pizarro protected the Inca, receiving a wound himself. He was the only Spaniard wounded in the massacre, while thousands of Indians died.

When the fighting had ended, Atahuallpa was a prisoner of the Spanish invaders—and Pizarro was master of Peru. The Incan soldiers lost heart at the capture of the Inca, and there was no leader to take his place.

Atahuallpa attempted to bargain for his freedom. He offered to fill a room full of gold to a height of nine feet above the floor for his release, and his courtiers began to collect the ransom.

Not long afterward, in February 1533, Pizarro's partner Almagro arrived with reinforcements of one hundred fifty foot soldiers and fifty cavalrymen. The third partner, Luque, had died in Panama. Although the added strength made Pizarro feel more comfortable about his position in Peru, it also began to cause friction in the Spanish camp about the future and the division of the loot.

With an immense quantity of gold flowing into Pizarro's headquarters, the Spanish melted most of it down into gold bars. The first tally came to a value of 1,326,539 pesos of gold, a staggering amount for those days. One-fifth was sent to the king, with large amounts retained by Pizarro and his officers, making them rich men, although some thought they should have had more.

With most of his ransom paid, Atahuallpa demanded his freedom. Pizarro faced a dilemma. To free the Inca meant probable revolt; to maintain him as a prisoner meant using many soldiers. Worried about an uprising of the Peruvians to rescue their king, many of the Spanish officers felt Atahuallpa should be killed. Others, including de Soto, said there was no evidence that justified his execution.

Pizarro dispatched de Soto to find out if there were any signs of an uprising. While he was gone, Pizarro called a trial of Atahuallpa on several charges—that he had usurped the throne, that he was guilty of idolatry, that he had assassinated his brother, Huascar, and that he had attempted to organize a revolt against the Spanish.

With the Spanish acting as judges, Atahuallpa was found guilty and sentenced to be burned at the stake in the great square of Caxamalca on the night of August 29, 1533. Chained hand and foot, the Inca was led to the stake, with the fagots ready to be set ablaze.

Friar Valverde, holding a cross, told Atahuallpa that if he became a Christian, the Spanish would be merciful—they would strangle him so that he would die quickly and not be subject to the lengthy process of dying in the flames. Pizarro confirmed this promise. So, a few minutes before his death, Atahuallpa accepted baptism as a Christian. Then he was strangled to death.

"The treatment of Atahuallpa, from start to finish, forms undoubtedly one of the darkest chapters in Spanish colonial history" is the verdict of William H. Prescott in his famous book *The Conquest of Peru*. "From the moment Pizarro and his men entered Peru, the hand of friendship had been extended to them. Their answer was to kidnap the Inca, massacre his unarmed people, murder him, and plunder the country."

Pizarro had conquered Peru. He entered the capital city of Cuzco in triumph on November 15, 1533. Grateful for the riches that he received, King Charles of Spain raised Pizarro, who had started life as a swineherd, to the rank of nobleman, with the title marquess de los Atavillos, named after a province in Peru.

But the conquest, the title, and the gold did not result in peace and prosperity. Instead, it brought rebellion, civil war, and death to Pizarro and his chief lieutenants.

In addition to his honors to Pizarro, King Charles also granted Almagro, Pizarro's partner, power to discover and occupy the lands to the south of Peru. Marching south, Almagro found mountains, snow, and freezing cold weather, but no evidence of gold or other riches. He decided to return to Cuzco, which he felt fell within his domain.

During his absence, the Peruvians, under the command of the new Inca, Manco, had finally rebelled against Pizarro's rule. Thousands of Indian soldier fought the Spaniards in the mountains around Cuzco and finally trapped them in the city early in 1536. There they remained, surrounded by hostile Indians, for months.

When Almagro approached Cuzco, he found it under the command of Hernando Pizarro, who claimed the city for his brother. Unable to reach an agreement with Hernando, Almagro entered the city under cover of darkness on April 8, 1537, taking control of it. He put Hernando Pizarro in jail but refused to execute him, as some of his officers suggested.

Meanwhile, Francisco Pizarro, who had established a new capital of Peru in the city called Lima near the seacoast to the north, sent an emissary to try to work out an amicable arrangement. He failed. The two rival chiefs, once partners, met on November 13, 1537, to work out a settlement, but that failed, too.

At this point, Almagro made a fatal mistake. He freed Hernando Pizarro, accepting his word as a knight that he would leave the country in six weeks. Instead, Hernando Pizarro joined his brother and marched with an army of seven hundred men to attack Almagro.

On the morning of April 16, 1538, Spaniard fought Spaniard for control of Peru. Pizarro's men charged, crying *"El Rey y Pizarro!"* ("The King and Pizarro!"), while Almagro's defenders shouted, *"El Rey y Almagro!"* In two hours, the battle was over. Hernando Pizarro had triumphed, taking Almagro prisoner.

Immediately, he put Almagro on trial for levying war against the crown and dispossessing the royal governor of Cuzco, his brother Francisco. Hernando stonily refused to return the favor of freedom that he himself had received from Almagro. Almagro was found guilty and executed. Almagro had trusted Pizarro; he paid for it with his life.

Almagro's followers did not forgive the Pizarro brothers. They waited patiently, and on June 26, 1541, eighteen or twenty of them entered Francisco Pizarro's house and killed him. They ran into the streets, crying, "The tyrant is dead! The laws are restored! Long live our master the emperor and his governor, Almagro!" The rebels proclaimed Almagro's son the governor and captain-general of Peru.

Francisco Pizarro, the conqueror of Peru, died at the age of about seventy. A courageous soldier motivated by greed and ambition, he had discovered and conquered a rich new empire for Spain. In doing so, he betrayed the Indians who had greeted him in a friendly way, murdered thousands of them, and destroyed their way of life.

৩৫18৩৫

Children of the Sun

THE STORY OF THE EUROPEAN DISCOVERY OF WHAT IS NOW THE SOUTH-western part of the United States begins with a man with the most unusual name of Cabeza de Vaca. Translated into English, his name means "head of a cow." Peculiar as it may sound, it was a proud name for the family, dating back to 1212.

In that year, the army of the Christian king of Spain fought against the Moorish occupants of the country in the mountains north of Seville. Unable to attack through the mountains, the king of Navarre decided that he had to turn back.

But a Spanish shepherd, Martin Alhaja, told the king's men about a remote pass through the hills behind the enemy forces. Alhaja marked the entrance to the road with a cow's skull. By using the pass, the king gained a great victory. He rewarded the shepherd by making him a nobleman, with the name Cabeza de Vaca.

One of his descendants, Álvar Núñez Cabeza de Vaca, the oldest of four children, was born in about 1490, in the city of Jerez de la Frontera in southern Spain, not far from the sea and the port of Cadiz. He grew up hearing tales of his illustrious ancestors—not only the original Cabeza de Vaca, but of his grandfather, Pedro de Vera, the conqueror of the Canary Islands. His father, Francisco de Vera, served as an alderman of Jerez. His mother, Dona Teresa Cabeza de Vaca, came from a background of captains, mayors, and knights.

Nothing much is known of his early years, except that he served with a Spanish army in Italy in 1511, when he was about twenty-one years old. A big, brawny man with a red beard, he rose to the rank of lieutenant before returning to Spain in 1523. For several years he served the duke of Medina Sidonia as a military man and as a steward of his estates. During that time, he presumably married, but there is no record of his wife's name nor any children.

The later Cabeza de Vaca enters the pages of history in 1527, when he was named treasurer of an expedition to conquer and settle Florida, a clear indication that he was an honest, able administrator as well as a military man. The leader of the expedition was Panfilo de Narvaez, who had helped to conquer Cuba.

On June 17, 1527, the expedition left Spain in five small ships. After spending the winter in Cuba, the fleet sailed for Florida, arriving on the west coast on Good Friday, April 10, 1528. Narvaez's force, consisting of four hundred men and eighty-two horses, landed just north of what is now St. Petersburg on a sandy beach. In front of them stood a small Indian village that appeared to be vacant. The Indians had fled into the interior upon sighting the strangers.

In the empty village, Narvaez raised the flag of Spain, read a proclamation taking possession of the land in the name of the king, and took part in a solemn Mass of thanksgiving. A group of Indians approached, making signs that obviously meant "go away." But the Spaniards, who had found a gold rattle in one of the Indian huts, had no intention of leaving before they found more gold.

Holding objects of gold, they asked the Indians where they could find more. The Indians pointed north and said, "Appalachen."

Narvaez decided to march inland to reach the city of gold, ordering the ships to sail to meet him at the mouth of the Rio Grande—he thought it was nearby, but it was really far to the west. He never saw the ships again. One was lost at sea. The others spent nearly a year looking for Narvaez along the coast without success, before returning to Mexico.

On May 1, leading three hundred men and forty horses, Narvaez started inland. For two weeks they marched without seeing an Indian or a village or even a house. The going was tough, through swamps and creeks tangled with fallen trees, with no food except the hardtack biscuits they brought with them. They came to the Suwanee River and crossed it in makeshift boats. At last, on June 25, they came in sight of their goal, in the panhandle of Florida, just south of the Georgia line.

Cabeza de Vaca led a party of foot soldiers into Appalachen. Instead of the glittering city of gold, it turned out to be a small village consisting of about forty thatched huts—no gold, no jewels. The women were dressed in tattered cloth and deerskin, the men wore nothing at all. Although there was an abundance of game, Appalachen was surrounded by marshes, swamps, lakes, fallen trees, and tangled underbrush. The Indians were hostile, too, shooting arrows at the invaders and then disappearing into the underbrush.

Discouraged and hungry, the Spanish left, marching south toward the sea. Attacked by flies, mosquitoes, and ticks, Narvaez's men hacked their way to the mouth of the Appalachicola River, under continual attack by Indians in the forest and bush. Narvaez decided to build boats to return to safety in Cuba or Mexico. But no one had any shipbuilding or sea experience; nor did they have any materials needed to build boats—no tools, iron, pitch, or rigging.

In six weeks, though, they managed to construct five rude boats, each thirty-three feet long, caulking the planks of the bottoms with the fiber of the palmetto tree. A horse was killed every third day to provide food for the boat builders. When they foraged for food in the wilderness, the Indians shot at them, killing ten. Forty men died of hunger and sickness.

The desperate Spaniards knew that they would all die if they did not succeed in leaving that desolate shore. Cabeza de Vaca later wrote:

From the tails and manes of the horses, we made ropes and rigging, from our shirts, sails; and from the junipers growing there we made the oars that appeared to us requisite. Such was the country our sins cast us into, that only by very great search could we find stone for ballast and anchors, since in it all we had seen none. We flayed the horses, taking the skin from their legs entire and tanning them to make canteens wherein to carry water.

In late September, the clumsy boats put out to sea, carrying 247 survivors. Their destination was Panuco, the northernmost Spanish settlement in Mexico, which they thought was only a short distance away (it is actually about thirteen hundred miles). Under a hot sun, they slowly moved westward close to the shoreline, occasionally meeting poor Indian fishermen.

Thirst was their greatest problem because the horseskin bags containing water soon rotted. Putting in to shore to replenish their water supply, they encountered mostly hostile Indians. Despite the difficulties, they slowly worked their way toward Pensacola Bay, farther west to Mobile Bay, and then to one of the mouths of the Mississippi River. Strong currents kept them from going ashore.

One stormy day at sea, Cabeza de Vaca rowed his boat toward the one led by Narvaez, asking for help in reaching land. Narvaez refused. As Cabeza de Vaca recalled later: "He answered that it was no longer a time in which one should command another; but that each should do what he thought best to save his own life; that he intended to so act; and saying this, he departed with his boat."

Thus abdicating his responsibilities as a commander, Narvaez disappeared. He was never heard from again, presumably lost at sea. But Cabeza de Vaca survived. Tossed by the waves for days, he and his shipmates were finally cast ashore somewhere on what is now Galveston Island on the Gulf of Mexico coast of Texas on November 6, 1528.

Half drowned, the Spaniards were in a pitiable condition. So emaciated that their bones could be counted, the sick and starving soldiers crawled on the sandy shore on their hands and knees. The stronger ones made a fire, roasted some corn, and found some rainwater. As the weary survivors slowly revived, some Indians appeared and provided food and water.

Cabeza de Vaca convinced his shipmates that their only chance for survival depended on food and shelter in the Indian camp. When they arrived there, they found that another Spanish boat, one led by Andres Dorantes, had also been washed ashore. Together, Cabeza de Vaca and his companions, numbering about eighty, were the first Europeans to set foot on the land that is now Texas—the discoverers of Texas.

As winter approached, food became scarce, mainly because there were too many Spaniards for the poor Indians to feed. "So protracted was the hunger we there experienced, that many times I was three days without eating," Cabeza de Vaca later recalled. With hunger came disease. In a short time, many of the weakened Spaniards died, so many that their number was reduced from eighty to fifteen. The Spaniards called their refuge La Isla de Mal Hado ("The Island of Bad Luck").

Many of the Indians also fell sick, possibly a form of cholera. Somehow the Indians came to the idea that the strange white men from the sea were sorcerers who possessed the secrets of healing. Cabeza de Vaca and the others, who knew only the basic first-aid rules of soldiers, were forced to try to heal the ailing. They followed the native custom of making a cut where pain was felt, then sucking blood from the incision. They knew how to cauterize wounds with fire, which soldiers in the field used. Above all, they prayed.

Somehow the Spaniards survived the first winter—not as guests of the Indians but rather as slaves. Cabeza de Vaca was put to work at a task usually reserved for women—pulling roots from some of the salt-marsh rushes. "From this employment I had my fingers so tender that at but a straw's touch they would bleed," he later wrote. "Many of the canes were broken, so they often tore my flesh."

In the spring of 1529, the Indians and their Spanish captives crossed from the island to the mainland of Texas. Here in the marshes of the swampy land where mosquitoes flourished, Cabeza de Vaca fell ill, probably with malaria. When he recovered, he found that the other Spaniards had gone on without him, believing that he would die.

Put to the most menial of tasks, he dug roots, picked up driftwood for fires, and carried the simple belongings of his masters as they moved about in search of food. In despair, the proud Spaniard accepted humility. As he later recalled, "Therefore I take pleasure in infirmities, in reproaches, in necessities, in persecutions, in distresses, for Christ's sake; for when I am weak, I am strong."

For more than a year, Cabeza de Vaca lived among the poor Indians of the Texas coast, working his way up to become a trader. From the beach, he brought shells for making beads and conchs for knives, trading them to Indians inland for deerskins and hard canes for making arrows. He wandered afield from the Galveston area in his trading ventures.

One day in 1532, near the Guadalupe River, he came across a band of Indians who said that not far away were two other white-faced men and a black man. When Cabeza de Vaca arrived there, he found Andres Dorantes, who had given him up for dead more than three years before. With him was a tall black man, Estebanico, Dorantes's slave, and Alonzo Castillo Maldonado, the son of a doctor in Seville. Those four were the only survivors of the four hundred men who had set out with Narvaez back in 1528 to colonize Florida.

Instead of being conquerors, though, they were slaves. Their masters were Indians who wandered with the change of seasons in search of berries, prickly pears, pecans, and walnuts, as well as to fish in the waters of the streams that ran down to the Gulf of Mexico.

"Because we are now eating these fine nuts, do not think you have come to a land of plenty," Dorantes told Cabeza de Vaca. "When winter comes we shall dig roots with much labor, and for dainties we shall eat snakes, lizards, mice, insects, frogs, and any reptile we find.''

With his health restored, Cabeza de Vaca became a keen observer of the Indians he served. He noticed that when men married, their wives were purchased from enemy tribes, the price usually being a bow with two arrows. He added:

They cast away their daughters at birth and cause them to be eaten by dogs. The reason of their doing this, as they state, is because all the nations of the country are their foes; and as they have unceasing war with them, if they were to marry away their daughters, they would so greatly multiply their enemies that they must be overcome and made slaves; thus they prefer to destroy the girls, rather than that from them should come a single enemy. We asked why they did not themselves marry them; and they said it would be a disgustful thing to marry among relatives, and far better to kill [them] than give them to either kindred or to their foes.

At the end of the summer, the warring tribes declared a truce, however, to gather in the land of the prickly pears, where the cacti produced fruit in such abundance that the hungry Indians ate as much as they wanted for the only time during the year. With the Indians feasting, the Spaniards decided that it would be a good time to escape and try to make their way south into Mexico.

In September 1534—six years after they had been cast ashore in rags—the quartet of three white men and one black man ran away from their Indian masters and began a new phase of their life in the wilderness. They met another band of Indians, who turned out to be friendly.

That night as they sat by a fire, some Indians approached. One said he suffered from a great pain in the head, which the medicine man could not drive away. Perhaps the white men could help him?

Cabeza de Vaca motioned to Castillo, the doctor's son. Castillo knelt and prayed. Then, following Indian tradition, he blew upon the seat of the man's pain. He traced on the Indian's head the sign of the cross, and he uttered a prayer in Latin.

The Indian rubbed his head and smiled. His pain had disappeared. The Indians flocked around the men who seemed to have magical powers, bringing them venison and other gifts. For three days, the Indians celebrated the miracle before moving on, asking the Spaniards to go with them.

For eight months, Cabeza de Vaca and his companions lived with the Indians, moving south from the Corpus Christi area to near the mouth of the Rio Grande River in Texas. Wherever they went, other local Indians heard of their healing powers and came for help. Even though they were well treated by the Indians, food was still scarce and the living difficult. Cabeza de Vaca described their life at this time:

Throughout the country we went naked, and as we were unaccustomed to being so, twice a year we cast our skins like serpents. The sun and air produced great sores on our breasts and shoulders, giving us sharp pain; and the large loads we had, being very heavy, caused the cords to cut into our arms. The country is so broken and thickset that often after getting our wood in the forests, the blood flowed from us in many places, caused by the obstruction of thorns and shrubs that tore our flesh wherever we went. At times, when my turn came to get wood, after it had cost me so much blood, I could not bring it out either on my back or dragging. In these labors, my only solace and relief were in thinking of the sufferings of our Redeemer, Jesus Christ, and in the blood he shed for me, in considering how much greater must have been the torment he sustained by the thorns, than that I there received.

After crossing the Rio Grande south into what is now Mexico (although they did not know it), Cabeza de Vaca and his companions moved west. In that arid land, they met many tribes of Indians, most friendly and helpful. Everywhere they went, they were called upon to heal the sick, which they often did. Because of their apparent powers, they were called "the children of the sun" and regarded as holy men.

For months they moved westward with the sun, over mountains

and across deserts. They crossed the Rio Grande again into what is now the region around Alpine, Texas, always accompanied by hundreds of friendly Indians. Many of the Indians were sick and infirm, awaiting treatment by the strange medicine men.

Like all Spanish explorers of the day, Cabeza de Vaca believed that one of his missions was to convert the natives to Christianity. He wrote:

> We taught all the inhabitants by signs, which they understood, that in Heaven was a Man we called God, who had created the sky and the earth; him we worshipped and had for our master; that we did what he commanded and from his hand came all good; and would they do as we did, all would be well with them.

Following the Rio Grande for a time, the four strange men led an army of Indians back into Mexico, crossing the river at El Paso, into the thriving farming valley of Sonora. The Indians there gave them many presents—food, cotton shawls, beads of coral, and, to Cabeza de Vaca's astonishment, five emeralds made into arrowheads. It was the first time since they had left Florida eight years earlier that they saw any signs of the wealth that they had come to seek.

"Whence do these come?" he asked.

"From the high mountains to the north, where are great pueblo cities and tall houses," the Indians replied. "These people sell us these emeralds in return for the feathers of the Guacamayo, our green parrot."

A few days later while traveling south, Cabeza de Vaca noticed an Indian wearing a curious necklace with a horse nail dangling from a buckle of a sword belt.

"Where did you get this?" Cabeza de Vaca asked.

"From men who wore beards like you," the Indians replied.

With news that other Spaniards might be close, Cabeza de Vaca and his three companions hurried south. As they advanced they found a horrible wasteland. Even though the land was fertile, with flowing water, it was empty. The people had fled to the mountains, where they scratched out an existence by eating the bark of trees and other humble food.

When Cabeza de Vaca asked why, the Indians replied that Christians had come from the south, burning houses, destroying crops, and taking away men, women, and children as slaves. In Cabeza de Vaca's own words:

> We passed through many territories and found them vacant; their inhabitants wandered fleeing among the mountains, without daring to have houses or till the earth for fear of the Christians. The sight was one of infinite pain to us, a land very fertile and beautiful, abounding in springs and streams, the hamlets deserted and burned, the people thin and weak, all fleeing or in concealment. As they did not plant, they appeased their keen hunger by eating roots and the bark of trees.

For Cabeza de Vaca, the news was both good and bad. Bad because his fellow Christians were causing so much suffering among the Indians; good because rescue was near. Followed by hundreds of Indians who regarded him as a holy man, he continued south until he found the trail of the Spanish raiding party. Then, to travel more quickly, he, Estebanico, and eleven Indians went forward to search for his fellow Spaniards.

Two days later, early in March 1536, near the Sinola River in northern Mexico not far from the Gulf of California, they emerged from the bush. In front of them were four men on horses. The mounted men looked with amazement at the white man and the black man, heavily bearded, standing in front of a small group of Indians.

Speaking Spanish for the first time in years, Cabeza de Vaca asked the mounted men to take him to their leader. His first words were "Give me a certificate of the year, month, and day I arrived here and of the manner of my coming."

By his own calculations, he and his companions—Andres Dorantes, Alonzo Castillo Maldonado, and Estebanico—had journeyed six thousand miles on water and land since they had landed on the Florida coast in 1528. After years of suffering, they had come out of the wilderness, returning to the outposts of Spanish civilization.

They arrived in Mexico City on July 23, 1536, and were greeted there by the two leading figures of the colony, the viceroy, Antonio de Mendoza, and Hernando Cortés, the marquess of the Valley of Oaxaca, the conqueror of the Aztec empire.

Mendoza showed a great interest in the tale of the men who had been the first Christians to penetrate the remote areas north of Mexico. After hearing about the gift of emeralds they had received, he questioned them about gold. They had not seen any, but they told him they had heard stories of great cities to the north beyond the deserts. Mendoza had already heard about those fabulous cities—seven of them, filled with gold and silver, rivaling the rich cities of Mexico and Peru that had made so many Spaniards wealthy.

For Mendoza, this was a golden opportunity. He asked Cabeza de Vaca to lead an expedition back to find the seven cities that would make them all rich. But the weary wanderer was interested only in returning to Spain to report to the king. Neither of the other two Spanish gentlemen who had accompanied him, Andres Dorantes or Alonzo Castillo Maldonado, would go back, either. They remained in Mexico, marrying rich widows.

That left only the black slave, Estebanico, who had seen everything that his master, Dorantes, and Cabeza de Vaca had witnessed. But a slave could not be entrusted to head any expedition, so Mendoza appointed Father Marcos of Nice, a Franciscan friar, to make a preliminary trip to the north in the interests of religion and the king—in reality, to find the seven cities of gold. Estebanico would be his guide.

That expedition led to another remarkable exploration of the American Southwest by Francisco Vasquez Coronado.

~19~

The Seven Cities of Gold

IN MEXICO, THE BLACK MAN ESTEBANICO WAS A SLAVE. WE KNOW very little about his early life except that he was captured by the Spanish in Morocco in 1513 and taken to the New World shortly thereafter. Even his name, which translates into Stephen in English, is given differently by many historians—Esteban, Estevanico, Estevan, and Estebancito.

Obviously he was a strong man, because he had survived eight years in the wilderness with Cabeza de Vaca (see chapter 18). Despite that remarkable story, he was still a slave in Mexico. But in 1539, an opportunity opened up for him—to guide a new Spanish expedition back into the desert to the north to find the fabulous cities of gold that he and Cabeza de Vaca had heard about from the Indians.

On March 7, 1539, the expedition left Culiacan, the northern outpost of the Spanish in Mexico, under the command of Father Marcos of Nice, a Franciscan monk (sometimes called Fray Marcos de Niza). Marching on foot, the white priest and the black slave presented a startling contrast. Father Marcos wore the traditional somber gray robe of his order; Estebanico wore bright colors, with jingling bells on his wrists and ankles and feathers in his black hair. At his side were his constant companions, two large grey-hounds.

For Estebanico, the trip into the wilderness was a liberation. Everywhere he went, his appearance created a sensation among the Indians, who had never seen a black man before. From his previous trip, word had spread of his reputation as a medicine man who could cure sickness. Now he took advantage of that reputation, collecting a large amount of turquoise jewelry from the Indians. He also made friends, especially among Indian women, who were free of any race prejudice.

In Sonora in northern Mexico, Marcos halted to celebrate Easter Sunday but sent Estebanico ahead to scout out the land. Since Estebanico could not read or write, Marcos devised a system whereby messages could be sent back by fleet Indian runners. If Estebanico found a country of moderate importance, he would send back a wooden cross the size of a man's hand; if the country was of great importance, the cross would be twice as large; and if it were bigger than New Spain, the cross should be very large.

With his greyhounds at his heels, Estebanico left in style, plumes in his hair and bells on his arms and legs. He also carried a feathered gourd rattle in his hand, to let all who heard it know that an important man was approaching. With a large group of Indians following him, he crossed what is now the United States-Mexico border into eastern Arizona, becoming the first non-Indian to enter that area of the future United States.

In four days, an Indian runner reached Father Marcos carrying a cross as tall as a man. He also brought word from Estebanico: Come immediately because "the greatest country in the world" lay ahead. Only thirty days away, he said, was the first city of the new country, Cibola. It was the first time any European had heard the magical name of Cibola.

The Indian messenger described the fabulous land ahead:

In the first province there are seven very large cities, all under one lord, with houses of stone and lime, large, the smallest ones of two stories and with a flat roof, and others of three or four stories, and that of the lord with five, all placed together in order; and on the door-sills and lintels of the principal houses many figures of turquoise stones.

Father Marcos was elated. He followed Estebanico's trail across the desert lands to the north, receiving additional crosses that confirmed the good news. Without waiting, though, Estebanico, dressed in his finery and leading a band of several hundred Indian followers, pushed ahead to Cibola.

For once, though, his seemingly magical powers failed. As he approached Cibola, which in reality was the Zuni village of Hawikuh in what is today western New Mexico, Estebanico sent a messenger bearing his magical gourd rattle, ornamented with two feathers, one red and the other white, and strings of small bells.

When the Zuni Indians received the gourd, they hurled it to the ground angrily. An elder of the village said the gourd represented enemies and warned the messenger that the approaching party would be killed if it tried to enter the city. When Estebanico heard the news, he rejected the warning. By now he was supremely confident of his powers to impress any Indian, no matter how hostile.

He was wrong. The Indians seized Estebanico, took away his trading goods, and threw him into a guarded house. They questioned him. Defiantly, he said he had many brothers who were not far away and who were well armed.

"I come to tell you," he said through an interpreter, "that you must prepare to receive two white-faced men, servants of a very great lord beyond the sunrise, who know all about the great things of heaven, and are coming to instruct you in these divine matters."

To the Zunis, his story sounded peculiar. They needed no instruction in divine matters. And here in front of them was a black man who said he represented white men. They concluded that Estebanico was a dangerous liar and should be killed.

In the morning, they permitted Estebanico and several of the captured Indians out of their hut for a drink. Estebanico began to run for his freedom. The Zunis showered arrows at him, hitting and killing him. One of the captured Indians escaped and ran to tell Father Marcos about it.

Despite the bad news, Father Marcos felt that he had to see the fabulous city of Cibola before returning to Mexico. He went forward cautiously, until he came within view of Cibola. In his own words, this is what he saw:

> It is situated on a level stretch on the brow of a roundish hill. It appears to be a very beautiful city, the best that I have seen in these parts. . . . The town is bigger than the city of Mexico. At times I was tempted to go to it because I knew that I risked nothing but my life, which I had offered to God the day I commenced the journey; finally I feared to do so, considering my danger and that if I died, I would not be able to give an account of this country, which seems to me to be the greatest and best of the discoveries.

Before starting back, he made a mound of stones, placed a cross on it, and laid claim to the seven cities and the country around them in the name of the viceroy and the king. He christened the land the New Kingdom of St. Francis and then turned back to Mexico City.

To this day, historians are divided about what Father Marcos really saw and how much he exaggerated. Apparently he did catch a glimpse of the buildings of Cibola, but quite obviously the town was not as large as Mexico City. Did he knowingly deceive his superiors, or did he merely magnify his observations to make a good story better? We don't know.

Marcos's story caused a sensation in the capital of New Spain. The tale of more riches to be discovered in the north found a receptive audience, and a large number of idle gentlemen volunteered to serve in an expedition organized by the viceroy of Mexico, Antonio de Mendoza.

To command the expedition, Mendoza appointed a trusted aide, Francisco Vasquez Coronado, whom he considered to be "wise, skillful, and intelligent, besides being a gentleman." Coronado had been born in Salamanca, Spain, in 1510, the son of Juan Vasquez de Coronado, a gentleman, and Isabel de Luxan. As a well-born young man, he served in the court of the king. There he met the man who became his mentor, Mendoza. When Mendoza went off to Mexico as viceroy in 1535, Coronado accompanied him.

At the age of twenty-five, backed by Mendoza's friendship and patronage, Coronado began a rise to prominence in Mexico. When black miners near the capital revolted in 1537, Coronado was dispatched to suppress them. He did so quickly. In 1538, he was named a member of the city council of Mexico.

Coronado stood out in the rough surroundings of New Spain as a handsome young man with blue eyes, dark blond hair, mustache, and beard. His prestige and fortune were helped by his marriage to a wealthy heiress, Beatriz de Estrada, daughter of the royal treasurer of New Spain, who was rumored to be an illegitimate son of the king of Spain. They had three children.

When Mendoza faced troubles in New Galicia, a wilderness outpost in northwestern Mexico, he sent Coronado there to straighten out matters. Coronado was appointed governor of the outpost in 1539. When Father Marcos came into New Galicia later that year with his tale of the riches of Cibola, the first official he told was Coronado. Together, they returned to Mexico to tell Mendoza the good news.

When the story of Cibola spread in Mexico, Mendoza had no trouble in recruiting an army. The troops gathered in February 1540 in Compostela, the capital of New Galicia, where Mendoza reviewed a glittering display of Spanish might. One onlooker described it as "the most brilliant review yet held in New Spain."

Leading the parade was the captain-general, Coronado, riding on horseback, his gilded armor gleaming in the sun. Following him came two hundred twenty-five men mounted on sturdy horses, then sixty foot soldiers carrying pikes and muskets. After them came several hundred Indian warriors in brilliant headdresses of parrot feathers, their naked bodies painted in black, ocher, and vermilion, armed with bows and arrows.

On February 23, 1540, the army, supported by a large number of cattle, sheep, and pigs taken along as a walking food supply, marched north—beginning one of the great adventures in American exploration. Father Marcos went as a guide.

It took Coronado and his men a month of hard marching to reach the northern outpost of New Spain in Culiacan. There, Coronado divided his army, leaving most of it behind to follow slowly, while he pushed ahead rapidly with a small party of eighty horsemen, twenty-five foot soldiers, and some Indians and slaves.

It was a rough trip through the deserts and mountains, with the trail so rocky that some horses died of exhaustion and some Indians deserted. They crossed what is now the United States-Mexico border into what is now Cochise County, about thirty miles west of Bisbee, Arizona, where the Coronado National Monument stands today as a memorial.

For weeks they marched north in the harsh, hot climate along the present-day Arizona-New Mexico border, crossing the Gila River, the Salt River, and mountains until they reached the Zuni River. With food supplies running short, they turned east in early July until they caught their first glimpse of Hawikuh (which is today on the Zuni Indian Reservation on the western border of New Mexico).

It was a shock. Instead of a splendid city gleaming with gold and silver, they saw a small village of stone. One of the men who was there wrote: "When they saw the first village, which was Cibola, such were the curses that some hurled at Friar Marcos that I pray God may protect him from them. It is a little crowded village, looking as if it had all been crumpled up together."

Moreover, the Zunis, who had killed Estebanico, showed their hostility toward the invaders with a shower of arrows. Coronado ordered his men to attack the Indians, who were massed in front of their houses. The charging cavalrymen forced the Indians to retreat to the rooftops, from which they showered rocks down on the Spaniards. Coronado, in his shining armor, was their prime target. One rock hit him on the helmet, others wounded him on the face, an arrow struck his foot, and he fell to the ground.

His men rallied, climbing ladders to the Indian stronghold, and the city fell to the Spaniards. "There we found something we prized more than gold or silver, namely, much maize, beans, and chickens larger than those of New Spain, and salt better and whiter than I have ever seen in my life," one soldier wrote.

With ample food supplies, Coronado spent several months in Zuni country. In August 1540, he sent a report back to Mendoza. He also sent back Father Marcos because he did not think it was safe for the priest to stay in Cibola, "seeing that his report had turned out to be entirely false, because the kingdoms he had told them about had not been found, nor the populous cities, nor the wealth of gold, nor the precious stones he had reported, nor the fine clothes, nor other things that had been proclaimed from the pulpits."

Coronado sent out several exploratory expeditions. In the first, Pedro de Tovar went north and discovered the pueblos of the Hopi Indians, who were friendly and offered gifts of clothing, maize, and turquoise. They also told Tovar of a great river to the west, which interested the Spaniards because it might offer a passageway to the Pacific Ocean.

Coronado sent Garcia Lopez de Cardenas to find that river. After a journey of twenty days, Cardenas made a great discovery— the Grand Canyon of the Colorado River in northern Arizona. Lacking water, for three days Cardenas and his men tried to get down to the river. They failed because of the steep, rocky sides and returned. (It was two hundred years before another white man gazed upon the Grand Canyon.)

While Cardenas was gone, an Indian delegation from the east visited Cibola to see what the strange white men looked like. The Spanish soldiers nicknamed the leader of the visitors Captain Bigotes ("Captain Whiskers") because he had a long mustache, something most uncommon among the Indians. He brought shields and headpieces made of the tough hide of a strange animal, something like a cow, as presents and invited the Spaniards to visit his country, which he called Cicuye.

In need of secure quarters for the winter, Coronado dispatched Hernando de Alvarado and twenty men to investigate Cicuye. Alvarado marched through a land of abandoned pueblos and rough desert dotted with black craters and lava flows. On September 7, he reached the banks of a large river. He christened it Rio de Nuestra Señora ("River of Our Lady"). We know it today as the Rio Grande.

The people there, living in a group of pueblos called Tiguex (between today's Sandia and Bernillo), were hospitable, greeting the Spaniards with flute music. It was a fertile land, producing corn, beans, and melons—obviously a better place in which to spend the winter than the harsh desert of Cibola. Alvarado immediately sent a courier to Coronado with the news.

Leaving Tiguex, Alvarado moved a little to the east to the home village of Captain Whiskers, the pueblo of Cicuye (now called Pecos, on the Pecos River), just under one thousand miles from the border crossing. Pedro de Castenada, who later accompanied Coronado, left this description of the pueblo:

> Cicuye is a village of nearly 500 warriors, who are feared throughout the country. It is square, situated on a rock, with a large court or yard in the middle. . . . The houses are all alike, four stories high. One can go over the whole top of the village without there being a street to hinder. There are corridors going around it at the first two stories, by which one can go around the whole village. These are like outside balconies, and they are able to protect themselves under there. The houses do not have doors below, but they use ladders, which can be lifted up like a drawbridge.

When Coronado and his men arrived in Tiguex, it was already winter. As they settled in, Alvarado brought in a peculiar-looking Indian slave who had a strange story to tell. The Spaniards named the Indian El Turco ("the Turk") because he wore something like a turban. Almost certainly he was a Pawnee Indian of the plains.

The Turk told a tale of a wonderful country to the east, where there were big cows, a river with fish bigger than horses, people who ate from golden dishes, and a king who spent his afternoon siestas under a great tree whose branches carried little golden bells that rang in the breeze. The Spanish, greedy for gold, believed him, perhaps because the story offered hope in a winter of troubles.

At first peaceable and friendly, the Indians of Tiguex turned against the Spanish because of a series of grievances. Coronado had seized Indian garments so his men could keep warm; that meant the Indians were cold. He had ejected the entire population of one village so that his soldiers could have shelter. And a Spanish soldier had violated an Indian woman.

The Indians rebelled. They seized the Spaniards' horses and retreated into one of their strongholds. The Spanish, led by Cardenas, stormed the pueblo and, after a bitter fight, offered a truce. The Indians accepted. Instead of peace, though, Cardenas ordered the Indian prisoners to be tied to stakes and burned alive as a punishment.

When the unarmed Indians saw men being tied to the stakes, they fought bare-handed against the Spanish soldiers, who were armed with swords and muskets. "It was one of the most terrible and cold-blooded massacres of southwestern Indians in all history," one historian has written. It was, he said, "a stain on the escutcheon of Francisco Vasquez Coronado to the end" even though he was not present at the massacre.

No wonder, then, that when the ice broke on the Rio Grande in the spring of 1541, Coronado was ready to move on to Quivira, the city of gold. As he and his men marched east through New Mexico into what is now the panhandle of Texas and western Oklahoma, they began to see "the cows," the first glimpses of the buffalo of the plains.

This is how he described the buffalo:

At first there was not a horse that did not run away upon seeing them, for their faces are short and narrow between the eyes, the forehead two spans wide. Their eyes bulge on the sides so that, when they run, they can see those who follow them. They are bearded like very large he-goats. When they run they carry their heads low, their beards touching the ground. From the middle of the body back, they are covered with very woolly hair like that of fine sheep. From the belly to the front they have very heavy hair like the mane of a wild lion. They had a hump larger than that of a camel. Their horns, which show a little through the hair, are short and heavy. During May, they shed the hair on the rear half of their body and look exactly like lions.

Aside from the dangerous buffalo, Coronado found the plains a problem, too. The prairie grass covered everything, showing no streams, no mountains, no trees, no bushes—nothing that could be a landmark. Men got lost in the thick grass and could not find their way back to camp. Some died, unable to find their companions.

Occasionally Coronado came across a band of wandering Indians. None of them confirmed the Turk's tale of gold and silver in Quivira. Near the end of May, the army had been on the prairie for more than a month, enduring hunger and thirst with no sign that they were reaching their destination. Coronado decided to send most of his men back to the Rio Grande. He would go forward with a small party, with the Turk, in chains, as a guide.

With thirty horsemen and half a dozen foot soldiers, Coronado rode on—on through the monotonous plains for thirty days. They crossed into what is today Kansas, east of Dodge City, up to the Kansas River. They found herds of buffalo, a fine rich black soil, and villages of the Wichita Indians, their huts thatched with grass— but no gold or silver or the fine kingdom that the Turk had described.

The exact spot in Kansas that Coronado reached is not known, but it was somewhere east of the present city of Salina in the central part of the state. Wherever they were, Coronado had failed to find the wealth he sought. Like so many other Spanish explorers greedy for gold, he had been misled by a smooth-talking liar.

Because it was apparent to all that he was lying, the Turk confessed that he had been encouraged by the Zunis to talk about the gold of Quivira to draw the Spaniards away from the pueblos. It was a pattern that the Indians learned almost everywhere to get rid of the invaders—tell them about gold in some other land so they would leave. Coronado ordered the Turk executed.

After almost a month in Kansas, the disappointed Coronado

started the long trek back to the Rio Grande. Blazing a path taken in later years by American traders, the Santa Fe Trail, he arrived back in Tiguex in the fall of 1541. He wrote a letter to the king, describing Quivira:

> The country itself is the best I have ever seen for producing all the products of Spain, for besides the land itself being very fat and black and being well-watered by the rivulets and springs and rivers, I found prunes like those of Spain and nuts and very good sweet grapes and mulberries. I have treated the natives of this province, and all the others whom I found wherever I went as well as possible, agreeable to what Your Majesty had commanded, and they have received no harm from me or from those who went in my company. . . . What I am sure of is that there is not any gold nor any other metal in all that country.

Disappointed, the Spaniards spent a second winter in Tiguex, suffering in the cold weather because of a lack of wood for fires and clothing for the men. One day, shortly after Christmas in 1541, Coronado was severely injured in a fall from his horse. That put him to bed at a time when his leadership was needed the most. Some of the men wanted to return to look for the gold of Quivira, others just wanted to return to the safety of Mexico.

Coronado refused to divide his forces, and so, early in April 1542, his army began an unhappy retreat from Tiguex. Many of his horses died along the way, some of his men deserted, and the enraged Indians attacked constantly. The remnants of the glittering army that had set out to conquer new lands two years before returned to Culiacan empty-handed and in tatters in June 1542. A few months later, Coronado reported to Mendoza in Mexico City that his mission had failed.

At the age of thirty-two, his rapid rise in the leadership of Mexico came to an end. He returned to his wife, his estates, and his governorship of New Galicia, but his career, for all practical purposes, was over. In 1544, he even faced a secret inquiry by high Spanish officials on charges of neglect of duty, favoritism in appointments, acceptance of bribes, and inhumane treatment of natives. He was cleared of the major charges but fined six hundred gold pesos for several minor infractions.

He spent the rest of his life with his wife and children in Mexico City, where he died on September 22, 1554, at the age of forty-four.

❧20❧

Discovery of the Mississippi: The Spanish

WHO DISCOVERED THE MISSISSIPPI RIVER? WAS IT HERNANDO DE Soto, who generally receives the credit? Or René-Robert Cavelier, sieur de la Salle, who was the first European to travel down the length of the Mississippi? Or Alonso Alvarez de Pineda, whose name is not even mentioned in most history books? Let's look at the record.

· I ·

Alonso Alvarez de Pineda

In late 1518, an expedition of three vessels set out from the island of Jamaica to conquer the northern area of Mexico. Its commander was Alonso Alvarez de Pineda, about whom we know very little. But he must have been an able mariner and soldier to lead such an expedition.

Its first landing was somewhere on the west coast of Florida, where the Spaniards met hostile Indians, just as Ponce de León had. But Pineda showed more common sense than his predecessor. He left and sailed west, hugging the coast of the Gulf of Mexico.

Soon, in early 1519, his ships came to a large river, pouring a huge volume of fresh water into the gulf. Pineda anchored in one

213

of the outlets of the river and did some trading with the local Indians, who acted friendly. He sailed up the river about twenty miles, counting at least forty Indian villages along its banks.

Interesting as the new river was, Pineda had another mission, though—to sail on to Mexico. So he returned down the Mississippi to the Gulf of Mexico and continued his voyage west along the coast of Texas. When he reached Mexico, his expedition turned into a disaster.

Landing near the mouth of the Panuco River where the present city of Tampico stands, he and his men were attacked by hostile Indians. Many of the Spaniards, including Pineda, were killed. Not only were they killed, but they were cut up and eaten by cannibalistic Indians, and their skins were hung in Aztec temples as trophies.

Only one of Pineda's ships, commanded by Diego de Camargo, managed to escape. He returned to Vera Cruz with the news, reporting the disaster to Hernando Cortés.

Despite his horrible death, Pineda, who was the first European to sail completely around the perimeter of the Gulf of Mexico, accomplished two things. First, he demonstrated that there was no passageway between the oceans in the gulf. More important, he discovered the mouth of the Mississippi River.

• II •
Hernando de Soto

In the same year that Pineda died, a handsome, eager, curly haired young man only nineteen years old arrived in Darien on the Isthmus of Panama. Hernando de Soto, like many other poor young men from Spain, came to seek fortune and fame in the New World, lured by tales of island paradises lapped by blue waters and shaded by palm trees. Above all, he and the others believed that gold was as common there as paving stones in the streets of the cities of Spain.

Nothing much is known about de Soto's early life, except that he was born in Jerez de los Caballeros in the Estremadura region of Spain, presumably in 1500, although some authorities place his birth in 1496. He attended the University of Salamanca at least for some time, with his expenses paid by his patron, Pedro Arias de Avila, more commonly known as Pedrarias, the governor of Darien. Pedrarias also paid for de Soto's passage to the New World and appointed his protégé a captain of dragoons, or cavalrymen, in his small army.

Darien was anything but an island paradise. A patch of low-lying land, it bordered on a swampy breeding place for ferocious mosquitoes. It was hot, humid, and unhealthy. So in 1519 Pedrarias moved the capital to Panama, on the Pacific Ocean side of the isthmus (now the western exit of the Panama Canal). That opened up a gateway for further exploration and discovery on the west coast of Central and South America.

Two years earlier, in 1517, Vasco Núñez de Balboa (see chapter 11) had been executed as a result of a feud with Pedrarias before he had had a chance to launch a fleet to look for a kingdom to the south where the Indians said gold abounded. In the following years, many plans were made for such a voyage, but disputes among quarreling Spaniards prevented any from leaving. De Soto in those years earned a reputation as a top-notch soldier, the best horseman and swordsman in the army.

Loyal to Pedrarias, de Soto helped him win the province of Nicaragua to the north against rival Spaniards who claimed it. He entered a business partnership with two other young men in the lucrative trade of selling captured Indians as slaves. De Soto and his partners prospered and soon owned three ships.

When Francisco Pizarro sailed on his expedition to Peru in 1531, he left behind in Panama many men without funds or shipping to join him. De Soto had the ships and the money. A deal was made. De Soto would take ships, bringing reinforcements to Pizarro. In return he would be named lieutenant governor of the lands to be conquered, the chief assistant to Pizarro.

In Peru, Pizarro landed on the island of Puna in the Gulf of Guayaquil, despite Indian attacks. Even though the Spaniards de-feated them, the Indians maintained a steady harassment of the invaders. At this crucial moment, de Soto arrived with two ships, carrying a hundred soldiers and their horses.

With these reinforcements, Pizarro crossed the water to the mainland in May 1532 and began his conquest of Peru. In the next three years, de Soto became prominent as commander of the advance forces of the small Spanish army. He was the first Spaniard to enter the city of Tumbez on the mainland, the first to meet Atahuallpa, the Inca, and the first to enter Cuzco, the rich capital of the Incan empire.

When Pizarro imprisoned Atahuallpa, de Soto, who was a conciliator as well as a brave soldier, became the Inca's best friend. Sent off on a military mission, de Soto was gone when Atahuallpa was sentenced to death by a court-martial for planning to gather his warriors to attack the invaders. De Soto returned a few days after the Inca's execution on August 29, 1533.

Angrily, he confronted Pizarro. "Sir," he said, "you have done a serious injustice. You should in any case have awaited our return. As a matter of fact, the accusation against Atahuallpa is false. There is no gathering of men."

Despite the death of the Inca, fighting continued for years between the Peruvians and the Spaniards. During that time de Soto found time for a romantic adventure. An Inca princess named Curicuillor ("Star of Gold") because of her beauty followed her lover into battle. When he was wounded, she nursed him back to health. On a trip to Cuzco, de Soto heard the romantic story and put the two lovers under his protection.

He converted them to Christianity and had them married according to the laws of the Church. Two years later, after her husband had died, de Soto made the beautiful young widow, now named Leonora, his mistress. They had a daughter, also named Leonora, who remained in Cuzco after de Soto left.

By 1535, quarrels among the rival greedy Spanish conquerors of Peru had reached such an intensity that de Soto decided to return to Spain. He arrived there later that year, a very wealthy man from his share of the loot of the riches of Peru.

At the age of thirty-five, de Soto became a favorite at the court of King Charles, telling tales of his adventures in the romantic kingdom of the Incas. A rich, handsome man, de Soto married Isabella de Bobadilla, a daughter of his mentor, Pedrarias, whose family was well connected at the royal court, in November 1536. But de Soto, who had been happy as a soldier in the field, soon tired of the splendors of the court and of the comfort of marriage.

He wrote to the king, asking permission to lead an expedition into the interior of South America. The king and his advisors were more interested in Florida, which had been discovered by Juan Ponce de León in 1513 (see chapter 12). Several Spanish attempts to plant a colony there had failed because of the hostility of the Indians. De Soto agreed to explore and pacify Florida, which at that time meant not only the peninsula that we know as the state but the entire region north of Cuba.

In April 1537, de Soto was named governor of Florida and a knight of Santiago. By agreement with the crown, he raised an army of eager volunteers, with the necessary arms, horses, munitions, and military stores. It included twelve priests to instruct the natives in Christianity but no lawyers, because, as they said at court, their presence always resulted in too much litigation. On November 6, 1537, with trumpets sounding, banners flying in the breeze, and guns firing, de Soto and six hundred twenty men sailed off in nine ships to conquer Florida.

First, however, they stopped in Cuba, where de Soto organized a base of supplies. He added more horses to his army, as well as packs of bloodhounds and wolfhounds to be used to pursue hostile Indians. He also bought a herd of thirteen pigs to take as a walking supply of meat for his troops. To prepare the way in Florida, he sent an advance guard to scout out a suitable landing place. It all took time, so it wasn't until May 18, 1539, that de Soto finally sailed to Florida.

On a beautiful Sunday later in May, de Soto landed at Charlotte Harbor, on the west coast of Florida, a little north of where Fort Myers is today. It took almost two weeks to unload all the soldiers, animals, and supplies. Onshore, the Spaniards got a foretaste of what they were to face for the next few years—active hostility from the Indians.

One of his soldiers recalled later:

> The Indians are exceedingly ready with their weapons, and so warlike and nimble, that they have no fear of footmen; for if these charge them they flee, and when they turn their backs are presently upon them. They never remain quiet, but are continually running, traversing from place to place, so that neither crossbow nor arquebus can be aimed at them. Before a Christian can make a single shot, an Indian will discharge three or four arrows; and he seldom misses a shot.

Despite the beauty of the countryside, the Spaniards found it difficult going. Marshes, swamps, dense bushes, and ponds—in addition to hostile Indians—impeded the progress of the invaders, some of them wearing heavy armor made of iron, and their animals. To add to the confusion, de Soto had little idea of the interior and no effective interpreters. Despite all that, de Soto took formal possession of Florida in the name of the king on June 3, 1539.

Soon after they landed, a squad of Spaniards attacked a small group of Indians in a swamp. Only one man, naked, painted, and tattooed like the rest, did not flee. He cried out in Spanish, "For the love of God and Holy Mary, do not kill me." His name was Juan Ortiz, the last survivor of an earlier expedition, who had been a prisoner of the Indians for eleven years. De Soto welcomed him, not only as a reclaimed Christian but as a guide.

Ortiz told a story that later became legendary to English readers in the tale of Pocahontas and Captain John Smith. When he was captured, Ortiz was bound by his hands and feet to four stakes, under which sticks were piled for a fire in which he would be roasted to death. The daughter of the chief took pity on him and begged her father for his life. Ortiz became her slave.

He knew nothing about gold, something that soon became de Soto's major obsession. When asked about gold, the Florida Indians, like Indians everywhere in America, took the obvious way to get rid of the greedy invaders—they pointed to someplace distant from their own land. They said that the warriors in that other area even wore golden hats.

Under a blazing summer sun, de Soto led his army north, with high-spirited young soldiers on horseback in front, his pigs trailing in the rear. The quest for gold proved fruitless; there were no signs of any Indians wearing golden hats. Moreover, everywhere they went the natives quite naturally resisted de Soto's attempts to make them into porters to carry his supplies. He took drastic measures for getting those porters—he captured the local Indian chiefs and held them until the necessary carriers were supplied.

For months, de Soto and his men slogged their way northward, crossing swamps and rivers, running out of food, skirmishing with hostile Indians, and losing men to arrows fired from the densely wooded country. He decided to spend the winter near the fine harbor now called Pensacola Bay, sending a ship back to Havana with orders to return with provisions in the spring.

Before that rendezvous, though, de Soto decided to follow up on an amazing story told by a captive Indian. Far off to the east, the Indian said, lay a province governed by a queen who received gold and furs as tribute from other Indian tribes in the neighborhood. The skeptical Spaniards were convinced only when the Indian described how gold was mined and refined there.

So in early March 1540, de Soto and his men marched through Georgia in a northeast direction. It was not easy, battling their way through the fierce Appalachin Indians before reaching the territories of the agricultural Creeks. They ran out of food several times and resorted to eating some of the pigs that accompanied them.

On May 1, they reached the banks of the Savannah River, some twenty-five miles south of the present city of Augusta. There four canoes crossed the river, bringing a beautiful young Indian woman to greet them. She was not the Indian queen, though, but her niece. A few minutes later, the queen herself, dressed in a delicate white cloth, came across the river in a stately canoe, under an awning. De Soto immediately noticed that she wore ropes of pearls around her neck but no gold.

Taking the pearl necklace off, she offered it to de Soto as a gesture of good will. In return, he took off a ruby ring and presented it to her. The Indian queen, called the *cacica* (or "woman chief") by the Spaniards, made polite conversation with de Soto, translated by Ortiz.

She gave the visitors comfortable accommodations in her village, with abundant supplies of wild turkeys, venison, maize, walnuts, and mulberries. When de Soto asked about gold, she replied she had a goodly supply and brought out some of it. To the Spaniards' disappointment, though, it was light in color, probably mixed with copper. But she had an ample amount of pearls.

De Soto was not satisfied. Spoiled by his discoveries and the riches he had found in Peru, he seemed, even to his own aides, to be seeking a similar treasure trove of gold. "He would not be content with good lands or pearls," said one of his assistants.

Impatient, de Soto decided to move on to the north, crossing the Savannah River into what is now South Carolina. Despite the kindness and courtesy of the *cacica*, he forced her to accompany him because only in that way could he obtain the services of her tribe as porters. It was certainly an evil deed, illustrating a blindness among the Spanish conquistadors to the rights of the native Americans. As they reached the Blue Ridge Mountains, the *cacica* managed to escape, taking along with her most of the pearls.

As the spring weather improved, de Soto's band marched on, through the southwestern tip of North Carolina and the southeastern edge of Tennessee into Alabama. Everywhere they went, they alienated the local Indians by their never-ending demand for porters to carry their supplies. It led to a disaster for the Spaniards.

Marching south along a riverbank, they came to an Indian village at Tuscaloosa, led by an Indian chief of the same name. A large man, he made an impressive appearance, standing about a foot taller than most of the other Indians. As usual, de Soto asked him for porters to continue the journey south. Tuscaloosa refused, saying he served no man. At that point, de Soto, following his custom, made the Indian chief a captive.

Tuscaloosa furnished four hundred carriers. He also secretly sent out word to his warriors to concentrate at Mabilla, an Indian village north of present-day Mobile. On October 18, 1541, de Soto arrived at the fortified village of Mabilla. Despite signs of Indian hostility, he decided to camp within the village instead of on the open fields outside.

As soon as he entered, the Indians attacked. De Soto fought his way out, under a barrage of arrows. His men surrounded the village and attacked, but the Indians repelled the Spaniards. Late in the afternoon, though, some of the Spanish soldiers got close enough to set fire to the wooden huts of the village. In less than an hour, the village was destroyed.

The Spanish had won, but they lost more than they gained. Although two thousand Indians lay dead on the battlefield and the Spanish casualties were comparatively light—twenty dead and one hundred forty-eight wounded—they had lost all their supplies—food, clothing, bedding, tents, and even the few pearls left from South Carolina.

With his men in rags, de Soto himself changed. In despair, he turned moody, but his determination to find gold, which would mean success for his expedition, never wavered. A reasonable man would have marched south a short distance to Mobile Bay, where boats would take him back to Florida, but de Soto turned northward again in a frantic search for the elusive treasure. Despite the hardships, his men did not question his decision.

North through Alabama and then west through Mississippi, the small army of Spaniards slowly marched, sometimes meeting friendly Indians but more often hostile ones. A series of small battles were fought as de Soto and his men advanced until he reached an Indian village with the peculiar name of Quizquiz in western Mississippi. There he learned that he was close to a great river.

On May 21, 1541, de Soto first set eyes on the river that he called Rio del Espíritu Santo ("River of the Holy Ghost") and that we know as the Mississippi. It is believed that the name *Mississippi*, which it received later, came from a combination of Indian words, *michi*, meaning "big," and *sippi*, meaning "water."

Historians do not agree on the exact location of de Soto's discovery of the Mississippi River. They believe it to be somewhat south of the present city of Memphis, either in the southwest corner of Tennessee or the northwest corner of Mississippi.

Despite many romantic paintings that show de Soto and his men in polished armor on the day of discovery, the reality was quite different. One biographer described the Spaniards on that day:

> The gaily-sashed doublets of taffeta had long ago yielded to shreds of Indian fibre-blankets or the skins of wild animals, bald with wear. Many had not even so much as these, but wore habilments somewhat similar to those assumed by Adam and Eve after the Fall, cloaks and aprons of pampas grass, Spanish moss or ivy. Few of them had any horses; those that remained were scrawny, poorly shod, and distempered. The bloodhounds and Irish greyhounds, savage from the scarcity of food, were held in leashes baying hoarsely. . . . The white habits of the Dominicans and the black cassocks of the priests were lost or torn to tatters. They were as wild and matted of hair and beard as the others, bare-legged, and wearing buckskin drawers. . . . Even to the Indians, the Spaniards must have seemed like savages.

What they saw was an enormous, wide mass of water, sprawling into bayous and inlets, filled with little islands of mud, choked with vegetation. The swift current carried uprooted trees and branches downstream in a never-ending procession. To de Soto and his men, it was not a major discovery, as it was when Balboa first caught sight of the Pacific Ocean. There were no speeches, no ceremonies.

For the weary Spaniards, the Mississippi loomed only as a major obstacle to be crossed—and they had no boats. Even though the chief of the Indians on the other side of the river appeared, with two hundred large war canoes carrying about two thousand warriors, de Soto knew he could expect no help from him. He set his men to building barges, using wood from the local trees.

A month later, on June 18, de Soto and his men crossed the Mississippi River into Arkansas. At first the local Indians were friendly to the Spaniards because, as one chief said, they looked like "men from heaven, whom their arrows could not harm." De Soto erected a cross at one village and attempted to convert the natives to Christianity.

Still searching for gold, de Soto moved north and then west in Arkansas, reaching the gorge of the Arkansas River. The Indians there told him that there might be gold to the south, so he turned in that direction to Louisiana. As winter approached, he faced the problem of finding quarters for his troops, but most of the Indians in the area were hostile. In December, he settled down near an Indian village.

As spring came, his scouting parties could find no good way through the mud and canebrake vegetation to the sea. By this time, even the indomitable de Soto had become convinced that his ragtag army, reduced in numbers and without supplies, could not continue the search for gold. His army had dwindled to about half, his horses were down to a few lame animals, his supplies were exhausted, and all around were unfriendly Indians.

In despair, de Soto came down with a fever, losing the will to live. He could not face returning home a failure. After appointing Luis de Moscoso as his successor, de Soto died on May 21, 1542, a year to the day after he had discovered the Mississippi River, at the age of forty-two.

His officers thought it necessary to conceal his death from the Indians because de Soto had told them that Christians were immortal. At first they buried him, but the Indians became curious about the grave site. So the Spaniards dug up the body, wrapped it in a shroud, and weighted the bundle with sand. They took it in a canoe to the middle of the Mississippi River and dropped it into the river.

With de Soto dead, his men had one idea—to get out as quickly as possible. After trying to find a waterway to the west that would give them access to the Gulf of Mexico, they finally decided that they had to build small boats to go with the current down the Mississippi. After several months, the Spaniards, who had little experience in boat building, finally constructed seven large barges.

On July 2, 1543, the barges were ready to depart. But there was no room for about four hundred Indian servants, many of whom had been converted to Christianity. Moscoso left them behind. For seventeen days, the ragged fleet floated down the Mississippi, under a constant barrage of arrows from the Indians on the shore, before they reached the sea.

There their troubles were not yet over. It took more than a month of sailing along the coast in the stormy waters of the Gulf of Mexico before they reached a Christian settlement and safety. Of the original 620 men who had left, only 311 returned. They had not found gold, as de Soto had promised, but he and they had rediscovered the Mississippi River—twenty-two years after Pineda.

𝒞𝓈21𝓈𝒟

Discovery of the Mississippi: The French

THE FRENCH CONNECTION WITH THE MISSISSIPPI RIVER BEGAN ALMOST a hundred years after de Soto, when they began to explore the Great Lakes, with mixed motives of expansion, trade, and religion. Unlike the Spanish, who sent armies to conquer new lands, the French sent individual traders, looking for furs. Like the Spanish, they also sent priests, seeking to persuade the Indians to accept Christ.

One of those French priests was a young Jesuit named Jacques Marquette. Born in 1637, he came to Canada in 1666, studied Indian languages until he became fluent in at least six of them, and then went out as a missionary. He founded missions at Sault Ste. Marie, where Lake Superior empties into Lake Huron, and at Point Ignace on the Straits of Mackinac, where Lakes Michigan and Huron meet.

There he heard stories from the Indians of a great river to the west that seemed to empty into the Gulf of California and possibly the Pacific Ocean. For the French governor of Canada, that was important news. The French objective was to extend their control of America by occupying the interior of the country. By doing so, they could hem England into the Atlantic seaboard and secure a sea outlet on the Gulf of Mexico, disputing Spanish possession.

225

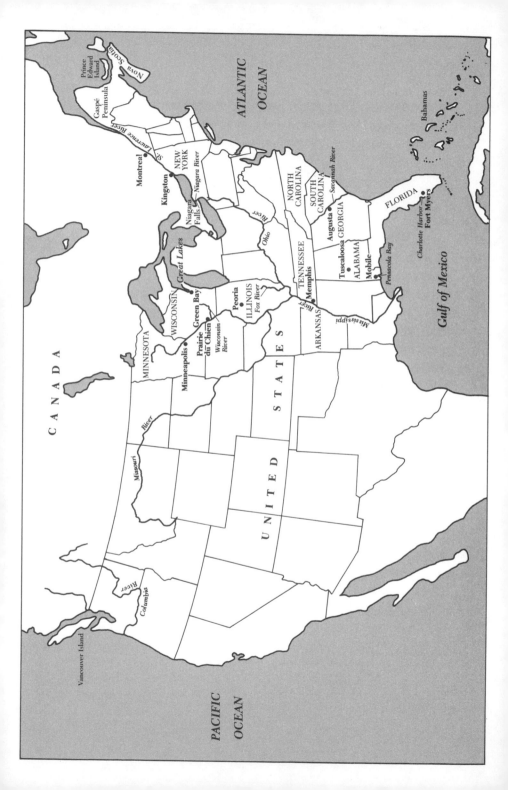

Louis de Baude, Count Frontenac, selected two men to explore the vast new region to the west. One was Marquette, often called Pere (Father) Marquette because of his religious affiliation. The other was Louis Joliet, a young man who had given up his studies for the priesthood to become an active fur trader. Like Marquette, Joliet had already traveled through parts of the wilderness in the upper Great Lakes area.

On May 17, 1673, the two travelers set out in birch-bark canoes, with a supply of smoked meat and Indian corn, accompanied by five other men. They canoed along the shores of Lake Michigan to Green Bay. The Indians along the lake tried to dissuade them from continuing. They said that the banks of the Mississippi were inhabited by ferocious tribes who tomahawked every stranger to death, its waters were filled with monsters that would devour them, and that the heat was so great they would die.

Ignoring the scare stories, the seven men paddled their way up the Fox River and crossed Lake Winnebago, gliding through fields of wild rice and visiting friendly villages of the Kickapoo, Miami, and Mascouten tribes. Under the guidance of the Indians, they carried their canoes over the marshes (near the modern city of Portage) to the Wisconsin River. By day they canoed slowly down the river; by night they camped on the shore.

Exactly a month after they started, on June 17, they entered a broad river, the Mississippi, near where the city of Prairie du Chien stands today. "With a joy I cannot express," Marquette wrote later, they had finally discovered the great river. For twenty days, they paddled south without seeing a human being. The Indians they met thereafter were all friendly, perhaps because the travelers came without guns.

They passed the mouth of the Illinois River, went by the torrential waters of the Missouri River, and soon came to the mouth of the Ohio River, the first white men to see all of them. At the junction of the Arkansas River, Joliet and Marquette agreed that they had gone far enough to conclude that the Mississippi flowed not toward the Pacific Ocean but south to the Gulf of Mexico.

On July 17, they turned back upriver and reached Green Bay

at the end of September. Marquette, who was ill, remained behind while Joliet returned to Quebec to report to Frontenac. Two years later, Marquette died in the wilderness he loved, at the age of thirty-eight. Joliet had a long career as an explorer and trader in Hudson Bay, the lower St. Lawrence River, and Labrador before his death in 1700 at the age of fifty-five.

Even though Joliet and Marquette did not complete the trip south to the gulf, they had found a practically continuous waterway from the cold St. Lawrence River through the heart of the continent to a warm-water port far to the south. To the French, that was a golden opportunity—to control middle America by a series of trading forts, which could monopolize the vast fur trade of the interior, while at the same time confine their major rivals, the English, to the Atlantic coast.

The next step in the French exploration of the Mississippi River fell to René-Robert Cavelier, sieur de la Salle. Called La Salle by everybody, he came to Canada in 1666 at the age of twenty-three. Born to a wealthy family in Rouen, France, he studied with the Jesuits for the priesthood but soon left, possibly because of his fierce ambition and dislike of discipline. In the new colony of Canada, he found scope for his desire for adventure and action.

On his arrival, he was given a tract of land at Lachine, above the falls of the same name, about eight miles west of Montreal. It was on the frontier of French civilization and hence open to Indian attack; but, on the other hand, it was close to the lucrative fur trade. La Salle carried on a flourishing trade with the Indians and in doing so became fluent in several Indian languages. From the Indians, La Salle learned of a great river to the west that flowed into the sea.

Before he could follow up on that lead, he had another job to perform. Count Frontenac called upon the young trader to set up a fort farther west, at the outlet of Lake Ontario into the St. Lawrence River, near the site of the present-day city of Kingston, Canada. Fort Frontenac was established in 1675.

In the following year, La Salle returned to France, petitioning the king for two things: a title of nobility and the lands around

Fort Frontenac. With both his requests granted, La Salle went back to Canada in a position to control the rich fur trade of the area.

"If he had preferred gain to glory, he had only to stay at his fort," a friend wrote. At Fort Frontenac, La Salle reigned as a lord of the forests around him, with buildings of stone, barracks for soldiers, a forge, a well, a mill, and a bakery, with a hundred acres of farmland to support them. From Fort Frontenac, tough Frenchmen in canoes went west to trade for furs.

La Salle, then thirty-three years old, was an ambitious man with vision. He saw in front of him a continent to be conquered. In his vision, the beautiful lands to the west, with fertile soil and friendly Indians, could prosper for both Church and king. And so he went back to France in 1678, with proposals to carry the French flag west.

In a formal note, the king replied:

Louis, by the grace of God King of France and Navarre, to our dear and well-beloved Robert Cavelier, sieur de la Salle, greeting. We have received with favor the very humble petition made us in your name, to permit you to labor at the discovery of the western parts of New France; and we have willingly entertained this proposal, since we have nothing more at heart than the exploration of this country, through which, to all appearance, a way may be found to Mexico.

In the fall of 1678, La Salle returned to Canada. With him was a new assistant, Henri de Tonty, an Italian military officer who became an invaluable ally in the wilderness. Tonty, an experienced soldier, had lost one hand in a grenade explosion, but this proved no handicap to him. In Quebec, La Salle gained another recruit for his expedition, Father Louis Hennepin, a Recollect (a branch of the Franciscan order) monk.

On a gusty day in November, Hennepin led an advance party up the St. Lawrence River into Lake Ontario in a small sailing ship, landing at the mouth of the Niagara River. In a canoe, Hennepin and several others went up the river until stopped by a mighty cataract, Niagara Falls.

Although the Indians of the area obviously knew about the falls and perhaps other wandering Frenchmen had seen them, Hennepin was the first European to see Niagara Falls and write about it. He is generally credited with being the discoverer of Niagara Falls. This is how he recalled that day later in the first written description of the falls:

On the 6th [December 6, 1678], St. Nicholas Day, we entered the beautiful river Niagara, which no bark had ever yet entered. . . . There is an incredible Cataract or Waterfall, which has no equal. The Niagara River near this place is only an eighth of a mile wide, but it is very deep in places, and so rapid above the great fall, that it hurries down all animals which try to cross it, without a single one being able to withstand its current. They plunge down a height of more than five hundred feet [in reality, about one hundred ninety feet], and its fall is composed of two sheets of water, with an island sloping down. In the middle these waters foam and boil in a fearful manner.

Meanwhile, La Motte began to construct a fort at the Niagara River. La Salle, who joined the advance party there, decided to build a sailing ship above the impassable cataracts. So his men hauled supplies on land around Niagara Falls and worked all winter to build the ship under the direction of Tonty.

As spring came, the ship, named the *Griffin* (sometimes spelled *Griffon*) after the coat of arms of Count Frontenac, was launched. The Indians looked with amazement at the largest vessel they had ever seen, with white sails flapping in the breeze and five small cannon peeking out of her portholes. They had never seen a sailing ship before.

On August 7, 1679, La Salle and his men boarded the ship and sailed westward on Lake Erie. Without any troubles, they sailed north through Lake St. Clair into Lake Huron and then proceeded into Lake Michigan. They cast anchor at Green Bay on the western shores of the lake, where they encountered a friendly Potawatomi chief and several of La Salle's advance party, who had collected a large store of beaver furs.

La Salle sent the *Griffin* back to Montreal, loaded with furs to be sold to pay his debts there. She was never seen again. Presumably she sank with all her hands during a Great Lakes storm—or perhaps she was scuttled by members of her crew, who divided the cargo for their own profit and then defected to the British.

With the fourteen men who remained, La Salle paddled south on Lake Michigan in four canoes, loaded with tools, merchandise, and arms. It was not an easy trip. Stormy weather, large waves, and rain buffeted the canoers by day. At night, they dragged their canoes through the breakers onto the steep shores to camp. Their food ran out, and the Indians they met seemed hostile. But La Salle, gifted in speaking to Indians, turned them into friends.

He and his men reached the southern end of Lake Michigan at the beginning of November. Joined by Tonty and some additional men, the party, now thirty-three strong in eight canoes, paddled down several small rivers until they reached the Kanakee River and then the Illinois River. Soon after New Year's Day, 1680, they arrived at Peoria Lake, where they saw about eighty Indian wigwams on both shores.

After an initial confrontation, with both sides afraid the other would attack, La Salle and his men were made welcome. La Salle said he had come to protect them against their enemies and to teach them to pray to God. If they were attacked, he said, he would stand by them and fight in their defense, if they would permit him to build a fort there. In the cold wintry weather, the Frenchmen built their fort, which they called Fort Crèvecoeur, near where Peoria is today. It was the first settlement of Europeans in what is now Illinois.

Once again, La Salle faced one of his most troubling problems—desertion. Many of his men, tough woodsmen unused to discipline, disliked La Salle, who was a stern captain. An aloof man, he could make friends with the strange Indians more easily than he could among his fellow Frenchemen. Six discontented men left in the night, obviously preferring the hardships of making their way through the snow and ice back to Canada to facing the unknown wilderness in front of them under the command of La Salle.

At Fort Crèvecoeur, La Salle divided the remaining members of his party. He sent Father Hennepin down the Illinois River to explore it. Unknown to La Salle, Hennepin made his way to the Mississippi River and then upstream as far as the present site of Minneapolis. He returned to Montreal and then to France, where he wrote a book exaggerating his trip, even claiming falsely that he had descended the entire length of the Mississippi River.

Meanwhile, La Salle, leaving Tonty in charge at Fort Crèvecoeur, left with four men to return to Montreal to obtain more supplies. It took them sixty-five days of paddling through icy waters and climbing through snow and ice, sometimes using snowshoes to walk while dragging their canoes, to reach Fort Frontenac. La Salle had traveled more than a thousand miles through the frigid, hostile country—a very tough journey.

La Salle obtained the supplies he needed, but before he left, stunning news reached him: Tonty wrote that soon after La Salle's departure from Fort Crèvecoeur, nearly all the men had deserted after burning the fort. La Salle's dream of a new French empire in the west seemed to be in ashes.

But like all successful explorers, La Salle had enormous confidence in himself and his mission. He organized another expedition, and in August 1680, just a year after his first trip, he followed his own water trail back to Illinois. He found a devastated area, strewn with charred poles bearing human skulls. A war party of the Iroquois Indians had massacred the Illinois Indians. La Salle continued down the river to the site of Fort Crèvecoeur, which had been demolished. There was no sign of the loyal Frenchmen.

Searching for Tonty and the survivors, La Salle went farther down the Illinois River until he reached the Mississippi River— the object of his dreams. With only four men, he obviously could not continue down the Mississippi, so he turned back, retracing his steps up the Illinois River, reaching Fort Miami on the shores of Lake Michigan.

Spending the winter at Fort Miami, La Salle began to organize the Indians of the area into a defensive alliance against the warlike Iroquois to the east. Called by one historian "the greatest orator in North America," he won them over by his skill as a speaker.

To the assembled Miami Indians of the area, he began with a gift of tobacco and of cloth to cover their dead, hatchets to build a scaffold in their honor, and beads, bells, and trinkets to decorate their relatives at a funeral feast. Then he spoke. He mentioned that one of the great chiefs had just been killed, but La Salle said he would raise him to life by taking his name and supporting his wife and children. The Indians applauded loudly.

At that moment, La Salle asked them to obey his chief, the king of France, and to live in peace with their neighbors. The next day, the Indians replied: "We make you the master of our beaver and our lands, of our minds and our bodies." With peace secured at his rear, La Salle felt that he could now proceed once more—for the third time—to achieve his ambition of reaching the mouth of the Mississippi.

First he had to go back to Montreal once more to pacify his creditors. He did so, and in May 1681, he returned by canoe to the top of Lake Michigan, where, to his great surprise and pleasure, he found that Tonty had arrived, too. Together they went back to Montreal, where they recruited more tough Frenchmen for the third expedition to the Mississippi River.

In the fall of 1681, La Salle reached Fort Miami once more. On December 21, the first day of winter, the expedition left—La Salle, Tonty, twenty-two other Frenchmen, and ten Indians. Using canoes, they paddled down the familiar waters of the Illinois River. On February 6, they reached the Mississippi River.

After all their troubles in reaching the Mississippi, their trip down the river was surprisingly uneventful. On their right, they passed the mouth of the Missouri River. Soon after, on their left, the mouth of the Ohio River appeared. They camped on the shore, hunting for food, and continued down the river, meeting friendly Indians at several places.

On April 9, 1682, La Salle reached the mouth of the Mississippi River at the Gulf of Mexico.

He planted a column in the ground and proclaimed:

In the name of the most high, mighty, invincible and victorious prince, Louis the Great, by the grace of God King of France and of Navarre, Fourteenth of that name, I, this ninth day of April, one thousand six hundred and eighty-two, in virtue of the commission of his Majesty, which I hold in my hand, and which may be seen, take in the name of his Majesty and of his successors to the crown, possession of this country of Louisiana, the seas, harbors, ports, bays, adjacent straits, and all the nations, peoples, provinces, cities, towns, villages, mines, minerals, fisheries, streams, and rivers, within the extent of the said Louisiana, from the mouth of the great river St. Louis, otherwise called the Ohio . . . as also along the river Colbert, or Mississippi, and the rivers which discharge themselves thereinto . . . as far as its mouth to the sea, or Gulf of Mexico.

On that day, La Salle acquired for France a stupendous amount of American land. With his voyage down the Mississippi River, the first by any European, La Salle established the French claim to the lands that stretched from the Allegheny Mountains to the Rocky Mountains, from the Gulf of Mexico north to the Missouri River—a vast territory that was to become part of the United States much later, in 1803, with the Louisiana Purchase.

La Salle had bold plans: to found a colony of French and their Indian allies on the Illinois River, to collect beaver skins and buffalo hides, and to ship them down the Mississippi to a fort at its mouth and then to France. By doing so, he could thwart his enemies and rivals in Montreal, jealous of his monopoly of trade in the Mississippi Valley. And, of course, he would become the lord of the enterprise.

He started out by building a large settlement on the Illinois River that he called Fort St. Louis. Thousands of Indians gathered around the fort—Illinois, Shawnees, Abnakis, Miamis, and others—as protection from expected attacks by the Iroquois. But La Salle ran into increasing debt. Not only was he unable to provide dividends for his financial backers, but he always seemed to need more money. At this crucial point in his enterprise, he lost his influential supporter, Count Frontenac, who had been replaced by a new governor who was not sympathetic to La Salle or his plans.

La Salle decided to return to France to seek support from the king. The moment was ripe for him. France was at war with Spain. King Louis was ready to support La Salle's plan to establish a colony and a fort at the mouth of the Mississippi River, from which he could attack the Spanish.

The king enthusiastically furnished four ships and two hundred soldiers, as well as settlers, including carpenters and other artisans, priests, and young women to become brides of the men. But the king was unwilling to give too much power to one man. He named Taneguy de Beaujeu to command the ships until they arrived in America.

Trouble between the two leaders broke out almost immediately after the ships sailed from France on July 24, 1684. They differed on the route to be taken, where to stop for water, and how to avoid the Spanish. Divided command was one of the reasons, of course, but another was La Salle's own personality. Convinced that his enemies were plotting against him, he was suspicious of everybody. He concealed his shyness with a cold and aloof manner, which alienated some, and made enemies of others by his severe punishments for breaches of discipline.

After almost six months at sea, in January 1685, the expedition finally arrived in the Gulf of Mexico. La Salle and his men landed, not near the Mississippi River, but four hundred miles beyond it, near Matagorda Island in what is now Texas. That mistake was the first in a series that led to a complete disaster.

One of the ships was wrecked on the reefs as they landed. Beaujeu, his mission complete, sailed away with two ships, leaving La Salle with only a small ship called the *Belle*. But the *Belle* was wrecked, too, leaving La Salle and his party stranded. As the men worked to erect a fort, many of them took sick and died. La Salle himself fell ill with a fever. But the fort was completed and named Fort St. Louis, the same name he had given earlier to a fort at the Illinois River.

By now La Salle realized that the Mississippi River was somewhere to the east. When he recovered from his illness, he decided to make his way through the marshes and bays to the Mississippi, traveling up the river back to Montreal to obtain more supplies for his sick and ailing men, a trip that he had made before.

Leaving behind twenty men, women, and children to hold the fort, La Salle with an equal number of men and five packhorses left in early January 1687. Day by day, they slogged their way through prairies and forests, crossing streams and gullies without number. In March, La Salle reached familiar ground in eastern Texas near the Trinity River. He sent a party ahead to find a cache of beans and corn that he had hidden years before.

But the men, who had feuded among themselves before, quarrelled bitterly again. Three of them were shot to death in their sleep by the others. They decided that their safety demanded the death of La Salle, the commander, who would certainly arrest them for murder.

They decided to ambush him as he approached. Crouching in the long, dry, reedlike grass, they waited. As La Salle came near, a shot was fired, instantly followed by another. Pierced through the brain, La Salle dropped. He died on March 18, 1687, at the age of forty-three.

The assassins stood over the body of their fallen leader. The historian Francis Parkman described the scene: "With mockery and insult, they stripped it naked, dragged it into the bushes, and left it there, a prey to the buzzards and the wolves."

Later, one of his loyal supporters wrote La Salle's epitaph:

His firmness, his courage, his great knowledge of the arts and sciences, which made him equal to every undertaking, and his untiring energy, which enabled him to surmount every obstacle, would have won at last a glorious success for his grand enterprise, had not all his fine qualities been counterbalanced by a haughtiness of manner which made him insupportable, and by a harshness towards those under his command, which drew upon him an implacable hatred, and was at last the cause of his death.

🪢22🪢

The Discovery of California

SPANISH SAILORS WERE FAMILIAR WITH THE WORD CALIFORNIA FROM a popular romance published in Spain in 1510 called *Las Sergas del Virtuoso Cavallero Esplandian* ("The Exploits of the Virtuous Cavalier Esplandian"). In it, a mythical emperor defending Constantinople is helped by an army of Amazons. One passage from that book reads:

> Know that, on the right hand of the Indies, there is an island called California, very near to the Terrestrial Paradise, which was peopled with black women. . . . Their arms were all of gold.

The legend of an island inhabited only by women fascinated almost all of the early Spanish explorers, including Columbus. None of them found it, but the dream led to the discovery of the real California. It started when a sea captain came back to a port on the west coast of Mexico in 1523 with still another tale about an island of warrior women somewhere out there.

Hernando Cortés, the conqueror of Mexico, listened with great interest. In May of 1532, he sent his kinsman, Diego Hurtado de Mendoza, north in two ships along the coast, looking for the fabulous island. A mutinous crew compelled Mendoza to send one of the ships back; he pushed north in the other ship and disappeared, never to be heard from again.

Fortuno Ximenes, a pilot, was sent to search for Mendoza. He landed on a bay in Baja (Lower) California, but the local Indians attacked and killed him and twenty of his men. The survivors made their way back to Acapulco and reported to Cortés the discovery of an island not inhabited by women but full of "the finest pearls."

After building two new ships, Cortés himself sailed north. He sighted the east coast of Lower California and landed in the bay of La Paz on May 3, 1535. Taking possession of the desolate, sandy land in the name of King Charles of Spain, he named the new territory Terra de Santa Cruz. But he found no pearls, no gold, no silver, no Amazon warrior women.

One might call that landing the discovery of California, even though Cortés landed on the eastern shores of Lower California, now the Mexican state of Baja California. The discovery of the land that is now the state of California in the United States came later.

For more than a year, Cortés stayed in the barren lands in and around La Paz. While there, he received some distressing news from Mexico City. The king had appointed Antonio de Mendoza as viceroy of the lands that Cortés had conquered. Although Cortés retained his title as captain-general of Mexico and marquess of the Valley of Oaxaca, Mendoza became the civilian head of the government of New Spain.

Cortés hurried back to Mexico City to protect his rights, leaving an aide, Francisco de Ulloa, in charge. When Cortés returned to Spain in 1539, Ulloa sailed north with three ships to make a survey of the coastline of the Gulf of California. After reaching the top near the mouth of the Colorado River, he called the gulf El Mar Vermejo ("the Vermillion Sea") because of the reddish hues in the water caused by the discharge of soil into it by the Colorado River.

He took possession of the land for Spain on September 18, 1539, this way, as described by a notary public on board:

The very magnificent Senor Francisco de Ulloa, governor's lieutenant and commanding this fleet for the very illustrious Senor
Marques del Valle de Oaxaca . . . took possession for the Marques in the name of the Emperor and our master, King of Castile,
actually and in reality placing his hand on his sword, and saying
that if any person disputed it, he was ready to defend it; cutting
trees with his sword, pulling up grass, moving stones from one
place to another . . . and taking water from the sea and throwing
it on the land, all in token of said possession.

Ulloa found the shoreline of the Gulf of California unattractive.
He described it as very poor, with mountains and rocks but without
trees or green except for cactus. When he arrived at the settlement
of La Paz, he found it in ruins. At the mouth of what is now called
the Colorado River, he reported seeing large numbers of sea lions.

Sailing south, he turned the cape at the southern end of Lower
California, going north for a short distance before returning to
Acapulco. His major accomplishment was discovering that Lower
California was a peninsula, not an island, as Cortés had thought.

With Cortés in Spain, the viceroy, Mendoza, had no rival in
further exploration of the Pacific area. In 1541, Mendoza sent
Francisco de Bolaños north in the Gulf of California once again
to the mouth of the Colorado River. Bolaños gave the name Puerto
de California to a small bay near the end of the Baja California
peninsula, the first use of the word *California* for the newly discovered land.

It was the next expedition, though, that brought the first Europeans to the land that is now the state of California. Its leader
was Juan Rodríguez Cabrillo, whose statue stands today at Point
Loma overlooking San Diego Bay as part of a national monument
in his honor.

Cabrillo is another one of the famous discoverers of America
whose birth and early life are not recorded. Although some historians have said he was of Portuguese descent working for the
Spanish, his latest biographer has concluded that he was born in
Spain, probably in Seville, in 1498 or 1500. We do know that

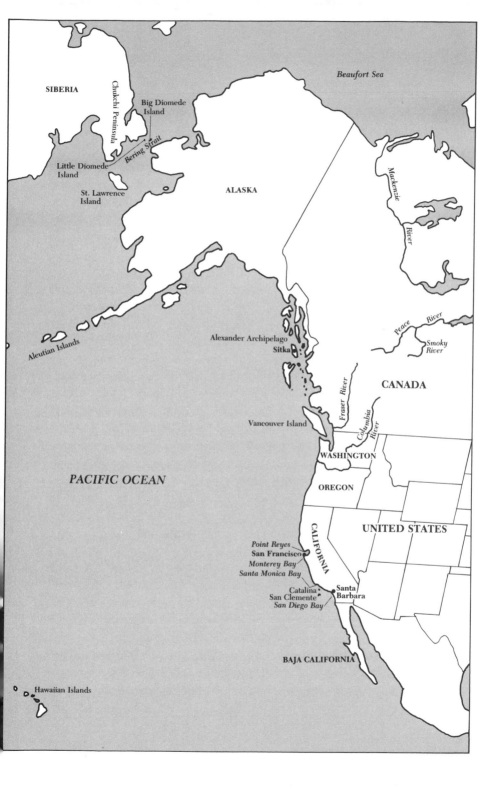

SIBERIA

Chukchi Peninsula

Beaufort Sea

Big Diomede
Island

Bering Strait

Little Diomede
Island

St. Lawrence
Island

ALASKA

Mackenzie
River

Aleutian Islands

Alexander Archipelago

Sitka

Peace River

Smoky
River

CANADA

Vancouver Island

Fraser River

Columbia River

WASHINGTON

PACIFIC OCEAN

OREGON

CALIFORNIA

UNITED STATES

Point Reyes
San Francisco
Monterey Bay
Santa Monica Bay

Catalina
San Clemente
San Diego Bay

**Santa
Barbara**

BAJA CALIFORNIA

Hawaiian Islands

Cabrillo made a friend in Seville, Diego Sanchez de Ortega, whose father was a merchant there, sending supplies to the New World. Nothing is known about Cabrillo's education or early years, but his later career demonstrates that he learned to read and write. There is evidence, too, that he came to the New World in 1510 or shortly thereafter with Sanchez. As a young man, he served with Panfilo de Narvaez in the conquest of Cuba, learning the soldier's trade. A skilled crossbowman, using bow and arrow, he also became something of a mariner. He worked for a time in the modest shipyards of Havana, where ships were hauled ashore for repairs and refitted for further use.

Cabrillo made his first mark in history in Mexico in 1520, when his superior, Narvaez, was sent there to bring Hernando Cortés back to Cuba on charges of disobeying orders (see chapter 13).

At the age of about twenty, Cabrillo served as a captain of crossbowmen in the Narvaez army. Despite its numbers, Narvaez's army stood no chance against Cortés. In a brilliant and daring night attack, Cortés routed Narvaez's army, capturing its commander.

Cortés treated the captured soldiers generously, promising them a share of the riches that would soon be available in Mexico City. Cabrillo joined his ranks, along with most of the other soldiers. Despite their increased numbers, the Spanish met an initial disaster in Mexico City. When the Aztecs attacked, killing hundreds of Spanish soldiers, Cabrillo was one of those who escaped with Cortés.

It was then that his training in shipbuilding became important. Cortés decided to return to Mexico City in a fleet of small vessels to attack the Aztecs from the lake around the city. Cabrillo became one of the carpenters working under the direction of Martin Lopez, an experienced shipbuilder. They built thirteen small ships that were carried in pieces over the mountains before being launched on the lake near Mexico City. In a series of battles, those ships destroyed the Aztec fleet of war canoes.

After the conquest of Mexico in 1521, Cabrillo served as a mounted officer in Spanish forces sent to put down rebellious Mexicans in various parts of the country. For a dozen years, Cabrillo fought in various campaigns in Central America, before he settled down in the city of Santiago in Guatemala.

Rewarded for his services, Cabrillo became a landed gentleman—and rich. He received large grants of land, which included the services of the Indians who lived there as virtual slaves. Gold was found on one of Cabrillo's properties, which resulted in his becoming one of the wealthiest men in Guatemala.

Settled in comfortable circumstances at the age of about thirty-two, he decided it was time to raise a family. He returned to Spain, where his friend and partner Sanchez had an unmarried sister, Beatriz Sanchez de Ortega. They were married in Spain in late 1532 or early 1533, returning to Santiago and settling down in the house that Cabrillo had built in Guatemala. They later had two sons.

In the late 1530s, Cabrillo became involved in shipbuilding along the western shores of Guatemala as a partner of the governor, Pedro de Alvarado, who was planning an expedition to Peru. Cabrillo built seven or eight sailing ships between the years of 1536 and 1540. But the expedition never reached Peru, and Alvarado died in 1541.

On September 11, 1541, a terrifying earthquake hit Santiago, covering the city with a flood of water, mud, and rocks. Most of the houses were destroyed, and hundreds of people died. Cabrillo wrote an account of the earthquake in a pamphlet that was published in Mexico later in 1541. The earliest nonreligious publication in the New World, it has been called the beginning of journalism in Spanish America.

Cabrillo was more interested, though, in a new expedition planned by the viceroy of Mexico, Antonio de Mendoza. Mendoza planned to send out two fleets, one to go south and the other north, to meet somehow in the Spice Islands of the western Pacific Ocean. Based on the crude maps of the day, Mendoza and the others believed that they were not far away. They expected the American coastline to run northwest all the way to China.

Following the death of his superior, Governor Alvarado, Cabrillo became the undisputed commander of the northern fleet, which was no surprise, because he owned the ships in it. One was called the *San Salvador* (sometimes referred to as the *Juan Rodriquez*) and another *La Victoria*.

With supplies aboard for two years, Cabrillo set sail on June 27, 1542. Within a week, the two ships had reached the tip of Baja California, following a sea lane previously charted by Ulloa and Bolaños. For two months, they sailed slowly along the western coast of Baja California, noting a generally barren land and very few Indians. In late August, they entered uncharted seas beyond the point reached by Ulloa and Bolaños.

On September 28, three months after his departure, Cabrillo discovered "a sheltered port and a very good one." He called it San Miguel; we now call it San Diego. Cabrillo had crossed the present international boundary between Baja California in Mexico and California in the United States—the first European to touch the shores of the west coast of what was to become the United States.

Remaining there five days, Cabrillo sent small boats out to explore the bay and the lands nearby. He found a few Indians on the shore and made the friendly gesture of presenting beads and shirts to them. From the Indians, Cabrillo heard stories of bearded men like themselves somewhere to the east. He did not know it, but the Indians were talking about the Coronado expedition in New Mexico (see chapter 19).

Cabrillo's ships sailed slowly up the coast, first to the islands now called Catalina and San Clemente, then to San Pedro Bay, noting the high mountains to the east. They anchored in what is now Santa Monica Bay. "We saw an Indian town on the land next to the sea, with large houses built much like those of New Spain," Cabrillo noted. He saw many fine canoes on the beach, each capable of carrying twelve or thirteen Indians.

During the months of October and November 1542, Cabrillo sailed slowly north, stopping frequently along the heavily populated coast. The Indians he met were friendly, coming aboard the ships to visit and bringing food. Cabrillo was impressed by the abundant food supplies of the Indians and their round houses.

Continuing north, Cabrillo sailed out to sea a bit to avoid the dangerous rocky coast. His men sighted what is now Point Reyes, but they missed the Golden Gate entrance to San Francisco, as almost all mariners did for the next two centuries. Sometimes the Golden Gate was shrouded in fog, at other times the narrow entrance was just difficult to see.

Cabrillo anchored in what is now called Drake's Bay, north of San Francisco. But the weather turned so cold that the sailors could hardly man the sails. So when the ships reached just a little farther north, in the area of Bodega Bay, Cabrillo ordered a return south.

In mid-November, Cabrillo once more passed the Golden Gate without noticing it and anchored to the south in Monterey Bay. After a short stay there, he sailed along the rugged mountains of California, looking for a place to stop and repair his leaky ships. He found a good harbor on the island on San Miguel, the westernmost island in the Santa Barbara channel.

Cabrillo decided to spend the winter in the sheltered Santa Barbara islands, repairing his ships. But the friendly Indians, who at first had welcomed visits from the Spanish explorers, soon tired of their continued presence. One of the Spanish crew later recalled, "all the time the armada was in the Isla Capitana [one of the Santa Barbara islands] the Indians there never stopped fighting us."

On Christmas Eve, Cabrillo sent some men ashore to fill water casks. The Indians attacked. Outnumbered, the Spaniards called to the ship for help. Cabrillo quickly gathered a relief party, which rowed to the island. "As he began to jump out of the boat, one foot struck a rocky ledge, and he splintered a shinbone," a shipmate recalled. Despite his injury, Cabrillo dragged himself to the island and refused to leave until all his men were rescued.

Back on ship, a surgeon treated Cabrillo's wound, but it quickly became infected. With the primitive shipboard medicine of that day, there was little that could be done. Cabrillo, knowing that his injury was fatal, gave command of the expedition to Bartolomé Ferrer, with instructions to make a complete report to the viceroy.

Cabrillo died on January 3, 1543, at the age of forty-three, and was buried on the island they called Capitana. No trace of his burial place has ever been found.

Two weeks later, Ferrer sailed north again in stormy seas. On the last day of February 1543, he reached the northernmost point of the voyage, probably off what is now Klamath, California, but possibly as far as southern Oregon. In a howling gale, Ferrer scudded south in ships that were battered and leaking. He arrived back at the starting point in Mexico on April 14, 1543—ending the first voyage of discovery to California.

Thirty-six years later, the next major expedition to the California coast was led by an Englishman, Francis Drake (before he became Sir Francis). Drake arrived there in his famous ship the *Golden Hind* after he had surprised, captured, and sacked Spanish ships and settlements along the western coast of South and Central America. Laden with gold and silver, Drake sailed north to escape retaliation—and arrived on the west coast of what is today the United States in June 1579.

Surprisingly, Drake explored the coast from the north to the south because he had made a wide sweep out into the Pacific Ocean before turning east toward land. He found a comfortable harbor south of Point Reyes in the bay named after him (without knowing that Cabrillo had been there before). Drake beached his ship to repair a leak and built a fortified camp on the shore.

The local Indians were friendly. Once the local chief came to visit, bringing a rustic crown for the visiting English captain. Drake interpreted that as a sign that the Indians were putting themselves under the protection of Queen Elizabeth. Shortly before leaving, Drake named the country Nova Albion, after the Greek name for England.

To commemorate the occasion, Drake, in his own words, "set up a monument of our being there . . . a plate of brass, fast nailed to a great and firm post," together with a sixpence bearing Queen

Elizabeth's name. In 1936, a brass plate was uncovered in the area, bearing the following inscription:

Be it known unto all men by these presents
June 17 1579
By the Grace of God and in the name of herr
Majesty Queen Elizabeth of England and herr
Successors forever I take possession of this
Kingdome whose king and people freely resign
Their right and title in the whole land unto herr
Majesties Keeping now named by me to bee
Known unto all men as Nova Albion
Francis Drake

Even though the plate is now displayed at the Bancroft Library in Berkeley, most historians think it is a forgery.

Drake sailed south, missing the entrance to San Francisco, just as Cabrillo had. He set his course to the west, starting out on the next leg of his voyage around the world. He arrived back in England in 1581, his ship heavily loaded with the loot he had taken from the Spanish off the coast of the Americas. On April 1, 1581, Queen Elizabeth made him a knight, Sir Francis Drake, on the deck of the *Golden Hind* at anchor in the Thames River.

Almost two hundred years later, in 1769, the magnificent harbor of San Francisco and its beautiful entrance, the Golden Gate, were discovered. Ironically, the discovery was made by land, not by sea.

In 1769, Captain Gaspar de Portolá set out overland from San Diego for Monterey Bay. Missing Monterey, he continued north. From the top of San Pedro Mountain, he sighted Point Reyes in the distance and sent a scouting party out to map the route. It returned with news that a large inland sea lay just over the hill.

Portolá marched northeast. From the summit, he and his men looked out on San Francisco Bay, one of the great harbors of the world. One of them noted in his diary, "It is a very large and fine harbor, such that not only the navy of our most Catholic Majesty but those of all Europe could take shelter in it." One of the priests with the party wrote: "If it could be well settled like Europe there would not be anything more beautiful in all the world, for it has the best advantages for founding in it a most beautiful city."

In 1776, the Spanish established their first settlement at San Francisco. To many, it has become just what that priest forecast— one of the most beautiful cities in the world.

๑๛23๛

The Discovery of Alaska

LOOK AT A MAP OF ALASKA AND YOU WILL FIND THE BERING STRAIT and the Bering Sea off to the west. And you may remember that thousands of years ago, the first Americans walked from Siberia over to Alaska on a land bridge that scientists call Beringia (see chapter 1). After whom were these geographic features named and why?

The story begins in the summer of 1681, when Vitus Jonassen Bering was born in the Jutland seaport town of Horsens in Denmark. Although his parents were associated with the leading families of the town, they were poor. Despite that, his father filled several civic positions of trust. His mother's family included a number of ministers and judicial officers.

We know little about Vitus's schooling and early life except that, like many others in that port city, he went to sea as a boy. He made at least one voyage to the East Indies. Returning in 1703, he came back just at the time that Peter the Great, the czar of Russia, formed a navy, recruiting able Danish and Norwegian sailors to help him. At the age of twenty-three, Bering joined the Russian navy with the rank of sublieutenant.

Bering was obviously a capable naval officer, rising in the ranks step by step until he received an appointment as fleet captain in

1724. In that same year, Czar Peter decided that the time had come to settle for once and for all whether Asia and America were tied together by land. Before his death in 1725, Peter appointed Bering, one of his most trusted naval officers, as commander of an expedition to find out the answer.

Another Dane, Martin Spanberg, was named his second in command, with Alexei Chirikov, a young Russian who was considered to be one of the best officers in the navy, as another aide. Bering's instructions were as follows:

1. To go to Kamchatka in eastern Siberia and build two boats.
2. To sail on those boats along the shore in a northerly direction.
3. To determine where Asia joins with America.

Despite the simplicity of the instructions, the task was difficult even to start. Kamchatka was six thousand miles from Moscow, across a wilderness of forest, mountains, swamps, mud, and steppes, with no bridges across its many great rivers. Bering had to transport all his shipbuilding supplies, except for lumber, across the vast stretches of Siberia by horse and wagon—and sometimes by sleds pulled by dogs—before he could sail.

Bering left St. Petersburg on February 5, 1725, on an overland trip that took more than two years. Day after day, week after week, his crew plodded through the rugged wilderness of Siberia, sometimes over snow that was seven feet deep. He and his men arrived at the shores of the Sea of Okhotsk in 1727. Before they could undertake their major task, though, they first had to build a boat to take them six hundred miles across that sea to the Kamchatka Peninsula.

On Kamchatka, they began construction of an oceangoing vessel sixty feet long and twenty feet wide. They finished the ship on July 10, 1728, and called it the *St. Gabriel*. For supplies, they loaded the *St. Gabriel* with liquor distilled from grass, salt boiled from the sea, and in place of meat took salted fish. Four days later, on July 14, Bering and forty-four officers and men sailed out of the Kamchatka River, following a course north along the coast of Siberia on the western edge of the sea later named for him.

On August 8, eight native men from the Chukchi Peninsula approached the *St. Gabriel*. Through an interpreter, they told Bering about a large island not far away. Several days later, Bering saw the island, which he named St. Lawrence Island (it is today part of the United States).

Bering then set sail due north to the strait that now bears his name. He was not the first to enter these waters; back in 1648 Semen Dezhnev had discovered the strait, but his discovery was forgotten until Bering rediscovered it. The strait is fifty-five miles wide, stretching from Cape Dezhnev on the Chukchi Peninsula in Siberia to Cape Prince of Wales on the Seward Peninsula of Alaska.

"By August 15, we came to latitude 67 degrees 18 minutes north and turned back because the coast did not extend farther north and no land was near the Chukchi or East Cape and therefore it seemed to me that the instructions of His Imperial Majesty of illustrious and immortal memory had been carried out," Bering wrote.

By passing the easternmost point of Asia, he had proved to his own satisfaction that Siberia was not connected to North America, even though he had not caught a glimpse of America. He did discover, though, Big Diomede Island, which belongs to the Soviet Union, and Little Diomede Island, which is part of the United States. Afraid of being trapped in the ice when winter came, Bering turned back to Kamchatka.

After spending the winter in Kamchatka, Bering started the long trip home. It took him a year and a half to reach St. Petersburg and report to the admiralty, which he did in the spring of 1730. Although Bering was welcomed warmly, he was also criticized for not really proving that the two continents were separated by water. Perhaps they were connected farther north. Why hadn't he sailed farther north until he reached the ice barrier in the polar regions?

To find the answers to the open questions, Bering proposed a second expedition, formally called the Great Northern Expedition, to explore the entire Pacific region—from Siberia to Japan and from Siberia to America. The expedition was approved in 1732.

Bering left St. Petersburg in 1733, but it took him four long and weary years to collect a crew, gather supplies, and transport them all to Okhotsk. The preliminaries to the expedition were hampered by a lack of cooperation from officials in both St. Petersburg and Siberia.

Surprisingly, even though they knew from experience how long and hard the trip across the vast stretches of Siberia would be, Bering and his officers took their wives and children with them. With Bering was his young wife, Anna Matveievna, and their two sons, Thomas and Unos. Chirikov took his wife and daughter and Spanberg his wife and daughter, too. The women and children returned to Moscow and St. Petersburg after the expedition had sailed.

In 1737, in Okhotsk, Bering and his men built barracks and warehouses before they started to construct two wooden ships. The new ships, called the *St. Peter* and the *St. Paul*, were each eighty feet long and twenty feet wide, drawing about nine feet of water, with two masts for sails. Bering himself commanded the *St. Peter*, with a crew of seventy-seven, including a German-born naturalist, George William Steller. Chirikov commanded the *St. Paul*, manned by seventy-five men.

Splitting from the main force, Spanberg left early, in 1738, on the southern leg of the expedition, on a separate voyage to the Kurile Islands and Japan. In miserable weather, he sailed along the length of the islands to Japan, completing that part of the exploration successfully before he returned safely.

In 1740—ten years after Bering had proposed the expedition— he finally sailed, but only on the first part of his exploration. He and Chirikov went across the sea of Okhotsk, around the tip of the Kamchatka Peninsula, and arrived at the excellent harbor in Avatcha Bay on the east coast of the peninsula in the fall. Bering gave the name of Petropavlosk to a base he constructed on Avatcha Bay.

By now Bering was sixty-one years old, discouraged and physically worn out. In May 1741, he called a meeting of his officers to discuss the coming voyage, as was the Russian custom. The organization of Russian expeditions was quite different from those under Spanish, Portuguese, or English flags, where the captain was a commander with complete, wide-ranging powers.

In St. Petersburg, Bering had received instructions to consult with and listen to his officers in all matters. A kind-hearted man, well liked by his subordinates, Bering led them, but he was unable to command as a Ferdinand Magellan or a Sir Francis Drake could. One of his officers later commented, "The only fault of which the brave man can be accused, is that his too great leniency was as detrimental as the spirited and often times inconsiderate conduct of his subordinates."

At the conference, Bering and his officers were certain that America lay to the east or northwest, but the map they had been given in St. Petersburg showed land to the southeast. They decided to follow their instructions, but if no land were found to turn north and east. The instructions were mistaken, based on an erroneous map. The route they chose put them well south of the Aleutian Islands and the Alaskan peninsula.

On June 4, 1741, with a gentle northwest wind behind them, the two vessels sailed from Avatcha Bay. For a week they followed the map, sailing southeast, finding nothing but open sea. When they turned north, they encountered fog. On June 20, the two ships lost sight of one another. From then on, they made their way separately, each trying to fulfill the objects of the expedition.

Chirikov in the *St. Paul* sighted land first. His log for July 15, 1741, reads:

At two in the morning, we distinguished some very high mountains, and, as the light at the time was not very good, we brought to. An hour later, the land stood out much better and we could make out trees. This must be America.

His landfall was the Alexander Archipelago in the panhandle of present-day Alaska, close to where the city of Sitka is now located. Unable to send out a landing party because of the fog, rain, and rocky shores, Chirikov sailed north. A few days later, on July 18, he sent a party of armed sailors ashore to find fresh water. They did not return.

Chirikov then dispatched his last remaining small boat, with four men, to look for the missing men. It, too, disappeared. They were obviously on a hostile shore. The next day, two small canoes manned by Indians appeared but were frightened away. The Russians became convinced that their shipmates had been captured and killed.

With his only small boats gone and his water supply running low, Chirikov decided to return to Kamchatka. He did not know it, but Chirikov, a man whose name is unknown to most Americans, had discovered America from the west a day before his commander, Bering, did.

Like Chirikov, Bering had sailed north when the two ships separated. On July 15, the same day that Chirikov sighted land, Steller, the naturalist who accompanied Bering, thought he saw land, too, but the other officers aboard the *St. Peter* disagreed. On the following day, July 16, the weather was clear and there was no mistake. The log of *St. Peter* recorded the event:

At 12:30 we sighted high snow-covered mountains and among them a high volcano N by W.

The landfall was called Mount St. Elias because it was discovered on St. Elias Day. The mountain, towering eighteen thousand feet in height, was clearly visible from the ship, about sixteen miles offshore. The coast, at the top of the Alaskan panhandle quite close to the present-day Canadian border, was indented with many bays and inlets.

The officers and men crowded around Bering, congratulating him on the discovery. But it was obviously not a happy occasion for Bering. Steller reported:

One can easily imagine how happy we all were to see land. No one failed to congratulate Bering, to whom above all others the honor of discovery belonged. Bering, however, heard all this not only with great indifference, but, looking toward the land, he even shrugged his shoulders in the presence of all aboard.

Prematurely aged, tired, and sick, Bering's only thought at the moment of his great triumph was how to get home safely. Not only were his provisions running short, but he himself did not feel well. Reluctantly because of possible danger, Bering permitted Steller, the German naturalist, to go ashore briefly on the island they called Kayak, just off the mainland, while sailors filled water casks.

Once ashore, Steller searched for signs of human settlement. Under a tree, he found a log hollowed out into the shape of a trough, in which he concluded that savages had cooked their meals by dropping hot stones into it. He also found caribou bones, pieces of dried fish, and other evidence that convinced him that the inhabitants of Kayak Island were similar to those of far-off Kamchatka.

Steller had only ten hours ashore for his observations. In his notebook, he wrote:

> The American continent (on this side) as far as climate is concerned, is notably better than the extreme northeastern part of Asia. For although the land, however it faces the sea, whether we looked at it from far or near, consists of amazingly high mountains, most of which had peaks covered with perpetual snow, yet these mountains, in comparison with those of Asia, are of a better nature and character.

Bering himself did not leave the ship even to set foot in America. Not only was he weary, but he seemed to be coming down with scurvy, that dread disease of sailors on long voyages without proper food. When a fair wind came up on July 21, Bering ordered the *St. Peter* out to sea, without even waiting for all the water casks to be filled.

It was slow going in the fog and mist. In late August, the ship anchored off a tiny island at the tip of the Alaskan peninsula. After taking aboard drinking water, the *St. Peter* once again attempted to sail west against strong head winds.

On September 4, the Russians encountered the first Americans in the Aleutian Islands. Two natives in kayaks paddled toward the ship but could not communicate because of language differences. The Aleuts presented the Russians with whale blubber; the Russians offered tobacco and whiskey.

From then on, the Russians sailed into trouble. Throughout September, they met stormy seas. Worse than that, scurvy spread among the crew so badly that a man died almost every day. On November 4, when only ten men in the entire crew could even move, land was sighted.

The navigators were sure that they had reached the Kamchatka Peninsula and that their long voyage was over safely. They were wrong. Instead of a haven, they had found a small desolate island, about a hundred miles northeast of Avatcha Bay. Bering wanted to continue on to Kamchatka. Following his orders, he called a conference of his officers. Unable to convince them to sail on, Bering permitted them to land on the island.

Two days later, the *St. Peter* crossed over a sandbar and the rocky reefs of an outer harbor and anchored in calm water. With winter approaching, the crew members who had enough strength set about building shelter—pits hollowed out of sand covered with canvas sails from the ship. The sick men were carried ashore.

Their major problem was survival. Their chief enemies were bold, ferocious blue foxes that showed no fear of men. The foxes darted about the camp, stealing any food left unguarded, carrying off clothing, tools, and anything else they could grab, even mutilating the bodies of sailors who had died.

In November and December, thirty men died. Bering himself lay dying in a miserable hut scooped out of the sand and covered with a few logs, half buried in the sand that drifted in. "The deeper in the ground I lie, the warmer I am," he told one of his lieutenants. "The part of my body that lies above the ground suffers from the cold."

Bering died on December 8, 1741, at the age of sixty-one, on the island that now bears his name. "Thus passed from the earth, as nameless ten thousands have done, the illustrious commander of the expeditions which had disclosed the separation of two worlds and discovered north-westernmost America"—so said the American historian Hubert Howe Bancroft.

On the island, one man, Steller, seemed unaffected by the scurvy that attacked all the others. For nine months, he studied the animal life of the island in detail, especially sea otters and sea cows. He was the only naturalist to examine live sea cows, because during the next few decades greedy fur hunters exterminated the species. But in Steller's time, the crew found that the flesh of the sea cow was edible. As they ate it, their health improved.

By spring, the men had improved so much that they built a new boat from the timbers of the *St. Peter*. On August 10, they launched a thirty-six-foot-long boat, also called the *St. Peter*, and three days later set sail from Bering Island. After an uneventful voyage, forty-six men landed back in Avatcha Bay on August 27, 1742, carrying with them a cargo of sea otter furs.

Thus ended the Russian voyage of discovery to America from the west, a voyage that followed roughly the same route taken by the first Americans more than fourteen thousand years earlier.

Bering's assistant, Alexei Chirikov, was actually the first Russian to see America, but Bering, the commander of the expedition, is given the credit. His name lives on in many geographical features of the north—the Bering Sea, the Bering Strait, and Bering Island.

With the rediscovery of Alaska—some fourteen thousand years after the first Asians crossed Beringia into America—the story of the "discoverers" of the New World is almost complete. But there is one more chapter that should be told—the "discovery" of the fiftieth state of the United States, in the Pacific Ocean far off the west coast of California.

‿24‿

The Discovery of Hawaii

AT THE AGE OF SEVENTEEN, JAMES COOK BECAME APPRENTICED TO a grocer and haberdasher in the tiny fishing port of Staithes on the northeastern coast of England. Day after day, he measured out raisins and ribbons for the customers of William Sanderson's store. The great lesson that James learned from all this was that he did not want to spend the rest of his life behind a store counter.

James was born on October 27, 1728, in the nearby village of Marton-in-Cleveland, the son of James Cook, a Scottish farm laborer, and his wife, Grace Pace, a Yorkshire village woman. He was the second of eight children, but most of them died as infants. As James grew up, he learned to read and write, first from a neighboring woman and then at a small nearby school.

Perhaps because he was good at arithmetic, he went to work at Mr. Sanderson's store. A responsible young man, James did not run away, even though the sea outside his windows strongly attracted him. He faithfully completed his eighteen months of apprenticeship before he turned to the sea. With the help of Mr. Sanderson, he went to the nearby city of Whitby, a major port, and became apprenticed to John Walker, a Quaker shipowner and coal shipper.

At that time, Whitby was the hub of a major coal trade, with hundreds of ships a year leaving for London, the Baltic, the Mediterranean, America, and even China and India. For a boy of eighteen, with a love of the sea, Whitby was an exciting place, even though the coal trade was not the most romantic of careers. He learned about the sea in ships that plied the waters along the rugged, rocky coast of England and sailed to Holland, Norway, and Ireland.

In 1750 Cook, after completing his second apprenticeship, became a full seaman. He spent the next five years on Walker coalers, learning his trade so well that Mr. Walker offered him command of one of his ships. At the age of twenty-seven, Cook was obviously a responsible young man, skillful in the maritime arts of navigation and ship-handling.

But Cook did something most unusual. He turned down the opportunity to become a captain of a merchant-marine ship to enlist in the Royal Navy as an ordinary seaman. On June 17, 1755, he volunteered for naval service. He never explained why, but one biographer said "he had always an ambition to go into the Navy."

For gentlemen or those with influence, becoming an officer in the Royal Navy was a chance for advancement and prestige. Ordinary seamen, though, faced a hard life, with terrible conditions, low pay, harsh discipline, and danger from drowning, disease, and brutality. "Manned by violence and maintained by cruelty"—that was the way one admiral described the fleets of Britain. Life was so bad that there were few volunteers; most of the Royal Navy's seamen were picked up on the streets and impressed into service against their will.

So it was a surprise to the officers of the *Eagle* when James Cook showed up at Spithead on June 25, 1755. He was obviously a valuable addition to the crew—mature, tall, healthy, intelligent, and experienced at sea. Within a month, he impressed the captain so much that he was promoted to a master's mate, a step up the ladder of rank at sea.

Cook served on various ships so well that when the Seven Years' War (1756–1763) began, he was promoted to the rank of master. It was a peculiar position in the Royal Navy. While the captain of

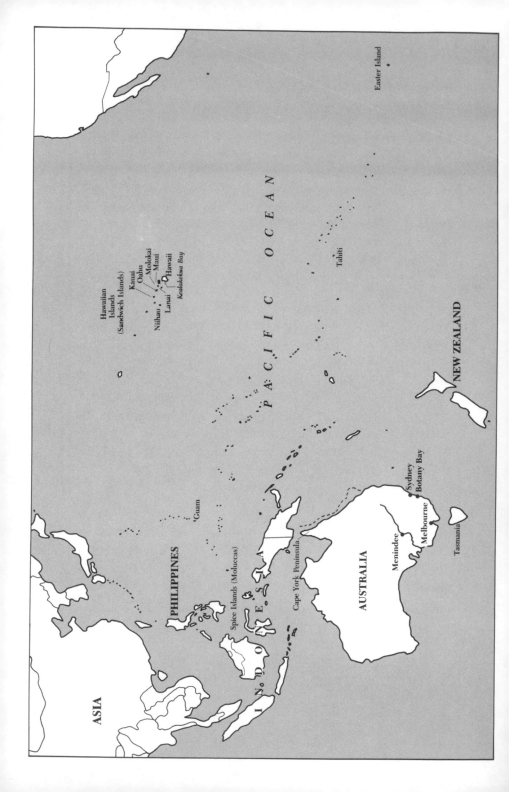

a ship was a naval officer responsible for its fighting ability, the master, who did not wear a naval uniform, supervised its navigation and general management of masts, sails, and supplies.

Cook's first assignment as master was aboard the *Soleby*, patrolling the coast of Scotland. His next post was on the *Pembroke*, a sixty-four-gun ship, one of England's largest. She was sent across the Atlantic Ocean in 1758 as part of a fleet to attack French strongholds in Canada. On July 26, the *Pembroke*, with Cook aboard, took part in the siege of Louisburg in Nova Scotia. When the French surrendered, the control of Canada began to shift from France to Britain.

The day after the surrender, while walking near the harbor, Cook noticed something peculiar. A man in the uniform of an army artillery officer carried a small table supported by a tripod. He set it down, squinted through a glass on it, and then wrote something in a pocket notebook. Curious, Cook approached the stranger and asked what he was doing.

The officer, Samuel Holland, was delighted to explain that he was using an instrument called a plane table, observing angles so that he could make a map of the harbor and its camps. Cook said he would like to learn how to do the same, and for the next few days, Holland taught him how to use the surveying instrument.

In the next few years, wherever the *Pembroke* sailed, Cook made charts of the seacoast of Nova Scotia and Newfoundland as well as of the St. Lawrence River. His commanders praised his map work in their dispatches to London.

Back in England, on December 21, 1762, Cook, then thirty-four years old, married Elizabeth Batts, twenty-one, and they settled down to live in Shadwell, on the riverside in London. In the following years, they had six children, two of whom followed their father into the Royal Navy.

Cook did not stay on land very long. His map work had impressed the lords of the admiralty so much that they assigned him to go back to Canada to make more accurate charts of Britain's newest possession. He sailed there in April 1763. After three years surveying the coastline of Newfoundland, he returned to London with charts that many years later were still regarded as some of the most accurate ever made.

His surveying work for the Royal Navy, not his seamanship, led to his next assignment—and his rise to fame. In 1769, the Royal Society, an organization of the nation's most learned men, planned several expeditions to take advantage of a rare celestial event. They called it the Transit of Venus, because on June 3 the planet Venus was to cross the face of the sun. By sending expeditions to Hudson Bay, Lapland, and the South Pacific Ocean, the scientists hoped to gather observations to compute the distance between the earth and the sun more accurately.

Since the Pacific observations required a long voyage, the Royal Navy supplied a ship, a converted coal ship—by coincidence from the port of Whitby, where Cook had learned the seaman's trade. She was renamed the *Endeavour*. Since it was unthinkable that a civilian could command a naval ship, the navy appointed James Cook to be its captain. With that appointment, he was promoted to the rank of first lieutenant.

A most unusual warship, the *Endeavour* had few guns. Her primary mission was to carry two civilian scientists, Charles Green, an astronomer, and Joseph Banks, a botanist, to the South Pacific. Banks, a rich young man, came aboard in style, with two artists, a secretary, four servants, and two dogs. Cook's instructions were first to make astronomical observations and second to look for what was thought to be an unknown continent in the South Pacific.

On August 25, 1768, Cook left England on the first of his three famous voyages of discovery. For weeks he sailed south in the Atlantic Ocean. It wasn't until January 1769 that he turned Cape Horn at the foot of South America into the Pacific Ocean. The *Endeavour* arrived in Tahiti on April 13, 1769—almost eight months after Cook had left England.

One of the most remarkable things about that long voyage— and Cook's other voyages—was that none of his men fell ill from scurvy, a common disease in early sailing ships. Even though he had no knowledge of scurvy's cause, Cook insisted on a diet of fresh vegetables and fruit when available and of sauerkraut at other times for all his men. He also required them to scour the decks regularly with vinegar to keep the ship clean and healthy—and these measures kept his crew healthy.

Cook established friendly relations with the Polynesian people who lived on Tahiti. After setting up their observation station and telescopes, Cook and Green recorded data on the little black spot that was Venus as it crawled across the face of the bright sun. With the first part of his mission completed, Cook set about the second.

He sailed south about fifteen hundred miles, but no continent appeared. With the weather worsening, Cook turned back north and west until he sighted New Zealand (which had been discovered by the Dutch navigator Abel Tasman in 1642). He mapped the coast of New Zealand and then sailed west to Australia. He put ashore at a harbor where Banks collected so many specimens that Cook named it Botany Bay (a little south of the present city of Sydney).

For four months, Cook sailed along the eastern coast of Australia, mapping it. On August 21, he reached the northern tip of Australia, Cape York Peninsula, and, in his own words:

> Nothwithstanding I had in the name of His Majesty taken possession of several places upon this coast, I now once more hoisted English Coulers and in the name of His Majesty King George the Third took possession of the whole Eastern Coast from the above latitude down to this place by the name of New South Wales, together with all the Bays, Harbours, Rivers and Islands situate on the said coast, after which we fired three volleys of small Arms which were Answered by the like number from the ship.

Sailing toward home, Cook stopped in Batavia in the Dutch-held island of Java to refit his ship before continuing around the Cape of Good Hope to the Atlantic Ocean. The *Endeavour* arrived back in England on July 12, 1770. Banks brought with him seventeen thousand plants never before seen in England, and Cook had made maps of more than five thousand miles of Australian and New Zealand coastline.

Cook was promoted to the rank of commander. Banks, who had

influential friends, introduced Cook to King George so that he could tell the king about the voyage and his new maps. Cook wrote to his mentor, John Walker of Whitby, in modest terms: "I however have made no very great discoveries yet I have exploar'd more of the Great South Sea than all who have gone before me so much that little remains now to be done to have a thorough knowledge of that part of the globe."

Despite that, both he and the admiralty agreed that more had to be done. Another expedition was necessary to prove that a major continent either was or was not somewhere in the South Atlantic or the South Pacific. Cook was given two ships for this expedition, the *Resolution* and the *Adventure*, with these instructions: sail around the world from the Cape of Good Hope to Cape Horn and back to the Cape of Good Hope, as far south as possible.

Cook left England on July 13, 1772, and arrived at the Cape of Good Hope on October 30. After taking on supplies of pickles, bread, and beef, Cook sailed into the icy waters of the South Atlantic Ocean. On January 17, 1773, his ships crossed the Antarctic Circle, the first European sailing vessels to do so.

Instead of land, though, Cook found icebergs—and fog so thick that the two ships lost sight of each other. According to plan, if separated they were to meet again in New Zealand. Cook arrived there on March 16 and found the *Adventure* waiting for him. Despite the beginning of winter, Cook plunged south again, down once more to the Antarctic Circle, where he faced a limitless expanse of ice. "We could not proceed one inch farther," he wrote.

Satisfied that there was no continent there, Cook turned back to New Zealand in late 1774, returning to England on July 30, 1775. "I have now done with the southern Pacific Ocean . . . and flatter myself that no one will think I have left it unexplored," he wrote.

Cook returned to high honors in his native land. The king received him and he was promoted to the rank of post-captain in the navy. He was also appointed fourth captain of the naval hospital at Greenwich, a post that would have permitted him to retire on an adequate pension.

Elected a member of the Royal Society, he received the society's Copley gold medal for the best paper presented to the society in 1776. His subject was the methods he used to preserve the health of his men on the long second voyage—a treatise on how to avoid scurvy.

He also prepared his journals for publication. They came out in 1777, with this modest introduction:

It is a work for information and not for amusement, written by a man, who has not the advantage of Education, acquired, nor Natural abilities for writing; but by one who has been constantly at sea from his youth, and who, with the Assistance of a few good friends gone through all the Stations belonging to a Seaman, from prentice boy in the Coal Trade to a Commander in the Navy. After such a Candid Confession he hopes the Public will not consider him an author, but a man Zealously employed in the Service of his country and obliged to give the best account of his proceedings.

At the age of forty-seven, Cook was not ready to give up the seafaring life. He volunteered to command another expedition planned by the Royal Society. Its aim was to seek out the dream of mariners from Columbus's day on—a northwest passage from the Atlantic Ocean to the Pacific Ocean. Since the Atlantic approaches to such a passage had baffled sailors for almost three centuries, it was decided to try to reach it from the Pacific Ocean side.

Once again, Cook had two ships under his command. His second in command was Lieutenant Charles Clerke, who had accompanied Cook on the two earlier expeditions. Cook sailed on the *Resolution*, with one hundred twelve men; Clerke commanded the second ship, the *Discovery*, with seventy men.

They sailed from England on July 12, 1776, on a familiar route around the Cape of Good Hope to New Zealand and then to Tahiti. Cook turned north and, at dawn on the morning of January 18, 1778, sighted two islands. For the natives of the islands, Cook's ships with their large white sails were a stunning sight. A Hawaiian legend describes their reactions:

One said to another, "What is that great thing with branches?" Others said, "It is a forest that has slid down into the sea," and the gabble and noise was great. Then the chiefs ordered some natives to go out in a canoe and observe and examine well that wonderful thing. They went, and when they came to the ship they saw the iron that was attached to the outside of the ship, and they greatly rejoiced at the quantity of iron.

Cook recorded his impressions:

I tied some brass medals to a rope and gave them to those in one of the canoes, who, in return, tied some small mackerel to the rope, as an equivalent. This was repeated, and some small nails, or bits of iron, which they valued more than any other article, were given them. For these, they exchanged more fish and sweet potato . . . a sure sign that they had some notion of bartering, or, at least, of returning one present for another.

It was the first encounter between Europeans and the people of the Hawaiian Islands, which lie in the eastern half of the Pacific Ocean, about two thousand miles west of San Francisco. The Hawaiian group consists of seven major inhabited islands—Hawaii, Maui, Oahu, Kauai, Molokai, Lanai, and Nuhau. Cook had landed on Kauai, where he found, to his astonishment, that the people spoke a language close to that in Tahiti.

Like their neighbors to the south, the Hawaiians were part of the Polynesian family. Thousands of years earlier, the ancestors of the Polynesians had migrated from southeastern Asia to Indonesia and then cross the islands of the Pacific to Tahiti, Easter Island, and Hawaii. Those first discoverers of Hawaii were obviously skilled navigators and explorers, guiding their canoes by the sun, the clouds, birds, currents, waves, and the stars at night.

Despite the pleasing climate and friendly reception, Cook spent only two weeks on the islands he had rediscovered. He named them the Sandwich Islands, after John Montagu, the earl of Sandwich, who was the first lord of the British admiralty. But his mission was elsewhere, and so on February 2, Cook left the warm, hospitable islands and sailed toward the icy waters of the north.

His first landfall was on the coast of what is today Oregon. He followed the coastline north, looking for an opening and finding none. He sailed through the Aleutian Islands into the Bering Strait, passing between America and Asia on August 9. But, just as he had been blocked by ice several years before in the Antarctic, he now encountered a solid wall of ice to the north—with no passageway through.

With winter approaching, Cook decided to sail south to Hawaii before another try at the Northwest Passage the following year. On January 17, 1779, his two ships anchored at Kealakeua Bay on the Kona coast of Hawaii. An excited crowd estimated at ten thousand people greeted his arrival, treating him as a god.

"The ancestral god has come back, for this is the time of the annual consecration," the Hawaiians said. Every day the Hawaiians sent vegetables, fruit, pigs, and other food to the ship. King Kalei'opu'u visited Cook, bringing with him feather cloaks, which were symbols of royalty. In turn, Cook gave the king a linen shirt, a sword, and a tool chest.

The pleasant interlude ended in early February when Cook's ships, refitted and supplied, sailed north for another attempt to find the northwest passage. But they were back within a week. The ships had run into a gale, which damaged the foremast of the *Resolution* so badly that Cook had to return.

This time the welcome was not as warm. Feeding the Englishmen had put a strain on the food supply of the Hawaiians, and their awe at the first sight of the white men had dwindled. For the first few days, as Cook and his men started repairs to the mast, all went well, but then irritations mounted over a series of thefts from the ship.

For the Hawaiians, taking things from the strange ship was a game; if caught, a Hawaiian would give up his valuable and go about his business laughing. For the Englishmen, though, it was a theft to be punished. In the past, Cook had permitted the thieves to go if the loot were returned. This time, though, Cook called for punishment. A man who had seized a pair of tongs, for example, was given forty lashes.

Despite that, the Hawaiian game of taking things from the strangers continued. Cook became more and more angry. The misunderstandings came to a head when some of the bold Hawaiians stole the *Discovery*'s small cutter, presumably to take it apart and salvage the iron in it. It was a serious blow to Cook, because the cutter was a necessary small boat in which to make trips ashore.

Cook, who had always been careful and restrained when dealing with strange people, made a major mistake here—a mistake that cost him his life. He decided to go ashore himself, accompanied by armed marines, to seize Kalei'opu'u, the chief, as a hostage until the cutter was returned.

Ashore, Cook and the marines marched to the village, where Kalei'opu'u, who knew nothing about the theft, readily consented to go on board the *Resolution*. He and his sons accompanied Cook and his men to the beach. Once there, though, some of the other chiefs and his wife argued that he should not go because he would be killed if he did.

A large crowd gathered at the shore, alarmed at what they thought was a threat to their chief. Many of the Hawaiians were armed with spears and stones and some of them carried daggers. Prudently, Cook decided to retire back to the *Resolution* without the chief.

As he made his way to the small boat, one of the Hawaiians threatened Cook with a dagger and a stone. They obviously no longer thought that Cook was a god. This is what happened next, according to his biographer:

> Cook fired one barrel of his musket, loaded with small shot, at this person, and, at that moment, we must think, the strained cord of his temper snapped, he lost the initiative. The man, being

protected by his heavy war mat, the shot did no damage—except that it further enraged the Hawaiians.

A wave of Hawaiians rushed toward the Englishmen. Stones were hurled, a marine was knocked down, and the other marines fired at the onrushing Hawaiians.

"Take to the boats," Cook yelled.

It was too late. Cook stood on the shore, waving for small boats to come in, when he was hit from behind with a club. While he staggered from the blow, he was stabbed just under the shoulder with an iron dagger—ironically, one of those presented to the Hawaiians as gifts by the Englishmen earlier. He fell face down into the water.

Some of the Englishmen escaped, but Cook and four marines died in the fury of the Hawaiian attack. The *Resolution* fired its guns at the shore, but the Hawaiians retreated to safety.

A few days later, under a flag of truce, the Hawaiians returned Cook's bones. He was buried at sea.

Lieutenant Charles Clerke assumed command of the expedition. After another unsuccessful attempt to find the Northwest Passage, the *Resolution* and the *Discovery* returned to England on October 4, 1779.

Cook, who died on February 4, 1779, at the age of fifty, is known today as the great explorer of the Pacific Ocean. But he should also be remembered as the man who discovered the Hawaiian Islands, the westernmost state of the United States.

With the discovery of Hawaii, which became the fiftieth state in the United States on August 21, 1959, our story of the "discoverers" of America is complete.

Important Dates in
the Discoveries of America

ca. 25,000 Wandering hunting tribes from Asia cross the frozen Bering Sea area into America.

 985 Biarni Heriulfson discovers Labrador and Baffin Island.

1000 Leif Ericsson discovers Newfoundland.

1492–1493 Christopher Columbus discovers America, landing either on Samana Cay or Watlings Island.

1493–1496 Columbus, on his second voyage, discovers Jamaica and other islands in the Caribbean.

1494 Treaty of Tordesillas, which separates Spanish and Portuguese spheres in the New World, is signed.

1497 John Cabot rediscovers Newfoundland.

1498–1500 Columbus, on his third voyage, discovers South America, landing in Venezuela.

1499 Amerigo Vespucci makes his first voyage to America.

1500 Vincente Yáñez Pinzón discovers the Amazon River.

1500–1501 Pedro Álvares Cabral discovers Brazil.

1501 Amerigo Vespucci makes his second voyage to America.

1502–1504 Columbus, on this fourth voyage, discovers Central America.

1507 Martin Waldseemüller drafts a map using the word *America* for the first time.

1513 Juan Ponce de León discovers Florida.

1513 Juan Ponce de León discovers Mexico.

1513 Vasco Núñez de Balboa discovers the Pacific Ocean.

1519 Hernando Cortés conquers Mexico.

1519 Alonso de Pineda discovers the mouth of the Mississippi River.

1519–1522 Ferdinand Magellan discovers the Strait of Magellan in the first circumnavigation of the earth.

1524 Giovanni da Verrazzano discovers New York harbor.

1528 Álvar Núñez Cabeza de Vaca discovers Texas.

1532 Francisco Pizarro discovers and conquers Peru.

1534 Jacques Cartier discovers the St. Lawrence River.

1539 Francisco de Maldonado discovers Mobile Bay.

1539 Estebanico discovers Arizona.

1540 Garcia Lopez de Cardenas discovers the Grand Canyon.

1540–1541 Francisco Vasquez Coronado explores the Southwest.

1541 Hernando de Soto crosses the Mississippi River.

1541–1542 Francisco de Orellana crosses South America.

1542 Juan Rodríguez Cabrillo discovers California.

1602 Bartholomew Gosnold discovers Cape Cod.

1609 Samuel de Champlain discovers Lake Champlain.

1609 Henry Hudson sails up the Hudson River.

1610 Henry Hudson discovers the bay in Canada that bears his name.

1611 Étienne Brûlé discovers Lake Huron.

1612 Étienne Brûlé discovers Lake Superior.

1616 Isaak Le Maire and William Schouter discover Cape Horn.

1673   Louis Joliet and Jacques Marquette discover the upper Mississippi River.

1678   Louis Hennepin discovers Niagara Falls.

1682   René-Robert Cavelier, sieur de la Salle, reaches the mouth of the Mississippi River.

1741   Vitus Jonassen Bering discovers Alaska.

1776   James Cook discovers Hawaii.

1792   Robert Gray discovers the Columbia River.

1792–1793   Alexander Mackenzie crosses Canada for the first time.

1803–1805   Meriwether Lewis and William Clark cross the United States to the Pacific Ocean for the first time.

Notes on Sources

THE STARTING POINT FOR ANY STUDY OF THE DISCOVERIES OF AMERICA is in the works of the eminent historian Samuel Eliot Morison. As a sailor, he followed the course of the *Nina*, the *Pinta*, and the *Santa Maria* at sea before writing his Pulitzer Prize-winning biography of Christopher Columbus. He also wrote two other books about the European discovery of America, emphasizing the harsh life at sea of the early explorers.

Luckily for those of us who are not fluent in Spanish, Portuguese, and Latin, many other scholars have combed the archives and libraries in Spain and Portugal for official documents, papers, and reports of the great voyages of discovery. Even if we can't read them in the original, numerous translations and summaries are available in English.

One of the major sources of primary information can be found in the numerous translations of the letters and documents written by Columbus himself. I used the Hakluyt Society's *Christopher Columbus: Four Voyages to the New World*, originally published in 1847, reproduced for American readers in 1961. It presents the discoveries of Columbus in his own words, both in Spanish and an English translation.

In modern times, many authors have written about the negative impact of the European discovery of America on the native Americans. One of the best is by Francis Jennings, *The Invasion of America*, with the title reflecting his viewpoint. The classic work on the devastating destruction of the civilizations of the Aztecs in Mexico and the Incas in Peru is still William H. Prescott's twin books *The Conquest of Mexico* and *The Conquest of Peru*.

Since the spelling of Spanish, Portuguese, and Indian names—and the accents on them—vary in many of the historical works and biographies, I have relied on Morison and Prescott for the spellings of those names in this book.

Many of these books—and the books cited in the following bibliography—are available at public libraries. I would like to thank the librarians at the following institutions where I did most of my research: the Pine Plains, New York, Free Library; the Vassar College library in Poughkeepsie, N.Y.; the Reading Room of the British Museum in London; the Barbican Library in London; the State Library in Albany, N.Y.; the New York Public Library in New York City, N.Y.; the Mid-Hudson Library System in Poughkeepsie, N.Y.; the Columbia-Greene Community College Library in Hudson, N.Y.; and the Library of Congress in Washington, D.C.

Bibliography

Titles marked by an asterisk are most suitable for young readers.

Arciniegas, German. *America in Europe*. New York: Harcourt Brace, Jovanovich, 1975.

———. *Amerigo and the New World*. New York: Knopf, 1955.

*Bakeless, John. *America as Seen by Its First Explorers*. New York: Dover, 1961.

Bancroft, Hubert Howe. *History of California*. San Francisco: A. L. Bancroft, 1884.

———. *History of Arizona and New Mexico*. San Francisco: A. L. Bancroft, 1889.

———. *History of Alaska*. San Francisco: A. L. Bancroft, 1886.

Baxter, James Phinney. *A Memoir of Jacques Cartier*. New York: Dodd Mead, 1906.

Beaglehole, J. C. *The Life of Captain James Cook*. Stanford: Stanford University Press, 1974.

Bishop, Morris. *Samuel Champlain, The Life of Fortitude*. New York: Knopf, 1948.

———. *The Odyssey of Cabeza de Vaca*. New York: Century, 1933.

*Blacker, Irwin R., editor. *The Portable Prescott*. New York: Viking, 1966.

Bolton, Herbert E. *Coronado, Knight of Pueblos and Plains*. Albuquerque: University of New Mexico Press, 1990.

————. *The Spanish Borderlands*. New Haven: Yale University Press, 1921.

Bourne, Edward Gaylord, editor. *The Northmen: Columbus and Cabot*. New York: Scribner's, 1925.

Bourne, Edward Gaylord. *Spain in America*. New York: Harper, 1904.

Boyle, Robert H. *The Hudson River*. New York: Norton, 1969.

Braider, Donald. *The Niagara*. New York: Holt, Rinehart and Winston, 1972.

Brebner, John Bartlet. *The Explorers of North America*. New York: Macmillan, 1933.

Brown, Lloyd A. *The Story of Maps*. Boston: Little, Brown, 1949.

Butterfield, Consul Willshire. *History of Brûlé's Discoveries and Explorations*. Cleveland: Helman-Taylor, 1898.

*Carmer, Carl. *The Hudson*. New York: Grosset and Dunlap, 1968.

Carter, Hodding. *Lower Mississippi*. New York: Farrar and Rinehart, 1942.

Castenada, Pedro de, editor. *The Journey of Coronado*. New York: Dover, 1990.

*Ceram, C. W. *The First American*. New York: Harcourt, Brace, Jovanovich, 1981.

*Claiborne, Robert. *The First Americans*. New York: Little, Brown, 1973.

*Coe, Michael, with Dean Simon and Elizabeth Benson. *Atlas of Ancient America*. New York: Facts on File, 1986.

Cohen, J. M. *The Four Voyages of Christopher Columbus*. London: Cresset, 1969.

Collier, John. *Indians of the Americas*. New York: Mentor, 1947.

Collis, Maurice. *Cortés and Montezuma*. London: Faber and Faber, 1954.

Cranston, James Herbert. *Étienne Brûlé, Immortal Scoundrel*. Toronto: Ryerson Press, 1949.

Crone, G. R. *The Discovery of America*. New York: Weybright and Talley, 1969.

Cronson, William. *Changes in the Land*. New York: Hill and Wang, 1983.

Crosby, Alfred W., Jr. *The Columbia Exchange*. Westport: Greenwood, 1973.

Day, A. Grove. *Coronado's Quest*. Berkeley: University of California, 1940.

————. *They Peopled the Pacific*. New York: Duell, Sloan and Pearce, 1964.

Diffie, Bailey W. *Latin-American Civilization*. Harrisburg: Stackpole, 1945.

Diffie, Bailey W., and George D. Winius. *Foundations of the Portuguese Empire, 1415–1580*. Minneapolis: University of Minnesota, 1977.

*Faber, Harold. *From Sea to Sea: The Growth of the United States*. New York: Farrar, Straus, 1967.

*Fagan, Brian M. *The Great Journey*. New York: Thames and Hudson, 1987.

Federal Writers Project. *California: A Guide to the Golden State*. New York: Hastings House, 1939.

*Ferris, Robert G., editor. *Explorers and Settlers*. Washington: National Park Service, 1966.

Flick, Alexander C., editor. *History of the State of New York*, volume one. Port Washington: Ira J. Friedman, 1962.

Granzotto, Gianni. *Christopher Columbus*. Garden City: Doubleday, 1985.

Hammond, George P., and Agapito Ray. *Narratives of the Coronado Expedition*. Albuquerque: University of Mexico, 1940.

Harlow, Vincent T., editor. *Voyages of Great Pioneers*. London: Oxford, 1929.

Harrisse, Henry. *John Cabot, the Discoverer of North America, and Sebastian, His Son*. London: Benjamin Franklin Stevens, 1896.

*Horgan, Paul. *The Conquistadors*. New York: Farrar, Straus, 1963.

Hunt, William R. *Arctic Passage*. New York: Scribner's, 1975.

Idell, Albert, editor. *The Bernal Diaz Chronicles*. Garden City: Doubleday, 1956.

Irving, Washington. *Voyages and Discoveries of the Companions of Columbus*. Boston: Twayne, 1986.

*Jennings, Francis. *The Invasion of America*. New York: Norton, 1975.

Kelsey, Harry. *Juan Rodríguez Cabrillo*. San Marino: Huntington, 1986.

*Kopper, Philip. *The Smithsonian Book of North American Indians Before the Coming of the Europeans*. Washington: Smithsonian, 1986.

*Lamb, Harold. *New Found World*. Garden City: Doubleday, 1955.

Lauridsen, Peter. *Vitus Bering: The Discoverer of Bering Strait*. Chicago: S. C. Griggs, 1889.

*Leacock, Stephen. *The Mariner of St. Malo*. Toronto: Glasgow, Brook, 1915.

Ledyard, John. *A Journal of Captain Cook's Last Voyage*. Chicago: Quadrangle, 1963.

*Lomask, Milton. *Great Lives: Exploration*. New York: Scribner's, 1988.

McAlister, Lyle N. *Spain and Portugal in the New World, 1492–1700*. Minneapolis: University of Minnesota, 1984.

Medina, Jose Toribo. *The Discovery of the Amazon*. New York: Dover, 1987.

*Morison, Samuel Eliot. *Admiral of the Ocean Sea*. Boston: Little, Brown, 1942.

*————. *The European Discovery of America: The Northern Voyages*. New York: Oxford, 1971.

*————. *The European Discovery of America: The Southern Voyages*. New York: Oxford, 1974.

————. *Portuguese Voyages to America in the Fifteenth Century*. Cambridge: Harvard University, 1940.

*Norman, James. *The Navy That Crossed the Mountains*. New York: G. P. Putnam and Sons, 1963.

Parkman, Francis. *La Salle and the Discovery of the Great West*. New York: Signet, 1963.

————. *Pioneers of France in the New World*. Boston: Little, Brown, 1924.

Parr, Charles McKew. *Ferdinand Magellan, Circumnavigator*. New York: Crowell, 1953.

Parry, J. H. *The Discovery of the Sea*. New York: Dial, 1974.

————. *The Discovery of South America*. London: Elek, 1979.

————. *The Spanish Seaborne Empire*. New York: Knopf, 1970.

Pohl, Frederick J. *Amerigo Vespucci, Pilot Major*. New York: Columbia University, 1944.

*Powys, Llewelyn. *Henry Hudson*. New York: Harper, 1928.

Prescott, William H. *The Conquest of Mexico and the Conquest of Peru*. New York: Modern Library, 1940.

Priestley, Herbert Ingram. *The Coming of the White Man, 1492–1848*. New York: Macmillan, 1929.

Quinn, David B. *North America: From Earliest Discovery to First Settlements*. New York: Harper and Row, 1977.

Rodman, Selden. *A Short History of Mexico*. New York: Stein and Day, 1982.

*Romoli, Kathleen. *Balboa of Darien: Discoverer of the Pacific*. New York: Doubleday, 1953.

Sale, Kirkpatrick. *The Conquest of Paradise*. New York: Knopf, 1990.

Scanlan, Marion S. *Trails of the French Explorers*. San Antonio: Naylor, 1956.

Sedgwick, Henry Dwight. *Cortés the Conqueror*. Indianapolis: Bobbs, Merrill, 1926.

Solomon, Louis. *The Mississippi: America's Mainstream*. New York: McGraw Hill, 1971.

*Stefansson, Vilhjalmur. *Great Adventures and Explorations*. New York: Dial Press, 1947.

Sullivan, James, editor. *History of the State of New York*, volume one. New York: Lewis, 1927.

Thwaites, Reuben Golden. *France in America*. New York: Haskell House, 1969.

*Tilden, Freeman. *The National Parks*. New York: Knopf, 1970.

*Viereck, Phillip. *The New Land*. New York: John Day, 1967.

Wilford, John Noble. *The Mapmakers*. New York: Knopf, 1981.

Williamson, John. *The Cabot Voyages and Bristol Discovery Under Henry VII*. Cambridge: Hakluyt Society, 1962.

Winsor, Justin, editor. *Narrative and Critical History of America*, volume 11. Boston: Houghton, Mifflin, 1889.

Wroth, Lawrence C. *The Voyages of Giovanni da Verrazzano*. New Haven: Yale, 1970.

Index